KATHERINE CHADDOCK REYNOLDS is assistant professor of education at the University of South Carolina.

D1714375

SOUTHERN BIOGRAPHY SERIES
BERTRAM WYATT-BROWN, EDITOR

VISIONS
AND VANITIES

VISIONS
AND VANITIES

John Andrew Rice of Black Mountain College

KATHERINE CHADDOCK REYNOLDS

LOUISIANA STATE UNIVERSITY PRESS
Baton Rouge

LA
2317
. R47
R49
1998

Frontispiece photograph of John Andrew Rice, *ca.* 1934, is reproduced courtesy of William C. Rice.

Grateful acknowledgment is made to William C. Rice for permission to reproduce small portions of the Doughten Cramer manuscript, the Olson-Rice correspondence, and the Katherine S. Warren report of Arthur Smith and descendants, all in Mr. Rice's private collection; to Richard Andrews for permission to use excerpts from his manuscript "John Rice and the Model Log Cabin"; to Sue Spayth Riley for permission to use excerpts from her manuscript "John Andrew Rice at Black Mountain College"; to the Harry Ransom Humanities Research Center, University of Texas at Austin, for permission to include excerpts from letters in the Harper's Collection; to the Rollins College Department of College Archives and Special Collections for permission to include excerpts from the Faculty Files; to the Friends Historical Library, Swarthmore College, for permission to include excerpts from the papers of Frank Aydelotte and from the folders of John A. Rice, Jr., and Nell Aydelotte Rice; and to Special Collections, Homer Babbidge Library, University of Connecticut, for permission to reproduce an excerpt from a letter of Charles Olson to Frances Boldereff.

Library of Congress Cataloging-in-Publication Data
Reynolds, Katherine Chaddock, 1945–
    Visions and vanities : John Andrew Rice of Black Mountain College
/ Katherine Chaddock Reynolds.
      p.   cm. — (Southern biography series)
    Includes bibliographical references (p.) and index.
      ISBN 0-8071-2203-3 (cloth : alk. paper)
    1. Rice, John Andrew, b. 1888. 2. Educators—United States—Biography.
3. Black Mountain College (Black Mountain, N.C.)—History.   I. Title.   II. Series.
LA2317.R47R49   1998
378.756'88'092—dc21
[B]   ·   97-51834
                                                  CIP

To my first teachers, my parents:

RICHARD EASTMAN CHADDOCK

AND KATHERINE MASSFELLER CHADDOCK

CONTENTS

ILLUSTRATIONS

ACKNOWLEDGMENTS

During the research and writing of this book I encountered individuals who shared their memories and personal documents, professionals who assisted in libraries and archives, colleagues and reviewers who critiqued my work as it progressed, and friends and family who offered crucial encouragement. To all I owe a debt of gratitude.

Family members of John Andrew Rice have been a vital part of this project by sharing information and impressions firsthand, particularly Rice's son Frank Aydelotte Rice, who reviewed the entire manuscript to offer suggestions and corrections and to add rich detail from his memories and records. Ann Rice, Peter and Karen Rice, Roger Marshall, Marilyn Rice, and Richard Carruthers also freely shared their recollections; and Dikka Moen Rice, the widow of John Andrew Rice, reviewed later chapters and added valuable perspective. However, my greatest gratitude to the family of John Andrew Rice is owed to grandson William C. Rice. His immediate encouragement to a stranger who phoned him without warning provided much of the inspiration for this project. His invaluable assistance continued as he gave lengthy interviews, offered suggestions for locating other interviewees, provided documents and photographs, and critiqued several drafts. His candor and objectivity were unimpeachable, far exceeding what biographers anticipate of family members.

Among early Black Mountain colleagues of John Andrew Rice, Ted and Barbara Dreier were particularly helpful in granting interviews and reviewing the manuscript. Peggy Loram Bailey of the original faculty also granted an interview and provided documentary information. Some of Rice's former students who shared their memories and thoughts were Richard Andrews, Hope Stephens Foote, John R. P. French, Jr., Sophie French, Jane Mayhall, Don Page, Sue Spayth Riley, Dorothy Shepherd Smith, Barbara Hill Steinau, Morton Steinau, Robert Sunley, Marian Nacke Teeter, David Way, Norman Weston, Betty Young Williams, and Emil Willimetz. I thank them, as well as others who provided advice and information, including Donna H. Bryan, Robert Chambers, Martin Duberman, Mary Harris, Philip Johnson, Mervin Lane, Willard Lockwood, and Helen McGraw.

Among the many archivists and librarians who assisted me in document review and collection, several who hosted me on multiple occasions and helped me sift through their voluminous materials are due special thanks: Kathleen Reich and Gertrude LaFrambois of the Rollins College Archives, in Winter Park, Florida; and Bill Brown, Steven Massengill, and others at the North Carolina State Archives in Raleigh. G. Thomas Tanselle of the John Simon Guggenheim Memorial Foundation reviewed and shared twenty years of materials on my behalf. Staff members at other institutions that provided important documentation include those at the College of Charleston, Columbia College, Fisk University, Howard University, the Montgomery County (Maryland) Historical Society, the New York Museum of Modern Art, Princeton University, the South Carolina Department of Archives and History, Southern Methodist University, Swarthmore College, Tulane University, the University of Chicago, the University of Connecticut, the University of Florida, the University of Nebraska, the University of South Carolina, the University of Texas, and Yale University.

I owe much to colleagues at both the University of Utah and the University of South Carolina who gave generously of their time and attention to earlier versions of this book. Principal among those at the first institution are Frederick Buchanan, Anthony Morgan, Carolyn Shields, Ann Hart, and Diana Pounder. In addition, Robert Bliss, former dean of the University of Utah School of Architecture, offered extensive insight as a friend and colleague who had also been a student at Black Mountain College. His interest in the project greatly influenced its progress. To my University of Utah mentor and friend L. Jackson Newell I extend an extra thanks for his suggestion that I should undertake this study, his willingness to listen and gently guide, and his humor when I most needed it, all of which continued well after my departure from Utah and his move to the presidency of Deep Springs College in California. Craig Kridel, an immediate source of encouragement and advice at the University of South Carolina, gave the project renewed momentum as I changed locations; and support continued from Lorin Anderson, Catherine Fry, Leonard Pellicer, James Sears, Jack Sproat, and James Wallace. I also received expert research assistance from Ronald Garrick, who tackled the detective work of solving discrepancies and tying up loose ends.

At Louisiana State University Press, John Easterly was encouraging from the start and wise enough to send my manuscript to two superb reviewers whose insightful comments greatly enhanced the final work: Bertram Wyatt-Brown of the University of Florida, and Fred Hobson of the University of North Carolina at Chapel Hill.

Finally, my family provided crucial support. My sister, Emilie Egan, combed through microfilm with me. My children, Brett and Adrienne Reynolds, were not only interested and enthusiastic, but also took an active part in endeavors such as labeling files and sorting correspondence. My husband Roy donated his time, patience, and applause. He is greatly responsible for my ability to complete this volume.

VISIONS
AND VANITIES

INTRODUCTION

Educator and author John Andrew Rice, best known as founder of the mete-
oric experiment in education called Black Mountain College, was an im-
probable patriarch of any enterprise. More iconoclastic than inspired, Rice
observed, experienced, and criticized American higher education of the
early twentieth century. In conversation and in print, he eloquently fumed
about dictatorial college administrators, bumbling trustees, and systems that
emphasized credit hours over learning and facts over meaning. But as the
driving force behind a college that would become one of the most highly renowned American models of distinctive processes in liberal education, John
Andrew Rice seemed peculiarly lacking in strategic savvy or organizational
acumen. It was characteristic of this paunchy and rumpled man, trailing a
ready supply of ashes from his pipe, to admit when appealing for funds from
wealthy patrons or foundation directors, "I don't know how this thing's going to work out. If I drew up any kind of plan, I'd feel under an obligation to
carry it through. I'm not going to do that."[1]

Since its distinguished journey from 1933 to 1956, Black Mountain College has been variously recounted as an experiment in general education, in
progressive education, in art education, and in utopian community building.
For John Andrew Rice, the small coeducational college located among the
scenic slopes of western North Carolina started as none of these. In the spirit
of William James, whom he greatly admired, and John Dewey, whom he
counted among his acquaintances, Rice viewed his academic endeavor not as
a controlled experiment to test educational theories, but simply as a prag-

<hr/>

1. John Andrew Rice, interview with Martin Duberman, June 10, 1967, audiotape in Martin
Duberman Papers, Personal Collection 1678, North Carolina State Division of Archives and History, Department of Cultural Resources, Raleigh.

matic means for implementing ideas about how to improve on the existing
fare of American institutions of higher education. Essential among those
founding ideas were: the centrality of artistic experience to support learning
in any discipline; the adaptation of emotional development as an important
educational aim; the value of experiential learning; the need for democratic
governance shared among faculty and students; the absence of oversight
from outside trustees; the contribution of social and cultural community
outside the classroom; and the efficiency of lean and loosely structured college administration.

After Rice's unbroken string of stormy resignations and terminations
from faculty positions at other universities and colleges, Black Mountain also
offered him a platform for personal expression. There with relative freedom
he could vent his often corrosive candor, exercise his remarkable talent for
Socratic classroom dialogue, and enjoy the absence of a heavy-handed upper
administration. With his audacity and his masterful command of communication unchecked, Rice met with both notable professional success and personal failure at Black Mountain. His experiences present us not only with an
occasion to learn from ideas tested in action, but also with an opportunity to
ponder the fascinating dynamics that occur when the possibilities of human
thought meet the frailties of human behavior.

The college that Rice nudged into existence, as its founder and then as its
head for five years, was swept to prominence in the history of American education by an unusual confluence of fortuitous timing and pioneering individuals. The ideals of progressive education, with its emphasis on classroom
community and individual student interests, had captured the vision of elementary and secondary educators and were ready for adaptation at the higher
level. During the 1920s, progressive curricular innovations, such as honors
programs and work-study courses, were tested at well-established colleges
like Swarthmore and Antioch. An experiment in combining scholarship and
self-sustenance took hold in California, where Deep Springs College students established a working ranch and a rigorous curriculum. On widely
scattered campuses faculty began to explore the methods of progressive education within their classrooms by encouraging interdisciplinary and collaborative learning. In Europe, the 1933 closing of the Bauhaus harbingered the
dark war years ahead and stimulated some of that continent's finest intellectuals and artists to consider careers in America. In the United States, the
Great Depression created an environment in which new and financially unstable ventures like Black Mountain College seemed no more risky than so
many other endeavors of the time.

This context offered Rice and his colleagues the opportunity to gather not only students and faculty seeking to redefine the operating norms of American higher education, but also an unusual array of creative and scholarly individuals committed to the free exchange of ideas and experimentation. Black Mountain became the place where Josef Albers worked magic with his vibrant colors and geometric lines; the site where Buckminster Fuller raised his geodesic domes; the space where Pulitzer Prize–winning composer Dante Fiorillo composed and rehearsed; and a retreat where visiting artists and intellectuals like John Dewey, Aldous Huxley, Henry Miller, and Thornton Wilder could withdraw.

Black Mountain built a legacy of achievement, especially in the arts, among those who taught and learned there. Furthermore, it demonstrated fairly quickly that the development of creative and mature thought might be more likely to occur in the context of a fully integrated and engaging process than to spring from a series of discrete curricular events. John Andrew Rice may have been recalling the dynamic and enigmatic nature of this process in later years when he frequently insisted, "Black Mountain College wasn't an experiment; it was an experience."[2]

Rice's ideas about education were collected from his own experience and sifted through a wellspring of natural cynicism. As a preacher's son whose boyhood was spent in small towns throughout South Carolina, he grew up to attend the highly disciplined southern preparatory school (Webb School, Bell Buckle, Tennessee), the large public university (Tulane University), the classic British university (Oxford, as a Rhodes scholar), and the acclaimed research institution (University of Chicago). As a faculty member who taught Greek and Latin language and classical philosophy, he managed stints at the Webb School, University of Nebraska, New Jersey College for Women (later part of Rutgers), and Rollins College (Winter Park, Florida), before the opening of Black Mountain College.

It was unlikely that Rice would locate his upstart venture in education anywhere other than the South. Although he recoiled against its isolationism and prejudices, he found enough comforting boyhood memories and fascinating human dramas to make the region both the place he loved to hate and the place he loved to love.

Yet the early-twentieth-century South seemed an unlikely venue for the establishment of a progressive experiment in higher education, when general acceptance still prevailed that the Northeast and Midwest were home to truly great seats of higher learning and forward-thinking educational innovations. The handful of distinctive and progressive colleges beginning to

---

2. Dikka Moen Rice to Katherine C. Reynolds, October 4, 1995, in author's possession.

commit to new approaches in teaching and learning were northern bred—including women's colleges Sarah Lawrence and Bennington, as well as experimental colleges within larger institutions at the University of Wisconsin and the University of Chicago. Only the classic texts program at St. John's College in Annapolis, Maryland, pushed curricular experimentation even as far south as a border state. The notable educational innovations in the South had taken another direction: toward extending the social and economic bases of postsecondary schooling. Berea College in Kentucky, Tuskegee University in Alabama, Bethune-Cookman College in Florida, a number of labor and farm colleges, and others made important inroads as early endeavors to assist minority and/or economically disadvantaged students in attending college. Black Mountain College, however, distinguished itself in the South as a new institution for the purpose of progressive curricular experimentation.

By adding a southern site to the collective urge for academic innovation, Black Mountain lent support to growing evidence that higher education would fully participate in what could be loosely labeled "the new South." Among the scattered pockets of excellence providing indications of a cultural and intellectual awakening was, for example, the gathering of "fugitive" southern literary genius in and around Vanderbilt University, to include John Crowe Ransom, Allen Tate, Donald Davidson, and Robert Penn Warren. Championing their place as home to voices to be reckoned with was southern progressive Edwin Mims, an observer and writer who chaired the Vanderbilt English Department and whose 1925 volume, *The Advancing South,* did much to announce the region's new possibilities. Further north, but still well within the region H. L. Mencken caustically dismissed in 1920 as "the Sahara of the Bozart,"[3] an interdisciplinary group of scholars joined noted sociologist Howard Odum at the University of North Carolina, Chapel Hill, to study and report the fabric of the South and to found at that university the Institute for Research in Social Science. At the same institution, an impressive group of dramatists gathered around Frederick Koch to write and produce works as the Carolina Playmakers, among them Paul Green and Thomas Wolfe, as well as a group who gained national prominence by pioneering the idea of folk drama.

John Andrew Rice first garnered national attention in early 1933 when his public criticism of Rollins College and its administration, as well as his verbal attacks on some faculty and students, prompted the termination of his faculty contract. This dismissal sparked an investigation by the American Association of University Professors (AAUP) and touched off a highly publi-

---

3. H. L. Mencken, "The Sahara of the Bozart," in *Prejudices, Second Series* (New York, 1920).

cized dispute about academic freedom. With Arthur Lovejoy at the helm of its investigative arm, the AAUP exonerated Rice and censured Rollins; but by the time the group published its report on the case, Rice already had led a handful of dissident faculty and students from the Florida college to Black Mountain.

A wily critic, Rice viewed American higher education as admittedly imperfect when colonial settlers borrowed from Oxford and Cambridge, but edging toward fatally flawed when late-nineteenth- and early-twentieth-century Americans borrowed models from German research institutions. He accounted for the trend as follows: "The method of their [German universities'] scholarship was something an American could put his teeth into, this getting at truth through facts and facts alone, welcome release from the heavy hand of the theologian, to whom education in this country was still mortgaged and for whom the poet alone was a match. But poets were not frequent and could not be made, while scholars could, and Germany was the place; and until such time as the American graduate school could get into mass production, a degree from Berlin or Leipzig was a safe investment." Nor did Rice find comfort in the experimental liberal arts colleges that were fashioning new American responses to the German educational challenge. "St. John's College, in Annapolis, is a vocational school without a vocation," he quipped, referring to that institution's reliance on classic texts.[4]

Rice reserved particularly intemperate criticism for Robert Maynard Hutchins' experimental college within the University of Chicago and was appalled by Hutchins' appeal that higher education should concern itself with "the single-minded pursuit of intellectual virtues" and promote among students "a common stock of fundamental ideas." Rice exchanged barbs with Hutchins in *Harper's Monthly Magazine,* insisting in a 1937 piece: "We ought to begin to consider education as a thing concerned at least in part with how people feel. If we do not, somebody else will, and all our structure of thought will disappear as quickly as it has in Nazi Germany. There was a country where the universities were concerned with pure thought, where the keenest thinking of the modern world was being done. And yet not a word was heard from the seats of learning when the house painter appeared and roused the Germans to feeling. While intellection was being sharpened and polished, savagery was going its way, waiting for a chance."[5]

Rice had added his passionate, if strident, voice to the growing number of

---

4. John Andrew Rice, *I Came Out of the Eighteenth Century* (New York, 1942), 261, 265.
5. Robert Maynard Hutchins, "The Confusion in Higher Education," *Harper's,* CLXXIII (1936), 458; Hutchins, *The Higher Learning in America* (New Haven, 1936), 59; John Andrew Rice, "Fundamentalism and the Higher Learning," *Harper's,* CLXXIV (1937), 590.

early-twentieth-century educators who debated missions and methods of American higher education in response to the expansion of vocational education and research universities. They took issue not only with the aims of higher education, but also with the administration of the system. Thorstein Veblen, avid critic of capitalism, targeted his sardonic discourse at university governing boards in his 1918 volume *The Higher Learning in America: A Memorandum on the Conduct of Universities by Business Men.* In 1922 Upton Sinclair recounted his travels to dozens of seats of higher learning in *The Goose Step,* which named names and selected anecdotes to demonstrate the darkest face of university trusteeship and administration, concluding, "Our educational system today is in the hands of its last organized enemy, which is class greed and selfishness based upon economic privilege."[6]

Critics of American higher education early in the twentieth century not only noted the adoption and adaptation of various European models, but also kept an eye on European experiments not yet exported. Among those that would have particular relevance for John Andrew Rice was the German architecture and art institute called the Bauhaus. Rice was determined to find an individual who could establish and direct an art program that would instill valuable principles of discipline and creativity not only in budding art professionals, but also in economics majors and foreign language scholars. After an impressive search, he hired Josef Albers, a masterful artist and teacher who thereby became the first Bauhaus export to the United States. Albers' wife, Anni, initiated the weaving program at Black Mountain. Following Albers to Black Mountain was Bauhaus stage designer and graphic artist Xanti Schawinsky. Later, the only American to complete the full Bauhaus program, Howard Dearstyne, became an instructor of architecture at Black Mountain College. Bauhaus masters shared with many American progressive educators a pragmatic regard for direct classroom experience and with many educational experimenters a respect for close-knit relations between students and teachers that extended to out-of-class activities.

Fortunate in the timing of a pioneering educational venture and in his own capacity to steer Black Mountain College through its rocky early years, John Andrew Rice was less fortunate in his capacity to sustain his own relationship to the college. In a close community of fewer than one hundred faculty and students, his strong personality was inescapable and did not always wear well as a day-to-day presence. At Black Mountain and elsewhere, there were apparently two John Andrew Rices—the brilliant, inspiring, and caring teacher and the brilliant, insensitive, and sharp-tongued pedagogue.

6. Upton Sinclair, *The Goose Step* (Pasadena, Calif., 1922), 478.

Most who have mentioned him in print—generally in passing on their way to recount the post-Rice, postwar, pro-art years of Black Mountain College—seem to agree only on the brilliance.

Rice is less widely remembered as he was characterized by the first chronicler of Black Mountain College, author Louis Adamic: "a natural-born teacher, perhaps one of the great teachers of all time, and intensely human." In contrast, Black Mountain College alumnus Morton Steinau found Rice "opinionated and not at all restrained about what he thought—charismatic, direct and often demeaning of students and other faculty."[7]

A masterful conversationalist who could readily generate wise and humorous discussions, Rice also was impatient and arrogant in his commitment to the stinging verbal barbs that he viewed as frank expression. Without a blink of apology, he was able to look square into the eyes of a Black Mountain College professor of philosophy who was concerned about his teaching performance and say, "You know, you really should get out of teaching. I think you really ought to be a golf pro." Still unapologetic three decades later, Rice would shrug off the incident and the subsequent faculty uproar about it by explaining with an air of peevish innocence, "Well, I meant it. He was a wonderful teacher of golf. Hell, that's what he could do. But he was furious at me."[8]

Bravado aside, Rice undoubtedly recognized his effect on those receiving the brunt of his penchant for confrontation. But his own enjoyment in surfacing the unexpected, exercising his notable wit, proving a point, or provoking an argument urged him on—well past consideration for other individuals or future implications. The flaw in his genius was to use it for its own end. In doing so, he managed to tear down as well as to build up and to demonstrate abrasiveness as well as intellect.

It is possible that Rice never came to terms with his southern heritage. The role of the highly educated southern intellectual was an uneasy one in the early twentieth century, when "scholarly" and "manly" seemed opposite terms by definition. Nor was it easy to reconcile a genuine fondness for the region with a recognition of its capacity for racial bigotry, religious hypocrisy, and local demagoguery. Defensiveness and insecurity possibly fueled some of Rice's outbursts. An aggressive manner may have served as the cara-

7. Louis Adamic, "Education on a Mountain," *Harper's,* CLXXII (1936), 526; Morton Steinau, interview with the author, May 3, 1993.

8. J. Rice, interview with Duberman, June 10, 1967. Also see Faculty Meeting Minutes, December 6, 1936, Black Mountain College Papers, North Carolina State Division of Archives and History, Department of Cultural Resources, Raleigh; hereinafter cited as BMCP, N.C. Archives.

pace that shielded his doubts, as well as the megaphone that announced assuredness.

Although his legacy likely would have been larger if lodged in a persona of greater repose, Rice managed to leave a substantial imprint on higher education. His primary contribution was to create an environment for putting important and untried ideas into action and to draw nationwide attention to the possibilities of new and different approaches to postsecondary learning. Although the scope and durability of the enterprise would be impossible to measure accurately, Black Mountain College became a demonstration site for philosophies about teaching and learning that were later passed on to other institutions.

Rice's own placement at the forefront of American higher education endured only as long as he could rein in his tendency for turning his observations into weapons. During the first several years after the opening of the college, its founding father and rector occupied himself with a constant flurry of policy-making meetings, student interaction, faculty recruitment, and fund raising. His schedule was also weighted by conference attendance and speaking engagements that introduced Black Mountain College to educators and the general public. Bold and eloquent from the dais or at the dinner table, Rice readily attracted attention and admiration for the small college forging new paths in education.

After several years, however, Rice seemed to tire of the effort and began more and more frequently to sow discord among faculty and students. Or perhaps others simply tired of the tensions he created. His words could transform delicately balanced collegiality into bitter and self-defeating warfare. In 1938, encouraged by his colleagues, he took the first of several leaves of absence from the college. By early 1940, not seven years after Black Mountain College had opened its doors, the faculty requested that John Andrew Rice resign.

His departure from higher education was complete. Although he was only fifty-two years old, Rice never again returned to teaching. Instead, he forged a second career from his beloved southern roots by writing about the South. In the award-winning *I Came Out of the Eighteenth Century,* an episodic autobiography primarily recounting his boyhood and college years, and in numerous short stories, he wrote powerfully and vividly about social realities and human relations among classes and races. He became, in print, a forceful talent who was able to supplement philosophical and political arguments for racial equality by telling stories about people, white and black, that humanized the issues. He also established his credentials as a superb writer and an expert, if cynical, observer of American institutions and habits.

Because Rice's primary impact was as an educator and because his own book is the only comprehensive source for personal descriptions of his early life, this biography explores in detail only the progression of the professional life of John Andrew Rice. In this sense, it is an educational biography. As such, it examines Rice's years of involvement as a student, teacher, educational critic, college founder, and leader. It includes prior history and later history selectively, reporting only those events and incidents that contribute to an understanding of Rice's philosophy and actions as an educator and to an examination of his success, his failure, and his influence in that role.

Our knowledge of John Andrew Rice's life as an educator enhances our understanding of the roots and development of American experiments in higher education and our recognition of the ways in which the characteristics of individuals shape the forms that ideas assume as they are put into practice. Rice's experiences also add to our store of historical evidence about the efforts undertaken in the early twentieth century toward fashioning an American design for higher education.

Scoffing that any history is an imperfect record, Rice recalled just a year before his death in 1968, "I've always said you couldn't write history, but you could come close to it if you know all the people and know the way they behaved."[9] This biography is a way of knowing John Andrew Rice and recounting how he and others behaved in order to illuminate both an influential individual and a rare chapter in American higher education.

9. J. Rice, interview with Duberman, June 10, 1967.

1

A Scattering of Influences

John Andrew Rice began life straddling cultures. Born in Lynchburg, South Carolina, on February 1, 1888, not twenty-five years after Lee surrendered to Grant at Appomattox, Rice arrived when the post–Civil War South was of two minds: one that clung to the notion of plantation gentility and one that embraced the march of Reconstruction. Cotton farmers and carpetbaggers represented the extremes, but both were part of the inevitable and dramatic change spreading through the South.[1]

Change also had taken hold elsewhere, as a country once committed to the economic primacy of agriculture, logging, and mining began to switch its allegiance to industry and trade. Advances and inventions earlier in the century had sought better living off the land. The applauded breakthroughs of 1888, however, were George Eastman's box camera and J. B. Dunlop's pneumatic tire. Commerce and communication were enhanced that year by the adoption of standard gauge train rails and free rural mail delivery. Perhaps most indicative of the watershed quality of John Andrew Rice's birth year was the publication of a remarkable new book that quickly reached bestseller status: Edward Bellamy's *Looking Backward,* which proposed a utopian response to the dislocations of social structure and the distortions of economic systems. As if to punctuate just how much change could occur in the

1. J. Rice, *Eighteenth Century,* 10–26; Federal Census of South Carolina, Richland County, 1900, Vol. 42, in South Carolina Department of Archives and History, Columbia, S.C. For treatment of the South as confronted by southerners of the late nineteenth and early twentieth centuries, see, for example, W. J. Cash, *The Mind of the South* (New York, 1941), Katharine DuPre Lumpkin, *The Making of a Southerner* (Athens, Ga., 1946), Edwin Mims, *The Advancing South* (Garden City, N.Y., 1926), and William Alexander Percy, *Lanterns on the Levee: Recollections of a Planter's Son* (New York, 1941).

years since midcentury, sales of Bellamy's response to industrialization edged only a few hundred volumes short of the previous nineteenth-century top seller, *Uncle Tom's Cabin,* published in 1851.

John Andrew Rice's family at the time of his birth still reflected the Old South of his grandparents. His maternal grandfather, William H. Smith, an itinerant Methodist minister of English descent, built the family plantation near the town of Lynchburg sometime around 1850 on land that had been in the Smith family since 1747. Called "Smith's Grove" before the family opted for the more poetic "Tanglewood," the estate included a large frame house built by family slaves from boards and pegs milled from trees on the property. Its flat acreage, located in the rural area of north-central South Carolina, was favored with neither the natural beauty found in the rolling hills to the west nor the commercial advantages of ocean ports to the east; but it did manage to produce ample rice, sugar cane, and cotton. Rice's mother, Anna Bell Smith, was born at Tanglewood in 1862. Her childhood years were spent there with three brothers and a sister, all of whom later brought their own children back to the family plantation for summers and holidays. For John Andrew and his two younger brothers, Liston McLeod ("Mike") Rice and Coke Smith Rice, the plantation was the most favored locale of their childhood years. Its stately Greek Revival main house, fronted by a wide two-story portico supported by four thick columns, could appear awesome and wonderful to a child. Its numerous out-buildings, trees, and meadows offered ample opportunities for youthful exploration. And the cotton fields were still operating in adequate prosperity during his childhood, with former slaves making the switch in status to hired help.[2]

John Andrew's father, John Andrew Rice, Sr., was from comparatively poor stock in South Carolina's humid low country south and west of Charleston. His father, Richard Blake Rice, was a country medical doctor of Irish and Scottish descent. He married Rachel Jane Liston, also of Scottish descent, and settled on a small, plain farm near the Salkehatchie River to raise a large family, in which John Andrew arrived in 1862 as the eighth

2. Federal Census of South Carolina, Sumter District, 1880, Vol. 28, in South Carolina Department of Archives and History; "Inventory and Nomination Form: Tanglewood Plantation," September 22, 1977, National Register of Historic Places, U.S. Department of the Interior, Washington, D.C.; Katherine Smith Warren, "An Account of Arthur Smith, Sumter County, South Carolina, and Some of His Descendants," 1985 (Typescript in private collection of William C. Rice); "The Death of Reverand William H. Smith," *Southern Christian Advocate,* February 25, 1882, p. 4; Cassie Nicholes, *Historical Sketches of Sumter County: Its Birth and Growth* (Columbia, S.C., 1975), 230–35; John Andrew Rice, "Grandmother Smith's Plantation," Part 1, *Harper's,* CLXXVII (1938), 573–77.

child. Richard Blake Rice was a traveling practitioner of medicine whose only office was the one-horse buggy he drove throughout the rural, generally impoverished lowlands. John Andrew Rice, Sr., perhaps because of his meager boyhood circumstances, grew up with little nostalgia for a place called "home" and had no regrets when, as a Methodist minister, he and his family moved frequently as the Methodist church assigned him to parishes in various South Carolina towns. Winters were spent in the parish towns— generally in church-provided parsonage homes filled with furniture donated by parishioners.[3]

As the summer and holiday retreat for Anna Bell Rice and sons, Tanglewood better offered a sense of home. There the Rice boys were joined by a steady stream of cousins, uncles, and aunts who were presided over by grandmother Mary McLeod Smith, widowed in 1882. John Andrew Rice remembered his diminutive, pipe-smoking grandmother with awe and affection:

> She was little and old and dried up, and attention to looks stopped with cleanliness; a stranger would not have guessed, to see her sitting there, that so much power could be lodged in so little space. The split-bottom chair was her movable throne, placed to catch the warmth of the sun; here she sat quietly puffing her pipe, meditating upon the rights and privileges and duties of a matriarch.
>
> . . . Her head had settled down between her shoulders and her chin was not very far from her nose. But there was no laxness anywhere. She was whole, and the full expression of her wholeness could be seen in her face, where the tiny muscles around the mouth and between eyes and ears held the flat surfaces of forehead and cheeks together in an active harmony. No part of her face ever spoke alone.[4]

The plantation summers became John Andrew Rice's earliest source of education, especially in the complex interrelations of gender and race. He learned that the girl cousins would join in games of sliding down hills of cottonseed or fighting mock battles for only so long before they reverted to the less frenetic arts of southern femininity. He noticed that the children of the former slaves were equal with the white children as they played together by day, but far separate when they scurried back to their family cabins in the

3. Federal Census of South Carolina, Colleton District, III, 1860, and X, 1880, in South Carolina Department of Archives and History; Alfred D. Betts, *History of Southern Methodism* (Columbia, S.C., 1952); Watson B. Duncan, *Twentieth Century Sketches of the South Carolina Conference, Methodist Episcopal Church* (Columbia, S.C., 1901), 261–62; J. Rice, *Eighteenth Century,* 41–55, 110–12.

4. J. Rice, "Grandmother Smith's Plantation," Part 1, p. 572.

woods at night. In the late afternoon, after a day during which black and white youngsters joined together happily as the knights or Indians of invented dramas, the arrival of the watermelon wagon signaled the time to withdraw, according to color, to different picnic tables—the white table being bigger and first to get served.[5]

For talk, John Andrew singled out Uncle Melt, whom he credited with some of his earliest training in the art of dialogue. Uncle Melt's cabin, a wooden shack where the old former slave resided, was a place to go and converse in "the inconsequential talk of the very old and the very young." Unlike Uncle Remus, Uncle Melt (for Milton) told no stories, but he had a ready laugh and a readiness to listen to a young boy's patter. His gift was in asking interesting questions; then he sat down to listen, nod, and suck on his corncob pipe as John Andrew spun his answers.[6]

The Smith family was an active and energetic clan. One of John Andrew's aunts, his mother's sister Fannie Smith Koger, became a missionary to Brazil. Uncle Alexander Coke Smith earned a reputation as a brilliant preacher and became bishop of the Methodist Conference of South Carolina. Another uncle, his mother's brother Ellison Durant Smith, became well known as Senator "Cotton Ed" Smith, whose United States Senate tenure (1908–1944) was the longest yet to be held in that body.[7]

Conversation was the order of the day, every day, as the extended Smith family gathered on the wide front porch or in front of the fireplace. Young John Andrew became an avid listener, attuned to each turn of phrase, shrug of shoulder, or wrinkle of brow. Later, Rice frequently noted that conversation in the South was distinguished by its subject matter—more often than not, people. He credited his southern roots with cultivating his fascination with people and his lifelong inclination to observe their actions and ponder their thoughts, noting, "In the South of my childhood and youth life was intensely personal. Ideas induced a yawn, and things, excepting on occasion their extreme scarcity; but let a name be mentioned, my tribe was off. I listened to words, tone, gesture, and I learned, as other small boys and girls were listening and learning. (The southern writers bear witness.)"[8]

John Andrew Rice, Sr., was easily a match for his Smith in-laws in terms

5. John Andrew Rice, "Grandmother Smith's Plantation," Part 2, *Harper's,* CLXXVIII (1938), 88–91.

6. J. Rice, *Eighteenth Century,* 11.

7. "The Death of Reverend W. H. Smith," *Southern Christian Advocate,* February 25, 1882, p. 4; "Inventory and Nomination Form: Tanglewood Plantation," National Register of Historic Places; Warren, "An Account of Arthur Smith," in W. Rice private collection, Boston.

8. John Andrew Rice, "Black Mountain College Memoirs," ed. William C. Rice, *Southern Review,* XXV (1989), 579.

of energy and forcefulness. In 1878, when he was sixteen, his family had sent him to the Sheridan Classical Institute, a college preparatory academy in Orangeburg, South Carolina. There, he found he had a facility for logic and a love of debate. When he graduated from South Carolina College (later the University of South Carolina) in Columbia, as valedictorian of the class of 1885, he was a favorite among public debaters for the Clariosophic Society, a prestigious campus literary society. He joined the South Carolina Methodist Conference in 1886, married the following year, and soon proved outspoken from the pulpit, unmovable in an argument, and firmly doctrinaire with his wife and three sons. Tall for his day, with a full black beard and piercing blue eyes, the Reverend Rice was physically suited to his powerful personality. He reveled in perplexing his parishioners with controversial and enigmatic questions. His sermons were marked by debates and quandaries with himself, and often his opening salvo would be something such as, "I know what I said last week seemed right to me at the time, but I'm not sure I don't have some doubt about it now."[9]

Among his areas of doubt were overly literal interpretations of the Old Testament and the efficacy of attacks on the Darwinian theory of evolution. His reservations put him in fairly direct opposition to Methodist fundamentalists and conservatives, and he generally enjoyed the controversy. However, controversy did not always serve him well. Later in his life, when he wanted to stay on as pastor at St. John's Church in St. Louis, the congregation insisted on a change. The preacher's oldest son would later estimate, "Wherever he went, about a third of the congregation worshipped him as a saint; the rest feared and hated him."[10]

Church seminary leaders commissioned the outspoken senior Rice to write a book on the Old Testament, but it proved too controversial to publish without some revision. Refusing to eliminate sections in question, Rice found another publisher, Macmillan Company, for *The Old Testament in the Life of Today.* In the volume, Rice raised fundamentalist hackles by applying what was termed "higher criticism" to the literal translation of the Bible. He contended that it contained errors of science and history, although he noted these should not cause concern in light of the good book's inspiration for human spirit. When Rice's book was released in 1920, he had just begun serv-

9. Duncan, *Twentieth Century Sketches,* 261–62; Frank A. Rice, interview with the author, February 13, 1993; Commencement Celebration Invitation, June 23, 1885, in Euphradian and Clariosophic Societies, Joint Programs Files, Archives, University of South Carolina, Columbia, S.C.

10. John Andrew Rice, Sr., "Dr. Rice and the Bible," letter to *Texas Christian Advocate,* September 22, 1921, pp. 8–9; Duncan, *Twentieth Century Sketches,* 261–63; J. Rice, *Eighteenth Century,* 154.

ing as professor of Old Testament at Southern Methodist University. Letter writing campaigns to Southern Methodist University administrators and to the press ensued, with conservative Baptists joining the fray beside fundamentalist Methodists against this harbinger of modern scholarship. Although his supervising bishop and most students defended him, widespread outrage from the church's grass roots created pressure for his resignation, which was accepted without hesitation, although not without nationwide publicity concerning the status of academic freedom at church-affiliated institutions of higher education.[11]

Still, the senior Rice was able to leave a lasting legacy to the Methodist church as a stirring speaker, an author of four books (all controversial, but none more so than the monograph *Is Christ on Trial in Tennessee?*), and the energetic force who oversaw the building of the widely applauded Boston Avenue Church in Tulsa, Oklahoma. His doubts about something he read or preached constituted critical intellectual banter and never endangered his reputation for decisiveness in action. His son would later recall, "He showed one element of greatness: he never acknowledged his own mistakes, however overpowering the evidence."[12]

Young John Andrew Rice and his brothers found the religious overtones of their life tedious. As John Andrew later explained to his own son, "We got tired of sitting in the front pew of church every Sunday and listening to hearing the world saved over our heads." His general distaste for anything related to religion eventually prompted him to characterize the church as "that monster that hovered over and dipped down into our lives."[13]

Along with his mother, John Andrew was particularly annoyed by the lack of privacy provided by a parsonage life where parishioners dropped by any time, any day, seemingly to pry into the lives of their minister's family. The family lacked any particular material possessions, especially household items, in their various poorly furnished quarters—with one exception, books. Good books, although not generally good literature, were the minister's one luxury and could be found in abundance wherever the Rices re-

11. Lewis H. Grimes, *A History of the Perkins School of Theology* (Dallas, 1993), 41–45; Nolan B. Harmon, ed., *The Encyclopedia of World Methodism* (New York, 1974), II, 2011–12; Mary M. H. Thomas, *Southern Methodist University: Founding and Early Years* (Dallas, 1974), 92–98; "Resolution upon Death of Rev. John A. Rice," *Oklahoma Annual,* Methodist Episcopal Church, South (Tulsa, 1930), 45–46. For discussions of the Rice action at Southern Methodist University as a question of academic autonomy among institutions of higher education, see, for example, Edwin Mims, *The Advancing South* (Garden City, N.Y., 1926), 144–46, and Sinclair, *The Goose Step,* 352–53.
12. J. Rice, *Eighteenth Century,* 98.
13. F. Rice, interview with the author, February 13, 1993; J. Rice, *Eighteenth Century,* 55.

sided. However, the most serious factor lacking in their lives was what John Andrew would later refer to as "invitation." He explained, "There was no art; there was no poetry; there was no literature worth reading. The invitations were not there, and my sense of poverty is the lack of invitation—the lack of a thing being there to be grasped." In summing up the circumstances of stern piety and perceived poverty in his first family, the son later recalled his father as someone "whom I didn't like in lots of ways and was afraid of."[14]

John Andrew and his brother Mike (Liston McLeod) would eventually conclude that ambition was their father's fatal flaw. An often-repeated Rice family story told of a summer cabin in the Ozarks given to the senior Rice by a grateful parishioner. A spring on the property was downhill from the cabin, and there was not enough money to buy a pump to get water to the house. Regardless, Rice insisted on laying pipe from the spring to the cabin, convinced that somehow the water would run uphill on its own through it. As family legend goes, the water did run uphill to the house every summer until the minister died; then, a pump had to be installed. In telling the story, family members simply shrugged and reminded each other that the senior Rice was a very forceful man.[15]

When Reverend Rice's ministry had taken him to four different South Carolina towns in the first six years of his marriage, his wife was sufficiently weary of parsonage living to announce, "I'd rather die than move again." Young John Andrew, who was exceedingly close to his mother and sensitive to her feelings, agreed, but heard his father simply retort, "Well, Anna, you knew when you married a preacher that you'd have to move." John Andrew was not wholly surprised when he overheard his mother talking with female relatives about her unhappy marriage.[16] Fortunately, however, in 1894 Reverend Rice was appointed president of Columbia (South Carolina) Female College, a post which promised longer tenure than sundry circuits and parishes.

Columbia Female College already figured in the Rice family history. Anna Belle Smith was attending there when she met John Andrew Rice, Sr., who was at nearby South Carolina College. Numerous aunts and female cousins attended Columbia, and many near and distant relatives were still in attendance when Rice assumed the presidency.

Columbia Female College was young John Andrew's first brush with

14. Betts, *History of Southern Methodism;* J. Rice, interview with Duberman, June 10, 1967.
15. John Andrew Rice to Liston McLeod Rice, January 11, 1939, in Faculty Files, BMCP, N.C. Archives; Roger Marshall, interview with the author, February 23, 1993.
16. J. Rice, *Eighteenth Century,* 46.

higher education, and he later labeled it "an asylum to which the daughters of good Methodists were sent during the interval between childhood and marriage, primarily for safekeeping." It was one of many small church-operated colleges for women that dotted the South at the time, largely founded by Baptists, Methodists, Catholics, and Presbyterians. They would later be characterized by the son of the Columbia College president as "temporary burying grounds, from which graduates ought to be handed back as they had been handed in, innocent of thought or idea."[17]

The town of Columbia in the last decade of the nineteenth century was still committed to the Old South of hoop skirts and Confederate flags. The stately capitol building proudly bore scars from General Sherman's cannon-ball assault; and Confederate general Wade Hampton, retired from service as governor and U.S. senator, was living out his years there riding his horse through town and nodding to hero-worshipping citizens. The Columbia Female College campus was located in the central business district just a few blocks from the state capitol. It consisted of one main building, three stories plus a bell tower, that housed classroom, chapel, library, and dormitory space for nearly two hundred students. A wooden fence marked the campus boundary, and the young southern belles in attendance were accustomed to strolling just inside it each afternoon, making eyes at and passing notes to the gentlemen (generally students at South Carolina College) who walked along the outer perimeter. Newly appointed President Rice decided rather quickly (perhaps from his own student experiences) that this boundary was silly, and he ordered the fence torn down. Although that removal caused a stir among conservative Methodists, they found yet greater grounds for outrage when President Rice dropped the feminine label to change the name of the institution to Columbia College. On these issues, after listening while under beds and behind curtains to the dormitory talk of the students, young John Andrew found himself in agreement with his father: "I think I was getting ready to prefer coeducation, which for all that can be said against it—and there is plenty—at least does one thing; it curbs the imagination."[18]

President Rice also tackled the curriculum at the college, and is generally credited with rescuing it from its status as a girls' finishing school and putting its program on equal footing with male colleges of the day. During his administration, the college began to grant bachelor of arts, bachelor of En-

17. *Ibid.*, 69, 99.

18. Jerald J. Savory, *Columbia College: The Ariail Era* (Columbia, S.C., 1979), 100–17; David D. Wallace, *The History of South Carolina,* (3 vols.; New York, 1934), II, 400–13; J. Rice, *Eighteenth Century,* 75.

glish, bachelor of science, and master of arts degrees. Students pursued rigorous language studies (Latin, Greek, German, and French), a full complement of science and math (mathematics, physics, chemistry, botany, astronomy, biology, and geology), as well as literature, history, economics, and religious studies.[19]

Family life at Columbia College was little improvement over parsonage life. The president's family was supplied with four identical, furnished dormitory rooms, and along with other faculty lived on the first floor of the main building. John Andrew's mother found little happiness there, but valiantly struggled to make a home for the three boys and to urge her busy husband to pay more attention to them. The boys and their mother gradually became a close-knit, isolated group without much contact with the father. Young John Andrew viewed his mother as a source of affection, laughter, and invented family games, but sought little nurturing from his forceful father. The senior Rice was busy making decisions, giving orders, and traveling throughout the state. When he did try to join in family activities, the boys generally found him too gruff and fearsome to be enjoyable.[20]

John Andrew started grade school in Columbia, attending a private school where he quickly decided he was smarter and already more learned than the other students his age. He did not mix well with his fellow students, probably at both his preference and theirs. By any measure precocious and enthusiastic to learn, the young John Andrew tackled piano, painting, and French, as well as reading, writing, and arithmetic. Showing an early tendency toward impatience, he observed the educational arena to which he was exposed and found it sorely lacking. Later he recalled his early sense of problems in the teaching profession: "I went to some of the teachers in my hope of learning, quite unprepared for the attitude I found, the assumption that no one really wanted to know what they had to teach, and I began to suspect that they had never wanted to learn anything themselves."[21]

In 1899 the family's world began to turn upside down. Grandmother Smith, who had seemed such an invincible, ageless matriarch, died at age eighty. Later that year, in April, when John Andrew was eleven years old and his younger brothers eight and five, their mother died quickly and unexpectedly just days after her thirty-seventh birthday. John Andrew was given few details, but he later was told that the premature death was related to a fourth

19. Savory, *Columbia College,* 116–17.
20. J. Rice, *Eighteenth Century,* 70–99; F. Rice, interviews with the author, February 13, 1993, November 24, 1995.
21. J. Rice, *Eighteenth Century,* 79.

pregnancy. An aunt explained to him, "I think she just got tired of living. Your father was too much for her."[22]

John Andrew's father realized within days that he could not manage his sons and the college, and in a few more weeks he found that neither could he count on cousins called upon to serve as surrogate mothers. Furthermore, he had an idea that he might use this new-found bachelorhood most productively to further his education and seek the doctoral degree he had never obtained. In this way it developed that John Andrew, a wavering mixture of scared little boy and arrogant youth, was delivered first to a boardinghouse near Columbia College where his father's brother, Uncle Willie, resided and next to a Methodist orphanage on the outskirts of downtown Columbia. His brothers Mike and Coke also were plucked from their quarters at the college to be parceled out among relatives.[23]

While Rice did not dwell on this division or on his grief in his later writing or conversation, he obviously had lost the stable and supportive family that is so crucial to normal social and psychological development following the loss of a parent.[24] With his grandmother Smith gone, there would be no more treasured plantation summers. With his mother gone, there would be no more nurturing warmth. With his brothers gone, there would be no more instant and intimate playmates. All that was most familiar and most comforting in his life disappeared at the start of his adolescent years.

Young John Andrew actually was a paying guest at the orphanage, and he was treated to his own white-tiled room in the infirmary, rather than mixed with other orphans in dormitory rooms. He quickly became arrogant and insensitive toward his fellow orphans, and he could not resist telling them about the favors that distinguished him—a living father and a twenty-five-cent weekly allowance. Each week he spent ten cents of his allowance to hire one of the orphan boys to make an early morning fire in his room before he got out of bed. John Andrew had lived several months in this unlikely home, perched on a magnolia and pine-covered hilltop, when his father informed

22. South Carolina Southern Conference Minutes, December 6–11, 1899, in Presidential Files, Columbia College Library Archives, Columbia, S.C.; J. Rice, *Eighteenth Century,* 103–104.

23. William C. Rice, interview with the author, January 6, 1993; J. Rice, *Eighteenth Century,* 103–105; Federal Census of South Carolina, 1900, Volume 42, in South Carolina Department of Archives and History.

24. For discussion of the psychological effects of loss of a parent, see, for example, John Bowlby, *Loss, Sadness and Depression* (London, 1980), Vol. III of Bowlby, *Attachment and Loss,* 3 vols.; Jonathan Bloom-Feshbach and Sally Bloom-Feshbach, *The Psychology of Separation and Loss* (San Francisco, 1987); and George H. Pollock, *The Mourning-Liberation Process* (2 vols.; Madison, Wis., 1989), I.

him that he would soon resign as president of Columbia College, take a nominal appointment as conference secretary of missions, and begin graduate studies at the University of Chicago. He would study there under Old Testament scholars William Rainey Harper and J. M. Powis Smith. John Andrew and his brothers would be gathered back together and sent to their paternal grandmother's plantation in the lowlands of Colleton County, southwest of Charleston. There, John Andrew later recollected, "Everyone was poor and everyone accepted poverty as an act of God," and his father's family was "stuck in the double poverty that comes of having seen better days."[25]

The plantation of the widowed Grandmother Rice was a far cry from Grandmother Smith's prosperous estate and hardly a plantation at all anymore. The original house had burned down early in the century, and the first family of John Andrew, Sr., had retired to a four-bedroom (with the attic used as an additional dormitory) home surrounded by pine forests and swamps and located nineteen miles from the nearest town, Varnville. The cotton patch and corn rows that supported the place grew nearly up to the house, and from planting to harvest were worked by Jake, the one hired field hand, and the residents of the house.

When John Andrew and his two brothers arrived to spend two years at Grandmother Rice's, her three daughters were in residence. John Andrew found nothing approximating a surrogate mother in his aunts or grandmother. Aunt Mollie was the firstborn of the brood that included John Andrew, Sr. Toothless, mindless, and assigned to tend the kitchen, she gave voice to senseless mumbling and occasional loud diatribes. Aunt Lou was brilliant and once beautiful, but hoeing rows of corn and plucking cotton from its razor pods had left her aged beyond her years. Aunt Jinny, who had moved back in with four offspring after she was widowed, played the maternal role for all seven children in residence at the turn of the century.[26]

Grandmother Rice, in stark contrast to her grandson's beloved Grandmother Smith, was sour and sedentary, prompting John Andrew later to recall only her most undesirable qualities: "Grandmother Rice was a vegetable. In the morning after breakfast she planted herself in a split-bottom chair in the chimney corner and sat rooted there all the livelong day. . . . Some old people, while they sit waiting for death, give their account of a road once traveled, where it is rough and where it is smooth, and set up for the young

25. Duncan, *Twentieth Century Sketches,* 262; Richard J. Storr, *Harper's University: The Beginnings* (Chicago, 1966), 18–20; J. Rice, *Eighteenth Century,* 104–106, 109.

26. Federal Censuses of South Carolina, Colleton County, 1890 and 1900, South Carolina Department of History and Archives; J. Rice, *Eighteenth Century,* 113–27.

some contrast to their hurried present; but my grandmother simply sat, un-touched by regret or pleasant recollection, suspended in time, beyond a thing so positive as waiting. . . . She never laughed, nor even smiled, but turned to the world the thick look that, I believe, had always been there."[27] John An-drew Rice recalled that he, his brothers, and his boy cousins spent their time sharpening machinery, splitting shingles and rails, and repairing various broken-down parts and pieces of the plantation. In the fall they joined in cutting and stripping sugar cane, which was pressed and boiled into syrup at a small, crude mill on the property. Several times a year they joined in the slaughter of hogs and cattle. For all the effort put into the land and its issue, poverty on the run-down farm seemed an inevitable way of life. Only when Father, the family preacher, visited did the son recall special hams and canned goods brought out from their hiding places in the smokehouse and root cel-lar. Bellies sank a bit again as soon as he returned to Chicago.

Schooling for John Andrew and his brothers occurred in a one-room country school, which was a three-mile walk from Grandmother Rice's. One teacher presided over all grades and renewed John Andrew Rice's pro-found doubts about the state of the teaching art: "He had no imagination, his ignorance was profound, he needed the money to go to college . . . these were his qualifications. He was, in fact, the average teacher of his day."[28] This teacher was quick to grab a peach-tree switch and apply it liberally to whip errant students into submission. John Andrew, the smug student who quickly learned more algebra than the teacher could comprehend, was among the few who escaped the switch. While academic opportunities were lacking at the country school, thirteen-year-old John Andrew did undergo an adolescent passage with older classmates schooling him in swear words and hearsay about sexual relations.

The next year, however, John Andrew was sent to a Methodist boarding school in the town of Bamberg, forty miles north of his grandmother Rice's ramshackle plantation home. Thus began his first experience with going away for school, the only type of schooling he would know from then on. For a fourteen-year-old boy who was hard-pressed to call any of the resi-dences he'd known "home," the experience of leaving the plantation held little significance as a rite of passage. A more memorable watershed event was his father's return from the University of Chicago after slightly more than two years. Although he had not managed to finish the Ph.D. he coveted, he did bring with him the new wife he had met there, Launa Darnell, a school

27. J. Rice, *Eighteenth Century,* 121–22.
28. *Ibid.,* 146.

teacher from Tennessee. He also arrived with the news of his first pastorate appointment to one of the more significant southern Methodist churches, Court Street Church in Montgomery, Alabama.

John Andrew, much to his own surprise and that of his relatives, took to his stepmother immediately, deciding to transfer the sensitive protectiveness he had acquired for his own mother to Launa Darnell Rice. Older and at least a bit more worldly than he, however, the new Mrs. Rice hardly needed such assistance. Still, on her way to starting her own family (a half-brother and a half-sister for John Andrew), she was kind and wise with her stepsons. By happy coincidence, she arrived just in time to play a pivotal role in John Andrew's education.[29]

With perhaps more than ordinary teenage mistrust of conventions, fourteen-year-old John Andrew questioned his schooling and the entire notion of education. Later he would offer the following interpretation of the process by which his doubts developed:

> While he was an infant he absorbed knowledge, taking it in through his tissues, without thought or care. Then, in boyhood, he became a collector of birds' eggs, stamps, tobacco tags, baseball averages, dates—anything that can be arranged in series. But if he is to become a man—some do—he grows tired of counting and collecting, and a terrifying thing happens: he ceases to be a scientist; he begins to ask, "What does it mean?" and with the coming of this question there comes the first step into manhood. To know is not enough.
>
> It hit me about the time we moved to Montgomery. Until then I had been a whole, a self-contained universe; but now when voice and shape and thoughts began to change, this other change came, this disrelish for mere knowledge, this hesitant desire for meaning.[30]

When he arrived in Montgomery with his family in 1902, John Andrew was so ambivalent about school that the family agreed he could drop out and get a job. Employed as a collection agent for a furniture store, he received there another type of education from a network of veteran collection workers who knew how to overcharge and pocket money at will. In particular, John Andrew recalled, on this job he first began to understand the plight of the urban black American who was eager to buy on credit, but was a favored target of rip-offs and a central figure in crass jokes among bill collectors.

John Andrew's new stepmother, however, had a different type of education in mind for the youth in whom she readily recognized a capacity for

---

29. *Ibid.*, 153–57; F. Rice, interview with the author, November 24, 1995; W. Rice, interview with the author, January 6, 1993.

30. J. Rice, *Eighteenth Century*, 185.

scholarship. Launa Darnell Rice, as a teacher in Tennessee, had gotten to know Sawney and John Webb, founding brothers of the school that bore their name. Both John Andrew and his father needed to be convinced that this college preparatory school might be the place for the son to make another start at his formal education. Launa Darnell Rice turned out to be just the right person to do the convincing, and by the time he was sixteen, John Andrew was heading for Bell Buckle, Tennessee, and the Webb School.[31]

31. *Ibid.*, 200–201; Laurence McMillin, *The Schoolmaker: Sawney Webb and the Bell Buckle Story* (Chapel Hill, N.C., 1971), 9–11; W. Rice, interview with the author, January 6, 1993.

2

Educating the Educator:
Webb, Tulane, Oxford

William R. Webb, better known throughout his life as "Sawney" Webb, was a bearded, tobacco-spitting Confederate veteran and a rough-hewn product of rural North Carolina. His younger brother, John, was a gentle, almost frail sort who was too young for Civil War service and developed a tendency to wander along dirt roads talking to himself or the sky. The two became known as "Old Sawney" and "Old Jack" to the boys, and even a few girls, who came to Bell Buckle, Tennessee, from throughout the South to attend Webb School. By early in the twentieth century, the institution founded by these unlikely educators became a prestigious preparatory school, and by 1915 it had graduated more boys who went on to become Rhodes scholars than any other single secondary school. The Webb brothers and their school would have a profound and lasting influence on John Andrew Rice.[1]

Before the Civil War, the college preparatory school movement had only a scattered following in the South, although Andover and Exeter had set examples in the North since the eighteenth century. While church-affiliated academies eventually would experience impressive growth, elementary or secondary education in the South before the Civil War generally took place at all-grade boarding schools or among small gatherings of students and teachers who simply set up shop at home or in a small log or frame cabin. Sawney and John Webb confronted one such dwelling in northern North Carolina which their older sister Susan had organized into a school. By the time Sawney Webb was in his teens, another educational endeavor, the J. P. Bingham boarding school, had moved near enough to his home to accommodate the Webb brothers as day students and to provide the Webb family

---

1. McMillin, *The Schoolmaker*, 109–19; *The Handbook of Private Schools* (73rd ed.; Boston, 1992), 508–509.

with much-needed income from a steady stream of boarders among boys who came from miles away. Schools became a way of life for the Webb family.[2]

Sawney's schooling continued through the University of North Carolina. Before graduating from "the Hill," however, he joined one of the student companies being formed to fight for the Confederacy. He came back wounded a year later and continued his schooling a while longer before joining up again. By the time the war was over, he had traveled throughout the South, killed only one man that he knew of, survived malaria, watched his horse "Electricity" shot out from under him, and spent the final days before Appomattox crowded into a Union ship transporting prisoners of war from Virginia to New York. During his stay at the University of North Carolina as a returning veteran, Sawney managed to complete a bachelor's and a master's degree.

By 1869 Sawney Webb was putting his brother John through the University of North Carolina on his salary as a teacher, first back at the Bingham School, then by taking in students at his home, then at a boarding school in Oxford, North Carolina. John, who was the more scholarly of the brothers, had vowed with Sawney to start a school together someday; they came a step closer to doing so when Sawney moved to Tennessee in 1870 to become principal of Culleoka Institute. John joined him during his second year at Culleoka, and fifteen years later they were finally in their own school. The Webb School was located in Bell Buckle, a railroad town fifty miles southeast of Nashville marked by dirt roads and country stores surrounding the train station. The school, founded after that visionary town offered to donate land and to help erect a building, was said to be the first preparatory school west of the Allegheny Mountains.

Perhaps because the Webbs had statewide reputations as superb teachers even before the school ground was broken at Bell Buckle, they raised $12,000 to build their school, a phenomenal sum at the time. They spent $4,000 on constructing the buildings and $8,000 on stocking the library. Students boarded with local villagers, and there was always an overflow group boarding at the homes the Webb brothers had built for their wives and growing families.[3]

The new Webb School became the centerpiece of the town as soon as it

2. Lawrence A. Cremin, *American Education: The Metropolitan Experience, 1876–1980* (New York, 1988); McMillin, *The Schoolmaker,* 11–20.

3. John F. Ohles, ed., *Biographical Dictionary of American Educators* (3 vols.; Westport, Conn., 1978), III, 1361–62; Randolph Elliott, "Old Sawney's," *Atlantic Monthly,* CXXVI (1920), 231–36; McMillin, *The Schoolmaker,* 100–105.

was built on its several fenced acres. A large main building, complete with a two-story arch over the entryway and called "the big room," housed the freshman and sophomore wings. The junior and senior classrooms were situated in additional large wooden buildings on the campus. Sawney Webb most often could be found outdoors on a split-bottom chair leaned against a large beech tree, chewing and spitting and calling boys over to listen to his strings of advice and his homilies. He advised, "Character is an educated will," and appealed, "God gave you a spinal column. Have more backbone than a fishing worm, my son." With a boy who thought he could not learn from his mathematics book, Sawney Webb used what he knew of the author to cajole, "You take that old book, my son, shake your finger at it, and say: 'Professor Wentworth, you doggone old Yankee, there's nothing you can put on these pages that I can't learn!' "[4]

By the time John Andrew Rice arrived at Webb in 1905, the Webb name and traditions were well known. A favored principle was that every boy and girl deserved a chance, even if they could not afford to pay for it. To students who worried about their modest backgrounds, Old Sawney insisted that it was far more important to "go pedigree your ancestors." "Don't talk to me about blue bloods that sit at the foot of the class," students recalled their headmaster intoning. "I'd rather have soapsuds or frogspawn in my veins."[5]

Webb School was home to an eclectic mix of the offspring of farmers and mechanics, doctors and lawyers. Most of the boys who arrived at Webb with young John Andrew Rice were no strangers to fistfights, knives, and brass knuckles. In some reaches of Tennessee, Webb was reputed to be a reform school. However, under the watchful toughness of Sawney and the scholarly affection of John, the Webb School managed a successful combination of classical education and character building that earned it widespread admiration. Woodrow Wilson, when he was president of Princeton University, was so impressed by the students who came from Webb School that he spent a week there with Sawney and John to see what it was all about.[6]

What it was about, as John Andrew Rice came to realize, was a demanding curriculum, rules aimed at self-discipline, responsibility granted to each student for his or her learning, inspired teaching, a readiness for corporal punishment, and expulsion when necessary. A student caught climbing over a fence was required to build a stile where he had climbed; thus, stiles were found almost every twenty feet along the fenced campus. If a student

4. McMillin, *The Schoolmaker*, 112–15.
5. J. Rice, *Eighteenth Century*, 199–205; McMillin, *The Schoolmaker*, 141.
6. J. Rice, *Eighteenth Century*, 201–206; McMillin, *The Schoolmaker*, 156.

plucked a leaf off a tree, he was required to plant a new tree. Profanity was grounds for expulsion, as was telling a lie.

The official school motto became, and remains, "Noli res subdole facere" ("Never do anything on the sly"). As a Confederate veteran, Sawney Webb had shown some sympathy with the Ku Klux Klan; but when the local group pressed him to join, he decided he could not participate in a group that hid themselves behind sheets. The school's rules and stipulations were many, rigorous, and often eccentric. Most were devised by Old Sawney and enforced by an honor code among students. John Webb was more concerned with, and reputedly more adept at, the inspired teaching underlying the school's academic success.[7]

Bearded and blue-eyed, John Webb resembled a slightly less hearty version of his brother. A walnut-sized bump in the middle of his forehead, labeled a "wisdom bump" by some of his acquaintances, convinced students he was the more intellectual of the siblings. They may have been right, even though the bump was the result of a childhood encounter with the horn of a bull. Students generally did not meet up with John Webb in class until their junior and senior years, when he taught them their required two years of Greek, the upper reaches of their four years of Latin, their advanced mathematics (trigonometry and calculus), and history. These, along with English literature and composition and elective physics, comprised the curriculum taught by five teachers when John Andrew Rice attended Webb School along with approximately 150 students.

John Andrew Rice began as a junior at Webb, and he developed an almost immediate affection for Old Jack. Where he viewed Sawney Webb as an arrogant doctrinaire inclined to self-promotion, he found in brother John a teacher who approached his work as a high calling. Rice recalled the younger Webb brother's repeated insistence, "I believe I would have paid to be allowed to teach." Late in the afternoon, John Webb would call softly from his study window, "Books!" to the seniors studying in groups or pairs out on the lawn. They would grab the chairs they carried with them from class to class and create a circle around him. He might read from something seemingly unconnected to their studies and wait to hear whether they would make the connection; or, he might pursue a point from earlier lessons. Rice recalled, "Silence was also speech with him. He had the wisdom seldom to complete a thought for others."[8]

The seniors—approximately thirty in John Andrew Rice's class of 1908

7. W. Rice, interview with the author, January 6, 1993; J. Rice, *Eighteenth Century,* 209–13.
8. J. Rice, *Eighteenth Century,* 222, 208.

—spent virtually all their time under the personal tutelage of Old Jack. They went to his classes, met with him in his office, browsed his library, and engaged him in conversation out on the big field that surrounded the school buildings. Webb rarely tipped his hand about his own thoughts on a subject or the answer to a question, but insisted that his students formulate their own ideas. Rice recalled this example: "Up to that moment I had gobbled books the way a dog bolts his rations, and had just finished off another. 'Mr. Webb,' I said, 'What do you think of *The Clansman?*' He kept his eyes fixed on the window, patted his knee with his right hand, laughed three dry cackles, and said, 'Some people like that kind of thing.' From that time on, no book was my master." John Webb started a class by asking a question. He might be looking for an original idea or a rote recitation, but if what he got was far off the mark of competence, his face would crumble to near tears—some claimed they saw actual tears at times. "It would just break your heart to have Mr. Webb disappointed in you," claimed one senior. "I'd rather have a whipping from Old Sawney than have Mr. John laugh at me."[9]

In later years it would become apparent that John Andrew Rice learned both course content and educational processes at Webb School, and he learned them from both Webb brothers. Where the younger Webb opened young minds by personally connecting with students, his older brother Sawney captured interest by fascinating his pupils with the gifts of the born raconteur. Each morning, after gathering all students and the several teachers for scriptures and prayer, Sawney Webb embarked on a ritual called "morning talk" that might last only minutes or several hours. He turned his personal experiences into moral principles and drew from local example to comment on the state of the world, current events, philosophy, science, religion, or other themes that crossed his brow. In string tie and black coat, with his trademark red beard that eventually grayed, he nearly always held his audience at full attention; and since the various classes at the school simply started and ended when they started and ended, he had no set morning schedule to fit.[10]

By the time John Andrew Rice graduated from Webb, he had proved himself a student with exceptional talents in classical thought and languages, as well as an excellent mind for literature and mathematics. He had proved to himself a notion he would hold to steadfastly throughout his life: "In the process of educating, the teacher is the most important person. Teaching is an

9. Webb School class of 1908, photograph, in possession of W. Rice; J. Rice, *Eighteenth Century*, 209; McMillin, *The Schoolmaker*, 131.

10. Elliott, "Old Sawney's," 233–34.

art, and the teacher, to the degree to which he has acquired that art, is an artist." For Rice, who now believed he had experienced both unacceptable and
exceptional teachers, the activity of teaching had shown itself to be the crucial ingredient in learning; and learning appeared to take place both inside
and outside the classroom and the formal curriculum.[11]

The slow pace of small-town Bell Buckle and the community of scholars
at Webb School proved short-lived for Rice and a vivid contrast to the ca-
cophony of New Orleans, where he arrived shortly after his graduation. His
father had been appointed to a four-year pastorate at Rayne Memorial
Church there, and the two oldest sons were to enter Tulane University as day
students. Even when New Orleans itself appeared noisy and forbidding,
young John Andrew had high hope for his studies at the college. He later recalled his optimism: "Perhaps, although general talk stirred misgivings,
there would be another John Webb, some professor who would tilt his chair
and make a little circle of light."[12]

Tulane University had begun as the University of Louisiana in 1847, but
underwent a name change in 1884 in recognition of a gift from wealthy businessman Paul Tulane. By the time John Andrew Rice and his brother Mike
entered as freshmen in 1908, it was an urban institution populated primarily
with local students who lived at home. The students and the faculty reflected
the eclectic mix of cultures found from the Garden District to the French
Quarter of the bayou city where approximately a quarter million people resided. The primary force running the university consisted of Creole and
American merchants and educators, but these were joined by ample numbers
of German and Irish immigrants on the faculty and in the student body.

During the first decade of the twentieth century, Tulane, like so many
other large colleges and universities, embraced specialization within the disciplines, research endeavors by the faculty, and counting by Carnegie units
for a measure of student progress. The latter innovation prompted Rice to
claim later, "Tulane was my introduction to numerology in education."
While at Tulane, Rice developed his lifelong distaste for the role of registrars
in higher education. Admission, he was informed by the Tulane registrar,
was dependent on evidence of having specific numbers of units in previous
work. The Webb School had not kept track of time in seat or units per semester, but rather had concerned itself solely with learning at whatever pace.
Rice quickly discovered that a large research university might be quite

11. John Andrew Rice, "Appendix," in *Report on Teachers and Teacher Preparation,* Montgomery
County (Md.) Special Commission (Rockville, Md., 1961), 1.

12. J. Rice, *Eighteenth Century,* 225.

different. "In Webb School there had never been a hint that accomplishment could be measured by the clock," he recalled. "The question was, 'Do you know?' In Tulane the question was, 'Do you sit, and, if so, how long?' "[13]

Only by the grace and creativity of John Webb was Rice's preparation in Latin, Greek, German, algebra, geometry, and English reconstituted as units accepted for entrance into Tulane. Later, after a career in higher education that put many registrars in his path, Rice concluded, "If I went into an American institution of higher education to reform it, the first thing I would do would be to shoot the registrar—shoot him; not fire him; shoot him. He's the most awful pest in the whole lot." He was delighted when he eventually attended Oxford University and found only one tiny room housing all registrar functions.[14]

The Tulane that counted course units and time in seat was riding the same wave as the scores of other American universities that had, since the final two decades of the nineteenth century, adapted the German university model. Prior to that time, the American scholarly fare had been influenced by the classical curriculum found at Oxford and Cambridge and marked by instruction in ancient languages and literature, philosophy and theology, and natural science and mathematics. Higher learning reflected the liberal education originally envisioned by colonial colleges as ideal for educating clergy and elite professionals. However, by the mid-nineteenth century, American students had begun to seek out places such as Leipzig and Heidelberg as alternatives to university degrees in England or at home. They liked what they found in Germany, including disciplinary specialization, the central importance of faculty needs and preferences, research aimed at truth seeking, the security of academic freedom, and—compared to the British system—fewer years of study required for graduate degrees. By 1876 Daniel Coit Gilman assumed the presidency of the new Johns Hopkins University to initiate fully the German model at an American institution. The model soon spread to Harvard under Charles William Eliot, and to the state universities, with the University of Michigan and its president James Angell heading the charge.[15]

13. John P. Dyer, *Tulane: The Biography of a University* (New York, 1966), 20–46, 119–68; Edwin A. Davis, *Louisiana: The Pelican State* (Baton Rouge, 1959), 262–82; Bennett H. Wall, ed., *Louisiana: A History* (Arlington Heights, Ill., 1984), 234–56; J. Rice, *Eighteenth Century,* 225.

14. Official Record of John Andrew Rice, Jr., 1911, in Office of the Registrar, Tulane University, New Orleans; J. Rice, interview with Duberman, June 10, 1967; W. Rice, interview with the author, March 29, 1994.

15. For comprehensive discussions of trends in nineteenth-century American higher education, see, for example, John S. Brubacher and Willis Rudy, *Higher Education in Transition: A History of American Colleges and Universities, 1636–1968* (3rd ed.; New York, 1976); Frederick Rudolph, *The American College and University: A History* (2nd. ed.; Athens, Ga., 1990); and Laurence Veysey, *The Emergence of the American University* (Chicago, 1965).

Events at Tulane, while John Andrew Rice was a student there, aptly illustrated the directions of growth and curriculum revision common to many such institutions. The School of Medicine had recently created new departments in pharmacy, dentistry, tropical medicine, and postgraduate medicine. The engineering faculty divided itself among mechanical, chemical, civil, architectural, and sugar engineering. The College of Arts and Sciences, one of the few areas in which enrollment was not experiencing any significant growth, eliminated its Latin program of study, added sociology to its liberal education curriculum, established a chair of pedagogy (and hired for it a new professor with a University of Leipzig doctorate), and adopted a vastly expanded system of electives.[16]

Observing these and similar circumstances in higher education, Rice would later assert: "For a curriculum we have substituted a labyrinth. Few, I take it, regret the passing of the good old fortifying classical curriculum; but we have reason now to distrust the unrestricted elective system. . . . The field of knowledge has been cut up into allotments, some of them small and relatively unimportant to the matter of education, yet tenanted and assiduously cultivated by earnest and industrious young men; and in any attempt to reinstitute a curriculum, these infant industries have to be reckoned with." Rice not only railed against the methods of American higher education, but lamented losses in content that he found most troublesome during his undergraduate years. Later he would charge: "When I went to Tulane, I think American education was at its deadest, lowest point. I had my explanation for it. Classics had dominated. And as any dominant becomes, it had become dead. So they were no longer teaching Greek and Latin ideas, such as they had. They were teaching grammar and nothing else. They were grammarians. Then the scientists came along, and they were very exciting. And they swept the board clean. Classics was out. Then, the grammarians among the scientists took over. And by the time I went to college, they had complete charge, and science was as dead as the classics had ever been, and there was nothing to take its place."[17]

Nevertheless, Tulane provided rewarding opportunities for education by experience for a young man headquartered in a bustling city teeming with intrigue and diversity. Rice was especially eager to take advantage of these opportunities after the first year, when his father was transferred to Fort Worth, Texas, and no longer a resident watchful eye. He bought his first suit jacket, learned to dance, joined Sigma Alpha Epsilon fraternity, and explored

16. Dyer, *Tulane*, 127–45.
17. John Andrew Rice, "The Exceptional Student in the Middle West," *School and Society*, October 31, 1925, pp. 544; J. Rice, interview with Duberman, June 10, 1967.

the seamy side of New Orleans by taking a job as a tenement house inspector. He met the new rich (many of whom owned the tenements) and the chronically poor, including shanty Irish, former slaves, retired prostitutes, and burly stevedores. Eventually, he could almost understand Cajun and colloquial French as he bent an appreciative ear to the stories of tenement dwellers he met on the job.

Halfway into the Tulane bachelor of arts degree that he conquered in three years, Rice was singled out by the academic dean and advised to consider a trip to Baton Rouge the next day to take examinations for entrance to Oxford as a Rhodes scholar. He vaguely remembered an earlier reference to the scholarships when his father, recently returned from the University of Chicago, read a newspaper account of Cecil Rhodes's huge endowment and noted wistfully that he only wished the opportunity had been available when he was younger. He also added the characteristic advice that young John Andrew had learned to ignore: "If you're so smart, why don't you . . . ?"[18]

At the time he competed, John Andrew Rice knew nothing else of the scholarships set forth in the seventh and final will of Cecil Rhodes. Born in England in 1853 with chronic ill health, Rhodes sought the milder climate of South Africa by the time he was eighteen years old. There, in the Kimberly diamond fields, he began to amass the fortune he could only enjoy until he died at age forty-nine. As indicated in his earlier wills, Rhodes had first considered the idea of setting up British-style colleges in the British dominions, especially South Africa. Later he decided that South Africa would be better served if some students selected by competition were funded to attend three years at Oxford University. The natural extension was for other British dominions to be represented, and Rhodes soon included Australia, Canada, and New Zealand in a revised will. Finally, he foresaw a possible contribution of Great Britain to the welfare of all Anglo-Saxon nations and dreamed of uniting the British empire and the United States; and, with that in mind, the American Rhodes scholarships took shape. Rhodes's will directed that a scholar be selected with regard to character and social adeptness, as well as scholastic achievements.

In 1904 when the first Rhodes scholars were named, and for at least twelve years after, competition was not keen. German universities were favored by American scholars who were attracted by the growing prestige of graduate study in those institutions. Furthermore, at Oxford they could add a second bachelor's degree after three years of study, but at a German institution they

18. Official Record of J. Rice, Tulane; J. Rice, *Eighteenth Century,* 239; W. Rice, interview with the author, January 6, 1993.

could acquire a Ph.D. in the same period of time. In order to be considered for Oxford, applicants—including potential Rhodes scholars—needed to succeed in responsions, the Oxford entrance examination that covered Greek and Latin grammar and translation, as well as mathematics. From 1904 until the selection process was changed in 1918, the spaces available for American Rhodes scholars were completely filled in only one year.[19]

With his Webb School training in Greek and Latin and some cramming in arithmetic on the train to Baton Rouge, John Andrew Rice had a good chance of making the first cut in competing for the scholarship that he had not even considered two days prior to the examination. Indeed, he was in the minority that passed. The final hurdle, months later, was an appearance before a state selection committee made up of the presidents of the universities and colleges in the state. In Rice's case, this appearance, again in Baton Rouge, meant shaking hands with committee members and presenting a packet of reference letters obtained both from people who knew him well (John Webb and his father's church connections) and from people who did not know him at all, such as the mayor of New Orleans. He later explained this determined and wide-ranging solicitation of approximately one hundred letters by asserting, "At the time the committee of selection was comprised of college presidents, that is, politicians, and so I played according to the rules." After Rice offered his handshake and presented his letters, the committee deliberated between him and a finalist from Louisiana State University. Two hours later they pronounced Rice a Rhodes scholar.[20]

During the summer of 1911 on his way to England, Rice detoured into Germany to discover what he might be missing. He was struck by the German adherence to form, noticing, "Every time you turned around, if you didn't know something, a sign told you. There was a sign everywhere— 'keep off the grass,' 'leave this there,' whatever." He returned to Berlin and Dresden during some spring and summer breaks, but fumed in letters home that he could not understand why those places were so notable and that he found their orderliness and cleanliness annoying. Cynical about what he perceived of the German mentality and frustrated by the German influence on American higher education, he later charged: "You can't talk to a German about liberty. You just waste your breath. They don't know what the hell you

19. Frank Aydelotte, *The American Rhodes Scholarships* (Princeton, N.J., 1946), 12–19, 65–71; Francis Wylie, *The First Fifty Years of the Rhodes Trust and the Rhodes Scholarships, 1903–1953* (Oxford, Eng., 1955), 53–62; William W. Thayer, "Comments on Rhodes Scholarships in American Periodicals," *American Oxonian*, II (January, 1915), 35–48.

20. J. Rice, *Eighteenth Century*, 241.

mean." Undoubtedly, he arrived at Oxford convinced that he was one scholar who would not have preferred the highly regarded German system.[21]

At Oxford, Rice found a different approach to education than anything he had ever experienced or expected. There were no required textbooks, no prescribed courses, no units to be accumulated. There were, however, expectations about learning that were tested by preliminary examinations (referred to as "mods") at approximately the end of one year, and final examinations ("finals")—written and oral, six hours a day for six days—at the end of three to four years. Lectures and tutors were the heart of the system, with students selecting to attend whichever of dozens of lectures each day that they believed might assist them in their studies. Typically, each term started with students sampling numerous courses (series of lectures), but within weeks attending only the few that seemed most worthwhile. Large initial audiences often dwindled to only a few students by the end of a term.[22]

Each student met with his tutor once a week, invited advice on selection of lectures and book purchases, discussed learning directions and progress, received any reading or writing assignments the tutor might deem appropriate, and submitted a weekly paper. One early Rhodes scholar described the paper requirement in typifying the Oxford learning approach:

> Sometimes my tutor gave me a definite book or chapter to read, sometimes portions of several; he might give merely the titles of the works or leave their discovery wholly to myself. What he tried to obtain from me was a paper in good style dealing with my topic in an original manner in which I might make use of but not copy the ideas of the men I had read—their grist must go through the mill of my own personality. The purpose was, above all, to arouse a critical attitude upon the part of the student who would be given little or no credit for the parrot-like recital of what someone else had written. Not to amass but to elucidate and interpret were the ideals at which he aimed.[23]

John Andrew Rice was assigned to Queen's College, one of twenty-two Oxford colleges that housed the university's more than two thousand students, ranging in size from approximately seventy to three hundred. The colleges were units that were not academically arranged but drew students together by common housing and social and sporting events. Each college

---

21. J. Rice, interview with Duberman, June 10, 1967; John Andrew Rice to Launa Darnell Rice, July 23, 1913, in possession of William C. Rice.

22. Chase B. Mellen, "The Organization of the University of Oxford," *American Oxonian*, II (January, 1915), 16–20; Aydelotte, *Rhodes Scholarships*, 64–70.

23. William D. Wallis, "The Oxford System Versus Our Own," *Pedagogical Seminary* (June, 1912), 6–7.

fielded its own team in every sport and boasted its own tennis courts, athletic fields for cricket and football, and boathouse on the Thames River. Only track athletes had to train and compete on a university field. With small colleges and multiple teams, nearly all Oxford students were involved in some sport. Even John Andrew Rice, who was not naturally inclined toward athletics, participated in rowing, tennis, and golf.[24]

The unit of academic organization was the school. Nine honor schools admitted the most ambitious students to highly demanding study and eventually ranked them according to their performance on final examinations. The range of honors extended from the coveted first-class honors, referred to as a "first," to the dreaded fourth-class honors. All scholarship students, including Rhodes scholars, were required to compete for honors. Students who were not aspiring for an honors degree were considered for pass degrees. In England, the pass was viewed as sufficient only for a career in school teaching or business, while honors was required for a future in higher education, the clergy, or civil service.

When John Andrew Rice studied at Oxford, the honor schools were mathematics, natural sciences, modern languages, jurisprudence, history, theology, Oriental studies, English language and literature, and *literae humaniores* (Greek and Latin classics). In addition, there were degree studies in music, medicine, and surgery; and diploma studies in geography, education, economics, engineering, anthropology, and forestry.[25]

Rice's decision to study jurisprudence stemmed from motivation typical of his age and station. He explained: "I had long decided that I would become rich, but respectably, and so, sharing the Southerner's contempt for business, had fortunately elected to be a lawyer. . . . The School of Jurisprudence was the only one in which I could make an even start with the Englishman. I had better sense than to try 'Greats,' the Oxford word for Classics, in which the native was trained from birth. Also, law was easiest." Rice's initial estimation may have been accurate, as he won first-class honors in law when he was examined upon graduating in 1914. In doing so he became one of seven graduates to earn this highest honor in his class of forty-five Rhodes scholars.[26]

24. Lewis C. Hull, "Athletics at Oxford," *American Oxonian,* I (April, 1914), 21–26; John Andrew Rice, Résumé, Rice Faculty File, College Archives and Special Collections, Rollins College, Winter Park, Fla., 1.

25. Mellen, "The Organization of the University of Oxford," 17–19; Wallis, "The Oxford System Versus Our Own," 12.

26. J. Rice, *Eighteenth Century,* 247–48; "Personal News," *American Oxonian,* I (April, 1914), 114–23.

Although the various schools at Oxford appeared to promote academic specialization, the methods of instruction had the effect of directing students toward a broader course of study. For example, the study of French included relevant science, history, philosophy, sociology, speech physiology, and phonetics. Frank Aydelotte, an early Rhodes scholar who later became president of Swarthmore College, characterized the Oxford academic system as "wonderfully simple. The method is to prescribe not what the undergraduate is supposed to take, but what he is supposed to know, to allow him a certain length of time in which to acquire that knowledge, and then to examine him in order to see whether or not he has acquired it."[27]

That John Andrew Rice would later fondly refer to his Oxford years as "three wonderful years of loafing" was a reflection on the daily routine and deferential treatment of Oxford students. Rice valued the privacy of his two rooms in Queen's College—a "bedder" sparsely furnished with narrow bed, washstand, towel rack, and tin tub; and a "sitter" complete with cannel coal fire, armchairs, bookcases, and large table. And he enjoyed the conviviality of association with other scholars lodged in the great stone residence overlooking a tree-filled quadrangle. A porter took Rice's luggage when he arrived and popped up regularly to carry tennis rackets or book purchases into the student's room. An ever-present "scout" named John was on duty in the lodgings at Queen's to wake him each morning; serve breakfast, lunch, and tea in his rooms; set his fire blazing; and tidy up his rooms.[28]

Although the rather sedentary Rice considered the afternoon routine of rowing or field sports as an ordeal, he discovered ample relief in the remainder of a typical Oxford day. Breakfast, or "brekker" to the students, was the primary occasion for socializing. Two to five students frequently gathered in one sitting room around bacon and eggs, toast and marmalade, filet of sole, and coffee. Conversation, ranging in topics from college athletic events and social plans to good books and favorite lecturers, was the centerpiece of the morning meal. In this regard, John Andrew Rice felt at home, since talk, from gossip to storytelling, was a favorite pastime in his turn-of-the-century South. He had earlier acquired expertise in dialogue and debate, and he loved good conversation. As the beginning of a paunch told, he also loved good food.

Unlike the sociable leisure of breakfast, lunch was a rushed cold buffet to be gulped before an afternoon of rugby, rowing, cricket, or other sport. No

27. Aydelotte, *Rhodes Scholarships,* 66.
28. J. Rice, *Eighteenth Century,* 246; 248–50.

lectures or tutorial appointments were scheduled between 1 and 5 P.M. At 5 P.M. tea and scones punctuated more conversation, which terminated just in time for some individual study before dinner. After dinner there was perhaps a stroll through the streets of Oxford, with cap and gown required after dark, or a smoke with more conversation back at the sitting room. Rice took up the pipe. Weekends held the promise of hikes, dinners out, and wine parties, although some students managed to study more than they socialized. Scholarship required self-discipline and a capacity for independent study amidst numerous opportunities for relaxation, a lesson which may have been the most crucial of all for many Oxford undergraduates.[29]

By the third year at Oxford, however, the undergraduate's life changed dramatically. He was expected to spend his time preparing for final examinations and to back off some from the social tug of his college. Most third-year students retreated to housing off campus with groups of three or four, regulating their lives around independent study.

Rice's letters home, sent to Fort Worth where his father was pastor of the First Methodist Church, were addressed almost exclusively to his stepmother. They revealed a great deal of affection for the woman he now called "mother" and for his young half brother and half sister. He scolded her if she failed to write often enough; he encouraged her to give herself a vacation and join him for a while in England (which she never did); and he closed his letters to her with endearments like "love and kisses" and "kisses to the kids, and save a thousand for yourself." Launa Darnell Rice sent him gifts, small sums of money, and news of the family. In contrast, letters between son and father were exchanged only once or twice during the years young Rice was abroad.[30]

Typically, association with students expected to be future leaders in Great Britain and the United States afforded Rhodes scholars opportunities to establish valuable lifelong networks of friends and contacts. During John Andrew Rice's stay, such opportunities were ample. The Prince of Wales (future King Edward VIII and future Duke of Windsor) was at Magdalene College. Future novelist Christopher Morley was a Rhodes scholar at New College. Joining Rice at Queen's was Edwin Hubble, studying jurisprudence prior to finding his calling in astronomy. But Rice decided the "one brilliant man in

29. A. M. Stevens, "Social Phases of Oxford Life," *American Oxonian,* II (January, 1915), 21–27; Wallis, "The Oxford System Versus Our Own," 7–9.

30. J. Rice to L. Rice, January 13, February 2, 23, June 28, 1913, all in private collection of W. Rice.

Queen's by far was Elmer Davis," who would eventually claim fame as an author, radio commentator, and director of the U.S. Office of War Information during World War II.[31]

Rice enjoyed close enough associations with several British students to receive invitations to stay at their homes during holidays. He spent one particularly grand Christmas vacation at a large country estate, Clopton Manor, owned by the Buckley family. There he got his first experience with being part of the upper class, and he thoroughly enjoyed it. The manor dwellers put on a play for the townsfolk and several dozen manor employees on New Year's Eve, casting Rice as a comedian in his acting debut. Afterwards, close friends and family came into the home for a dance, while the others were treated to a dance in one of the outbuildings. Although he later would gravitate to the decidedly liberal side of any social or political issue, the young Rice observed without criticism this disparity among the classes, writing to his stepmother, "England, you know, is the place for the man who is well off. Everything is arranged for the one who can pay for it, while the one who can't must do the work. The whole country seems like that: plenty of servants at low wages."[32]

The young scholar also was impressed by the life style of the British woman, compared to her American counterpart, noting, "She may not get all the adoration an American is used to, but she doesn't slave herself to death. . . . They have learned that a woman who has had an education and learned something of what life holds shouldn't spend her days wracking her brain over household cares." It is impossible to know whether Rice found the preferred alternative to homemaking to be leisure, employment outside the home, or volunteer service. Considering later directions, his affinity was for educated women with interests—any interests—outside the home.[33]

Former Rhodes scholar Frank Aydelotte still made frequent trips to Oxford as American secretary to the Rhodes Trust and came to influence the course of Rice's life. Aydelotte, the son of a woolen mill owner in the small and prosperous town of Sullivan, Indiana, had easily made a name for himself as a bright scholar and talented football player at the University of Indiana. Arriving in England to begin his Rhodes scholarship in 1905, he had immediately embraced the Oxford ways of life and education. Eventually, as president of Swarthmore College, he would import some of the Oxford phi-

31. "Personal News," *American Oxonian,* I (April, 1914), 114–23; J. Rice, *Eighteenth Century,* 262.

32. J. Rice to L. Rice, December [?], 1912, in W. Rice collection.

33. J. Rice to L. Rice, February 2, 1913, in W. Rice collection.

losophy to the United States, most notably the honors system. Rice and Aydelotte first met when, during Rice's stay at Oxford, Frank Aydelotte arrived to undertake additional work toward a doctorate in literature. During a year-long leave of absence from a faculty position at the University of Indiana, he did not manage to complete his doctorate successfully at that time; but he did manage to pursue a variety of research projects and to become acquainted with the Rhodes scholars then in residence. The year abroad also provided him with an opportunity to invite his younger sister Nell to make a first trip to Europe as the guest of himself and his wife Marie.[34]

Aydelotte, a steady and serious young man, may have had second thoughts about encouraging his sister's visit when Nell fairly immediately captured the attention of the more impetuous and uncompromising John Andrew Rice. This attention was not difficult to explain, for Nell had unblemished, wholesome looks: wavy brown hair, straight white teeth, and creamy skin. Most memorable was her "penetrating gaze with those captivating eyes." Typical descriptions of Nell, over half a century later, mention very pale blue eyes that drew frequent and long gazes from anyone who met her.[35]

During the spring of 1913 Rice's romance with Nell Aydelotte bloomed. He knew for certain that he had met his lifelong partner, and in full bliss he displayed a capacity for sentiment that was almost amusing and decidedly uncharacteristic. "I have found the end of the rainbow at last, and it isn't a pot of gold at all, but the most wonderful girl in the world," he announced to his stepmother. He described Nell as "a glorious girl" of "great courage" who "has got all the qualities that I need in a wife." And he viewed himself as "the happiest and happiest looking man in Oxford."[36]

Waxing introspective about his romance and future with Nell, Rice maintained, "I do believe she will make a better man of me. I have always needed to be loyal to some thing or some person, and I have never yet succeeded in it; but I believe I can now." His unparalleled delight even prompted a rare and lengthy letter to his father, in which he demonstrated much greater respect and affection than he ever recalled, or perhaps admitted to, later in life. "You have always been the best of fathers," the younger Rice insisted, "and I know how much it will mean to have you for my best man friend." Surprisingly, he wrote that he and Nell would like to settle in Texas to be close to the family when he completed his three years at Oxford in 1914. At

34. Frances Blanshard, *Frank Aydelotte of Swarthmore* (Middletown, Conn., 1970), 108–12.

35. F. Rice, interview with the author, February 13, 1993; Richard Andrews, interview with the author, May 11, 1993; Donald Page, interview with the author, June 14, 1993.

36. J. Rice to L. Rice, [n.d.], June 9, July 23, 1913, all in W. Rice collection.

that point, he planned to try his hand at practicing law, although he realized he might need to teach in a high school or college while supplementing his British jurisprudence background with training in American law.[37]

Frank Aydelotte was not at all in favor of romance between Nell and John Andrew Rice, much less their eventual engagement. Although he was compiling an enviable academic record at Oxford, Rice was recognized as an outspoken critic and unpredictable rebel. The Aydelotte family, descended from proper Huguenot stock and valuing hard work and serious business pursuits, was unlikely to embrace the erratic Rice. Frank Aydelotte, especially, was a serious and cautious young man and protective of his sister. Later, family members decided of him, "His middle name was respectability."[38]

However, Nell Aydelotte proved more her mother's daughter in continuing her defiant relationship with John Andrew Rice. Mathilda Brunger Aydelotte was known best in the Aydelotte's adopted home town of Sullivan, Indiana, as a thoughtful nonbeliever—an atheist (uncommon in the late nineteenth century) who was intellectual enough to garner serious attention from local preachers for her ideas and opinions but who rarely joined her outgoing Kentucky-born husband in community social occasions. Nell was the youngest of her three children, with Frank the oldest and Will in the middle. Nell had followed in the footsteps of her revered oldest brother by graduating from the University of Indiana. Never the energetic achiever that his brother became, Will arrived home from World War I afflicted with what appeared to be chronic shell shock. Although Will was slow and dazed, rarely able to hold onto a job or engage in a conversation, John Andrew Rice would eventually decide, "He was the nicest person in the family."[39]

During the summer of 1913 Nell returned to Sullivan to work in the local library and later served briefly as the city librarian for Mount Vernon, Illinois. Undoubtedly, Rice's determination in 1914 to find respectable employment immediately upon receipt of his Oxford bachelor of arts degree was influenced by his decision to marry Nell. Regardless of his first honors in jurisprudence, however, he did not pursue his earlier ideas about preparing himself to practice American law. He felt that some of his most important learning to date had been in the area of education itself, and his high regard for fine teaching may have loomed large in his decision to try the academic life. He thought that perhaps like John Webb or the best of the Oxford

37. J. Rice to John Andrew Rice, Sr., May 24, 1913, in possession of William C. Rice.
38. William C. Rice to Katherine C. Reynolds, October 18, 1993, in author's possession.
39. Blanshard, *Frank Aydelotte,* 8–18, 84; F. Rice, interview with the author, February 13, 1993; Sullivan (Ind.) *Daily Times,* December 30, 1914, p. 18.

tutors and dons, he could illuminate young minds. In May, just before his graduation, he wrote to Webb School to ask if there might be an opening for him on the faculty for the coming year.[40]

40. William R. Webb, Jr., to John Andrew Rice, May 31, 1914, in William R. Webb, Jr., Correspondence, Webb School Archives, Bell Buckle, Tenn. In his letter to Rice, William Webb indicates that he is responding to a letter from Rice; however, this letter from Rice has not been located.

3

Upstart Teacher, Unlikely Scholar

As his Rhodes scholarship days drew to a close, Rice received a response to his inquiry about employment at Webb School. The return letter, however, came not from Sawney or John Webb, but from William Webb, Jr., Sawney Webb's son, who was widely known as "Son Will." This event in itself was a clear indicator that Webb School had changed substantially since Rice's departure six years before. Old Sawney Webb had gone to Washington, D.C., in 1913, appointed by the Tennessee legislature to serve out the United States Senate term of Robert L. Taylor, who had died in office. When Sawney arrived in the capital, he found a number of his former students already in residence, including Attorney General Watt Gregory, Under Secretary of State Norman Davis, and Commissioner of Education John Tigert. Another Webb graduate, Ned Carmack, had been the other senator of the Tennessee delegation until he was assassinated two years prior to Sawney's arrival. Senator Webb quickly became popular with the press and the public, mainly for his humble roots and plain speaking; nevertheless, he soon decided that this would be his one experience with public life.

Old Jack Webb was getting very old indeed. He was more than ever prone to wander the surrounding hills talking to himself. Sawney had relieved him of all administrative work and accompanied him on any travel. Son Will, never well liked by John Andrew Rice, had been made the third principal in 1908 and by 1914 was very much in charge.[1]

Son Will undoubtedly had his own reservations about employing John Andrew Rice, and he replied to Rice's inquiry with a mixed message of invitation and discouragement: "We have a vacancy in our own faculty next year

1. McMillin, *The Schoolmaker*, 148–203; Rice, *Eighteenth Century*, 218–22.

and will be very glad to have you fill it, if you wish to do so. The place pays only $1,000. As a matter of fact, I expect you can get more if you can only find the place." However, Rice did not find another place and instead began teaching at Webb School that fall.[2]

During Christmas break, Rice married Nell Aydelotte. Perhaps reflective of continuing disapproval from the Aydelotte family, the wedding was not held in Nell's hometown. Rather, the ceremony took place at St. John's Methodist Episcopal Church in St. Louis, Missouri, where Rice's father had been sent only months earlier as the new pastor. Of Nell's family, only her brother Frank and sister-in-law Marie traveled to St. Louis for the ceremony.[3]

Nell quickly won the hearts of Rice's faculty colleagues and their wives. She was considered as lovely as she was gracious, and she undoubtedly helped increase Rice's standing among his colleagues. The first year for the couple was a classic extended honeymoon that prompted Rice's stepmother, Launa Darnell Rice, to recall later that she had never seen two people so much in love as the young Rices during that time. Nell was adept at homemaking and socializing while also maintaining her own bright individuality. While at Bell Buckle, in 1916 she gave birth to John Andrew Rice III. To her great sorrow he died only days into his infancy.[4]

Rice himself was not unanimously well regarded at Webb. Son Will, in a letter to his brother Thompson, later recalled of him:

> When he taught here he was excessively lazy. There was an outbreak of sore eyes in school. The boys who had it were out of school two or three days and were then ready to work again. John Andrew also had the trouble. He stayed out of school entirely for a week. Every afternoon for the next four weeks he telephoned me that his eyes hurt so that he could not teach and requested me to take his afternoon work for him. I later found that he was spending those afternoons reading aloud to his wife.
>
> He had a class in algebra. Three-fourths of his boys failed on his examination. . . . I then discussed it with John Andrew. He told me that he hated algebra and to be very frank he had made no effort to teach the class, that he had used the time for other purposes.

From the earliest stages in his professional career, Rice's response to academic disinterest or disapproval vacillated between laziness and rebelliousness, or

2. W. Webb to J. Rice, May 31, 1914, in Webb Correspondence.

3. "Personal News," *American Oxonian,* II (April, 1915), 120; Sullivan (Ind.) *Daily Times,* December 30, 1914, p. 18.

4. Frank A. Rice to Katherine C. Reynolds, December 8, 1994, and William C. Rice to Katherine C. Reynolds, April 27, 1994, both in author's possession.

sometimes a combination of both. He had little stomach for teaching subjects that could not readily capitalize on his bias for Socratic questioning and urge students to examine their values and assumptions. He disparaged mathematics as "pure in the sense of being furthest removed from experience."[5]

On the other hand, Rice would have loved to have taken over John Webb's work with the seniors when, by 1916, Old Jack became too ill to teach. However, by this time he had alienated Son Will and Old Sawney on a number of counts. One of these, stemming from his protective affection for John Webb, was his conviction that the growing prominence of Sawney's activities outside school had led to self-aggrandizement at his younger brother's expense. Not one to let a personal conviction go unheralded, Rice undoubtedly gave ample notice of the view he later expressed in print: "John Webb never thought he knew enough. Sawney read the daily paper and became a prophet. . . . The actor became well known while the scholar's fame spread slowly. Sawney let it be known to him that he regarded him as 'only a teacher.' "[6]

As a fellow faculty member, Rice's heart poured out to the ailing Old Jack. They read together from volumes in John Webb's floor-to-ceiling, book-lined study, and they talked about ideas late into the night. Rice continued to listen intently to the wisdom of the man who had been his first real teacher; but he caught intimations that the Webb brothers' relationship was uneasy and that Sawney was nudging his brother John slowly but surely away from Webb School affairs. John Webb's wife, Lily, protective of her husband and angry with similar suspicions, no longer allowed Sawney into their house. Old Jack, who had never been known to carp or complain, let it slip to Rice, "I no longer have any voice in running the school."[7]

One day during the winter of 1916, when John Andrew Rice was taking a walk in Bell Buckle, he was summoned to come quickly to an emergency. He found John Webb stumbling alongside the railroad track, barely able to speak. The stroke he had suffered rendered him unable to continue teaching. By spring he was dead. Sawney Webb determined that his brother's partnership interest in the Webb School was never intended to survive his death; nothing had been put in writing to refute this claim. However, John Webb and his family had intended that one day his son Albert and son-in-law Stewart Mims would become principals. Since Son Will was not particularly

5. William R. Webb, Jr., to Thompson Webb, January 1, 1942, in Webb Correspondence; J. Rice, "Fundamentalism and the Higher Learning," 589.

6. J. Rice, *Eighteenth Century,* 218–19.

7. McMillin, *The Schoolmaker,* 155–59.

popular with students and with some faculty, Old Jack's family believed that Albert and Stewart were at least as deserving to be principal as he. When Sawney Webb offered John's widow five thousand dollars to resolve the dispute, Lily turned him down and hired the best lawyer she could find: Webb School graduate Walter Armstrong, who would later become president of the American Bar Association. The final settlement reputedly was fifteen thousand dollars to eliminate John Webb's family from Webb School.[8]

John Andrew Rice ended his teaching career at Webb School just two months after John Webb's death. The old teacher's influence remained with Rice throughout his life, not so much for what he taught or even how he taught it, but for what he demonstrated to Rice about the power of the relationship between teacher and students. Rice later explained, "By simply being what he was, he gave me the idea that teaching—pursuing ideas, working toward truth, wondering, talking in the give-and-take way—was the greatest, most thrilling and satisfying business in life. He taught all the time, especially when he was not holding class. We students followed him around; he talked with us, and the big question always was: what is it all about? . . . He was a hero to me then, and he remained heroic to the end of his days."[9] Perhaps to launch a more satisfactory teaching career with older students, or perhaps to face old resentments head on, John Andrew Rice next decided to enroll in the doctoral program in classics at the University of Chicago, the institution his own father had embraced while leaving him in the poverty of his paternal grandmother's home. Wasting no time at the close of the Webb school year, he arrived in Chicago with Nell in June to begin summer quarter classes.

John Andrew planned to be the first in his family to complete a Ph.D., and for a time it seemed he might accomplish this goal. The University of Chicago fostered the reputation for excellence in higher education that had begun twenty years earlier when William Rainey Harper was president and John Dewey headed the departments of philosophy and pedagogy. While Rice found there some of the same disciplinary partitioning and unit counting he had frowned upon at Tulane, he also found a high regard for classics, including an academic journal in that area published by the university. He interacted happily with learned faculty and challenging student peers, including his old Oxford friend Elmer Davis.

During his first year of study (1916–1917) Rice was granted a small student stipend of $180, but for his second year he was awarded a full graduate

8. *Ibid.,* 158–59; J. Rice, *Eighteenth Century,* 221–22.
9. Louis Adamic, *My America* (New York, 1938), 622.

fellowship of $320. With a bit of savings added, Nell and John Andrew Rice could just manage to survive. For John Andrew Rice, however, a life style of scraping by presented no real problem. The legacy of his boyhood on the move was a disdain for ownership of material items and little respect for any that happened to come his way.[10]

During 1917, the couple became parents of a son who would survive infancy and thrive. They named him Frank Aydelotte Rice. As his third year of graduate study commenced, along with election to another fellowship, John Andrew Rice was beginning to view the university less with scholarly fascination and more with impatience. He was taking three courses a quarter, including summer, in Greek and Latin grammar, literature, philosophy, and history. He read Homer, Plato, Catullus, and others; and he studied at length Greek and Latin tragedy and Roman comedy. He quickly compiled a record of all A's and B's in twenty-five courses taken in his Latin and Greek studies major.[11]

However, after nine academic quarters, the prescription of what still remained for him to obtain a degree—comprehensive examinations and a dissertation—loomed very large for Rice, a student who had little appreciation for scholarly research and little ability to persist in something he did not enjoy. Although energetic in thought and conversation, Rice proved lethargic when scholarly research and writing required him to perform rigorous legwork and precise investigation. Neither the joy of scholarship nor the possibility of personal accomplishment could motivate him to tackle a dissertation, although he did eventually select Latin professor C. H. Beeson as his dissertation chair and determined that his topic would be somewhere in the area of Roman law. However, academic tenacity was missing. Somewhat softening this judgment, H. W. Prescott, chairman of the Latin department, later mentioned in a reference letter for Rice, "His only defect is slowness in getting things done."[12]

World War I offered relief. At the end of the summer quarter in 1918, Rice decided to turn down his third-year fellowship offer in favor of a post in the War Department in Washington, D.C. There he was assigned to the

10. F. Rice, interview with the author, February 13, 1993; Fellowship Application of John Andrew Rice, November 10, 1926, in John Andrew Rice File, Archives of the John Simon Guggenheim Memorial Foundation, New York.

11. Official Record of John Andrew Rice, Jr., 1925, in Office of the Registrar, University of Chicago.

12. F. Rice, interview with the author, February 13, 1993; W. Rice, interview with the author, January 6, 1993; Fellowship Application of J. Rice, November 10, 1926, and of H. W. Prescott, November 22, 1926, both in J. Rice File, Guggenheim.

codes and ciphers branch of the military intelligence division. He stayed at this work until 1919, when he returned for a final summer quarter at University of Chicago. He finished his coursework at that time, but did not return again until 1925 to take and pass comprehensive examinations in his Latin and Greek major, as well as language examinations in French and German. While these examinations advanced him to Ph.D. candidacy, he never managed to tackle the dissertation that would complete his degree.[13] In this regard, Rice followed precisely in his father's footsteps. And like his father, who eventually joined the faculty of Southern Methodist University, he would find himself forging a career in higher education without the uppermost credential. Rice outwardly shrugged off the issue, knowing full well that the degree was no assurance of fine teaching or even continued scholarship. Undoubtedly, though, his lack of a doctorate would create some internal gnawing, however unconscious, and may very well have contributed to a diminished self-image.

After a year in military intelligence, Rice again found himself on the job market, with a preference for teaching but still without the credentials required by many colleges and universities. Through his father, he found a teaching position at Soldan High School in the St. Louis public school system and moved his small family to the city where the senior Rice still presided over the largest Methodist church in town. After only a few months, however, he received word of an offer of a teaching position he greatly desired: associate professor of classics at the University of Nebraska. Good luck and good timing had favored him. It was the first year in a decade that the University of Nebraska had seen fit to hire faculty members who had not earned any of their degrees there, and the classics department chair had dragged his feet about filling a vacancy until he was desperate. Competition was dulled by faculty salaries that were commensurate with western salaries but lower than those at eastern universities, and by the University of Nebraska's decision to decline participation in the faculty pension plan initiated and funded by Andrew Carnegie. After a fifteen-minute interview, Rice was appointed. His annual salary, at two thousand dollars, was below his pay for high-school teaching in St. Louis, but he found the opportunity to join a university faculty irresistible.[14]

13. Fellowship Application of J. Rice, November 10, 1926, in J. Rice File, Guggenheim; Official Record of J. Rice, 1925, University of Chicago.
14. Fellowship Application of J. Rice, November 10, 1926, in J. Rice File, Guggenheim; J. Rice, *Eighteenth Century,* 271–72; Robert N. Manley, *Centennial History of the University of Nebraska* (Lincoln, 1969), 229–33.

Lincoln, Nebraska, situated at a confluence of railroad lines that fed an agricultural empire, was still considered part of the new frontier by many east-
erners. With its wide, straight streets and flat, grassy terrain, it enjoyed the
economic good fortune of steady growth and the vibrancy of housing the
state government as well as the state university that had opened its doors in
1871. Sam Avery, chancellor of the University of Nebraska since 1908, was
a rugged individual from the Nebraska plains who had arrived in Lincoln via
a doctorate in chemistry at Heidelberg University and a faculty post at the
University of Idaho. Given to cheap and ill-fitting clothes, few words, and
no pretense (not even so much as pretending to like football or alumni dinners), he was a studious and shrewd observer of human character. Faculty
frequently complained of Avery's lack of polish and proudly provincial out-
look. They saw little of the scholar, or even of the laboratory chemist, in the
man who had first entered the work force as a farmer, a lumberyard hand, and
a school teacher.[15]

After Rice had been on campus for approximately three years, Avery recognized in him a kindred spirit in candor, humor, and earthiness. Rice recalled fondly occasions when the chancellor would phone late at night to
summon him to his study for hours of chat. Generally, Avery then recounted
to Rice past and present struggles with regents, legislatures, and faculty—all
of whom he usually handled with finesse, alternating well-timed candor
with silent maneuvering.[16]

Avery must have had his hands full. He was known to be highly supportive
of his faculty, yet he needed to satisfy a group of five very involved and very
conservative trustees skimmed from the top of Nebraska's wealthiest local
commercial interests and characterized by Upton Sinclair as "a small board
of the big insiders." After a visit to the campus in 1921, Sinclair observed,
"All of these gentlemen know money; they know nothing whatever about
education, yet they guide the thinking of some eight thousand students. A
study of promotions and salaries reveals the usual fact, that instructors who
deal with commercial subjects have been advanced far beyond those whose
humble task is the improving of the students' minds."[17]

Sam Avery's method of dealing with people—trustees, faculty, alumni,
and students—became a course in human behavior for John Andrew Rice.
Avery studied people by their actions, listened at length, asked a few well-

15. Manley, *Centennial History*, 187–88; J. Rice, *Eighteenth Century*, 270–71.
16. J. Rice, *Eighteenth Century*, 272–80.
17. Sinclair, *The Goose Step*, 334–35.

placed questions, and, when necessary, made strikingly candid observations about the situation at hand. Rice was impressed by Avery's flair for gathering information and forging consensus without divulging his own preferences. He recalled that Avery "never, as long as I knew him, said, 'This is what I believe and this not.' The process was inductive and gauged to the reception of the pupil, for that was what I soon became. . . . I was discovering something I had never known before, something that Methodism had never taught me: that a human act is a human being acting, and that what he is colors, tones, even transmutes, what he does."[18]

The University of Nebraska also provided Rice with his first forum as an adult for studying the undergraduate experience from the outside. The experience shaped his resolve that undergraduate education would be his life-long interest and involvement. In his Greek and Latin classes, he began to test his notions about the crucial role of the teacher in the development of the student. "My education didn't begin until I went to Nebraska," he later insisted. "Up to then, I sort of floated along—through Tulane, a stupid place; through Oxford, a wonderful place." Gradually, his classes became more and more conversational, with discussions continuing as students walked with him from the classroom or ventured to his office.[19]

Rice decided, somewhat to his own surprise, that students at Nebraska represented "the best native intelligence I have ever seen. . . . If the intelligence of Nebraska students had been trained to its best, they could easily have made over America." His ideas about students and education in the Cornhusker State represented a turning point for Rice, marking the first time he would apply his impressive talents for critical thought broadly to the issue of higher education, rather than narrowly to the subject of his own higher education. In a pattern that would become characteristic of Rice's speaking and writing, however, his critical thought more often led him to expose problems than to propose solutions. For example, he decided while he was at Nebraska that the promising midwestern undergraduates were being cheated by what he saw as tremendous shortcomings in university education, observing, "They had in them, many of them and some of the faculty, the toughness that had created the West, the spirit of the second great migration, and being tough and intelligent and ignorant, they, more than any students in America, would have known the meaning of an education in and for democracy. But they got neither. The curriculum was like a cafeteria table,

18. J. Rice, *Eighteenth Century,* 276.
19. J. Rice, interview with Duberman, June 10, 1967.

except in the proportion of unpalatable dishes. One thing was as good as another; that was what they were told. They found out for themselves that one thing was no better than another."[20]

In his first published article about the state of higher education, Rice extolled meritocracy. In a 1925 issue of the journal *School and Society,* he charged that typical university fare for undergraduates was treated as a menu marked by "a standard not of excellence, but of mediocrity." Based on a paper he had presented at a conference of educators at Iowa State University, the article contended: "We have, in our eagerness to preserve the good, sometimes forgotten that we also have a duty elsewhere, to the best. Not that one begrudges the mediocre man his chance; only, let his mediocrity be not quite so splendid. If we must sing the average, let us not call it divine."[21]

Rice was particularly aggrieved regarding exceptional students in the arts and humanities, which he referred to as "still the home of learning." In this case he did advocate a solution, one he had seen as successful at Oxford and that was recently adopted in the United States at Swarthmore College, where Frank Aydelotte had been named president in 1921. Students who might be ready for challenging scholarship in one or more areas he proposed should pursue honors work. Rice supported his brother-in-law's efforts to spread the honors concept nationwide, suggesting that exceptional students should not spend four years filling up hours and credits toward majors and minors. Instead, in their last two undergraduate years, they should be granted greater personal initiative to explore areas of scholarly interest. Rice envisioned this end result: "Caught at this point in his career, and allowed to work in an atmosphere of freedom, he [the student] may catch the spirit of adventure that is the real scholar's."[22]

Observing undergraduates, Rice suggested there were two types of exceptional students, both standing to benefit from honors work. He labeled one the "young grammarian," a student who enjoyed knowledge acquisition and truth seeking in a detached way that did not need philosophical integration. Undoubtedly, Rice viewed skilled science and mathematics students in this category. The other type he called the "young philosopher," a student "for whom ideas have a quality, as it were, of personality. . . . Life is to him an adventure."[23]

Classes in Greek and Latin with Professor Rice soon became well known

20. J. Rice, *Eighteenth Century,* 287–88.
21. J. Rice, "The Exceptional Student in the Middle West," 544.
22. *Ibid.,* 545.
23. *Ibid.*

throughout the University of Nebraska for thought-provoking discussions. He prompted students to grapple with issues that might begin with Plato or Socrates but were likely to range far from these thinkers. Discussions often continued with one or more students joining Rice in his office, which was located in the massive brick University Hall erected in 1871. His cubicle was the old belfry of this first building on campus, complete with a frayed bell rope swaying in a circle of pipe smoke that lingered above his head. His student following was a mixed lot. Students from numerous colleges selected Rice's Greek or Latin courses for electives. The number of departmental majors grew from several dozen to several hundred during his seven years at the University of Nebraska, far outstripping even the university's nearly threefold rise in matriculation during a postwar student boom.[24]

One student, Josephine Frisbie, later recalled that Rice was "perhaps the most stimulating student influence at the University of Nebraska during the late '20s. His classes in Greek attracted alert students from all the colleges. Other faculty members were always at a loss to analyze this student admiration. Privately, we students used to remark that we were sure, not that Mr. Rice looked like Socrates, but that Socrates must have looked like Mr. Rice."[25] Frisbie had taken only one freshman year class from the Socratic professor when she found she had to leave school for a spinal operation. Rice spent an afternoon meeting with her in his office and then taking her to the library to select twenty books to read during her recuperation.

Another University of Nebraska student was so impressed with Rice that she remembered him fifty years later when she was driving to Florida from the Midwest and saw a sign for Bell Buckle, Tennessee. When she arrived at Webb School, she entered the president's office announcing that "the man who was the greatest influence in my life, while I was at the University of Nebraska, used to talk about Webb School." When she was introduced to William Rice, grandson of John Andrew and then a teacher at Webb, she explained, "He had a way of teaching us to think for ourselves. Suddenly, we were reading the classics for real questions to be answered for oneself, not just for things to be studied for exams."[26]

The years in Lincoln were enjoyable for the Rice family. Their second child, Mary Aydelotte Rice, was born in 1920, blessed with Nell's stunning blue eyes. Nell and John Andrew Rice carved out an active social life, at-

24. Josephine Frisbie, "Rice v. Socrates," *Time,* December 14, 1942, p. 9; Manley, *Centennial History,* 229–33; F. Rice, interview with the author, February 13, 1993.

25. Frisbie, "Rice v. Socrates," 9.

26. W. Rice, interview with the author, January 6, 1993.

tending an endless round of dinner parties, dances, bridge parties, and faculty picnics. They were delighted that their children enjoyed good times with nearby playmates. The Rices later looked back upon the Nebraska years as the happiest times they knew as a family.[27]

Rice found that faculty life left ample time for family life, and he spent hours reading aloud to his children and entertaining them with stories about the South and about Webb School. He was a masterful storyteller, fond of dry humor and endings with a twist, and capable of leaving Frank and Mary spellbound. A memorable voice—smooth, low, and only softly southern, with lilt rather than drawl—was one of the more commanding features of this five-foot, seven-inch, slightly bulging and bespectacled professor. Favorite family reading included Joel Chandler Harris' Uncle Remus stories, with Rice expertly intonating the dialects of Brer Rabbit, Brer Fox, Mr. Possum, Old Man Tarrypin, and the others.[28]

John Andrew Rice and his brother-in-law Frank Aydelotte began to forge a professional relationship that promised to overcome the reservations Aydelotte had had about his sister's marriage. Aydelotte, still serving as American secretary to the Rhodes Trust, taught English at the Massachusetts Institute of Technology for six years prior to his advancement in 1921 to the presidency of Swarthmore College. The brothers-in-law corresponded throughout the first several years of Aydelotte's Swarthmore presidency, when Frank was first promoting there and nationwide the honors program modeled on Oxford. Typically, Rice was late in responding to Aydelotte's requests for information about planned family trips or for names of faculty members who might speak at conferences; Aydelotte had often to resort to a second letter or an appeal to Nell. Aydelotte and his wife were hospitable about sharing their large home outside Philadelphia, and the Rice family stopped there whenever they journeyed east. At Rice's request, the Aydelottes even entertained other University of Nebraska faculty members when they traveled in the area.[29]

Rice was promoted to chair of the Department of Classics at the University of Nebraska in 1925, perhaps in response to his gift for interesting students in Greek and Latin languages and philosophies and perhaps in recognition of his close relationship with Chancellor Avery. However, considering

27. F. Rice to Reynolds, December 8, 1994.
28. F. Rice, interview with the author, February 13, 1993.
29. Blanshard, *Frank Aydelotte,* 121–57; J. Rice, "The Exceptional Student in the Middle West," 543–47; Frank Aydelotte to John A. Rice, October 13, November 1, 13, 1924, John A. Rice to Frank Aydelotte, October 30, 1924, August 30, 1926, all in Personal Papers of Frank A. Aydelotte, Friends Historical Library, Swarthmore College, Swarthmore, Pa.

his stormy relations with many faculty colleagues and some trustees, the appointment was at least somewhat unusual. His caustic candor, so often aimed at demonstrating to others the shortsightedness of their ideas or the shortcomings of their institutions, was viewed as arrogant and abrasive by those on the receiving end of his frontal assaults. "I never had any tact in my life," Rice later accurately assessed; and he never wanted any.[30]

Rice's stinging remarks at faculty meetings were sometimes offered jokingly, but rarely received in that vein. Typical was a remark to a dean who had successfully pushed for an honorary degree to be bestowed on a deserving individual. "Well, what did you get out of it?" Rice asked him afterwards in an attempt at combining cynicism with humor. The dean, however, in reporting the exchange to Sam Avery, clearly viewed the remark as a charge rather than a chuckle.[31]

The polite respect of collegiality was something Rice could neither acquire nor feign. Instead, he readily resorted to unprompted and ill-mannered aggressiveness, as if frustration and anger boiling close to the surface of his personality suddenly overflowed. He enjoyed telling his colleagues that he had taken a survey among them and found most would prefer to be in an occupation that better suited them—real estate. Sam Avery, at wits' end with his erratic soul mate, suggested, "Why don't you keep your mouth shut, Rice? If you would just keep it shut for, say, six months or a year, I could raise your salary. You know I can't do it now the way you talk."[32]

Rice was not without friends on the faculty, however. Particularly, he enjoyed the company of literature professor and notable literary figure Louise Pound. Some faculty colleagues such as professor of philosophy Hartley Burr Alexander and professor of education Oscar H. Werner were drawn to Rice's outspoken candor and his willingness to confront directly anything of which he disapproved. For example, Rice risked his friendship with Sam Avery to join a small group of faculty friends who were conspiring against administration policies in order to win faculty pay raises. Later he understood that his relationship with Avery transcended academic politics and managerial realities, insisting, "I loved Sam Avery and he loved me."[33]

Oscar Werner joined the faculty four years after Rice and soon became chair of the Department of Elementary and Rural Education. His friendship with Rice, as well as his respect for Rice's classroom teaching ability and

---

30. J. Rice, interview with Duberman, June 10, 1967.
31. J. Rice, *Eighteenth Century,* 280.
32. F. Rice, interview with the author, February 13, 1993; J. Rice, *Eighteenth Century,* 280.
33. J. Rice, interview with Duberman, June 10, 1967.

scholarly grasp of his subject matter, enabled him to make allowances for his colleague's frequently eccentric and impolitic behavior. He defended Rice to an academic acquaintance who inquired about the classics professor's liberal attitudes on social and political issues, explaining, "The old Greeks and Romans lived under conditions which were much closer to nature than we do. The self-imposed controls which we have developed in matters of sex, economic and political relationships were not customary then. Hence I think it is quite to be expected that a professor of classics will preach free love, object to social bondage of any sort and believe in freedom of a type quite incompatible with our present notion of culture. This conception of ancient freedom is what caused most of Rice's trouble here [at University of Nebraska]."[34]

When Chancellor Avery became fatally ill in 1927 and requested an indefinite leave of absence, John Andrew Rice lost his protection from those colleagues and even trustees who were growing increasingly impatient with what they perceived as his arrogance and insult. He surmised that a new chancellor would make his life miserable if he stayed on. Additionally, he understood that many of his faculty colleagues, even some of his early defenders, had lost patience with his determination to bait, to shock, and generally to shake up the fragile concord so crucial to academic collegiality. While he could still enthrall his students, his effectiveness in department and university affairs was stymied by hostility from increasing numbers of other professors. One instance that convinced him of his growing disfavor was the announcement in 1927 of a "graduate faculty" selected by a faculty committee that had been appointed by the new dean of graduate studies. When Rice was not included among the select new group, he decided he was being penalized for his "attitude toward research," demonstrated in his numerous and open potshots at the research of colleagues whom he felt published insignificant pieces in esoteric journals read only by a handful of scholars. However, it is also likely that the appointing committee was influenced by Rice's continuing status as a Ph.D. candidate who had yet to complete the dissertation.[35]

One of Rice's options at the time of Avery's departure was to tackle some research that might allow him to complete his doctorate. In fact, he had begun working toward securing funding to support such an endeavor as early as 1925 when the John Simon Guggenheim Memorial Foundation was formed

---

34. Oscar H. Werner to Willard Wattles, May 10, 1933, in John A. Rice Faculty File, Special Collections, University Archives, University of Nebraska, Lincoln.

35. John A. Rice to Henry Allen Moe, April 1, 1927, in J. Rice File, Guggenheim.

to support research and creative projects of established scholars and artists wishing to work abroad. Frank Aydelotte was Senator John Simon Guggenheim's first choice to head the foundation built on a family fortune accumulated in the nineteenth-century copper industry. Aydelotte opted to remain at Swarthmore and to accept only the chairmanship of the foundation's educational advisory board; but he suggested Henry Allen Moe, a Rhodes scholar from the class of 1919, for the directorship. Within a month after the availability of Guggenheim fellowships was announced in February, 1925, Sam Avery corresponded with Aydelotte and Moe to suggest they consider John Andrew Rice for support of a research year abroad. Appropriately wary that Aydelotte would want to avoid the appearance of giving special treatment to his brother-in-law, Avery appealed to him, "I hope that you will not discriminate against Mr. Rice on account of the family connection. There is such a thing as being too upright in such matters. Besides, the initiative was entirely my own, and Mr. Rice would be the last one to ask you for any special favors."[36]

Avery's fond hope was to set Rice on a stable academic career that might soften his impolitic nature. He considered Rice one of the brightest faculty members at the University of Nebraska, recognized his exceptional ability to inspire students, and cared enough to want to help Rice realize his academic potential. But he also knew that Rice had not yet demonstrated the patience or perseverance required of a real scholar. Perhaps a year in Rome, supported by a combination of Guggenheim funding and partial pay from the University of Nebraska, would inspire him to do scholarship and complete a Ph.D. in classics.[37]

By the time the Guggenheim Foundation was ready to recruit its first group of fellows in 1926, Rice had taken an interest, quite by accident, in a new area of scholarship: eighteenth-century British literature. During a trip to Omaha, he had visited the rare book collection of Dr. and Mrs. LeRoy Crummer. There he found a first edition of Jonathan Swift's *A Tale of a Tub* that originally had belonged to the author's cousin Thomas Swift and included the cousin's 1704 marginal manuscript notes. Examining the handwritten notes, Rice determined that the story generally attributed to Dean Swift in fact may have been written by or in collaboration with his cousin, and he longed to investigate that possibility. Although it was doubtful that re-

36. Blanshard, *Frank Aydelotte*, 244–54; Sam Avery to Frank Aydelotte, March 31, 1925, in J. Rice File, Guggenheim.

37. Avery to Aydelotte, March 31, 1925, and Sam Avery to David A. Robertson, March 31, 1925, both in J. Rice File, Guggenheim.

search in English literature could result in a dissertation acceptable for a Ph.D. in Greek and Latin, Rice had long enjoyed Swift's writing and was intrigued by the idea of detective work among Swift papers and manuscripts. Oddly, as if almost deliberately to avoid putting into place the final puzzle piece that would define him as a scholar and academic, Rice had little concern about dissertation bridges burned when he veered off the certain path to completing his degree in classics. Displaying an unfortunate tendency that would mark other life choices, he sabotaged long-term achievement that might have led to greater personal definition and self-fulfillment.

When Henry Allen Moe heard from Frank Aydelotte of Rice's Swift discovery, he wrote to Rice to suggest that the topic might merit application for a Guggenheim Fellowship. Rice's sudden change of scholarly discipline complicated his application process, since references from his university contacts in Greek and Latin could attest only to his general abilities, but not to the efficacy of the proposed Swift project. Moe and Aydelotte, however, worked hard behind the scenes on Rice's behalf, searching for experts who could estimate the potential contribution of the study of the authorship of *A Tale of a Tub*, help Rice shape the details of his research process, and write letters of recommendation to the fellowship selection committee. Eventually, Rice traveled to the University of Chicago and the University of Illinois (Urbana) to meet with English literature scholars Ronald S. Crane and Ernest Bernbaum. Their reports to the Guggenheim Foundation were favorable enough to secure Rice a fellowship, with $2,500 stipend for the 1927–1928 academic year. Sam Avery assured the foundation that he would provide leave time and search for funds to allow the University of Nebraska to supplement the fellowship amount with part-time pay.[38]

When Rice did not receive supplementary funding and realized that Avery, ill and on leave since the spring of 1927, was unlikely ever to resume the university presidency, he decided to defer his Guggenheim Fellowship. He understood that without the protection of Avery, he was left with deans and vice-presidents who would immediately work toward his forced resignation. So he accepted an offer as head of the Department of Classical Languages at the New Jersey College for Women, affiliated with Rutgers University in New Brunswick, New Jersey.

---

38. Fellowship Application, John Andrew Rice, November 10, 1926, Henry Allen Moe to J. Rice, September 14, 1926, Frank Aydelotte to Henry Allen Moe, October 22, 26, December 31, 1926, Henry Allen Moe to Frank Aydelotte, October 25, 1926, Henry Allen Moe to John L. Lowes, December 27, 1926, Ernest Bernbaum to Henry Allen Moe, February 26, 1927, Ronald S. Crane to Henry Moe, February 26, 1927, Henry Allen Moe to J. Rice, March 9, 1927, all in J. Rice File, Guggenheim.

The family moved to New Brunswick in the fall of 1927 and found nothing of the congeniality they enjoyed in Nebraska. They lived in cramped and plain faculty housing where young Frank and Mary found no friends. Frank took to skipping school, which brought frequent visits from the truant officer. Nell took to her bed with a bout of pleurisy. It seemed that at any given time, one or more family members had a cold or a flu. "The entire family was wretched," concluded Frank Rice, who later viewed the move to New Jersey as the beginning point of faltering relations between his mother and father. The following year, the Rice family moved across the Raritan River to suburban Highland Park, New Jersey. With the onset of health and marital problems, Nell retreated for several months of that year to her family home in Sullivan, Indiana, taking her daughter Mary with her.[39]

Annoyed at finding himself in New Jersey and unhappy at home, Rice became impatient with the New Jersey College administration and with a number of his colleagues soon after his arrival. The source of his most vehement and very vocal objections was Mabel Smith Douglass, dean of the college. A New Jersey native who had graduated from Barnard College, Dean Douglass became a New York City schoolteacher and, when widowed at age forty, a successful businesswoman. In 1914 she organized a powerful citizen lobby to make Rutgers University coeducational and even ran a highly successful subscription drive to raise funds for necessary new construction. Eventually, she compromised with trustees on a Rutgers-affiliated college, the New Jersey College for Women, which opened its doors in 1918 with Mrs. Douglass at the helm.[40]

By the time John Andrew Rice arrived on campus, a number of faculty and trustees already objected to the powerful Dean Douglass. She was a skilled negotiator, especially with state agencies and legislators, and she enjoyed excellent relationships with students; but some viewed her as stubborn and arrogant in her commitment to "*my* college, *my* faculty, *my* students." Rice soon became one of the more visible members of the faction that could not get along with Dean Douglass, finding in her neither the mentorship he had known in Sam Avery nor the admiration he had found in at least a few faculty friends at Nebraska. He bridled at her inability to find genius in his outspoken views or to excuse his eccentricities and abrasiveness. Rather than

39. F. Rice to Reynolds, December 8, 1994, Frank Aydelotte to Nell A. Rice, October 4, 1928, in Aydelotte Papers, Swarthmore.
40. William H. S. Demarest, *A History of Rutgers College, 1766–1924* (New Brunswick, N.J., 1924), 184–207; George P. Schmidt, *Douglass College: A History* (New Brunswick, N.J., 1968), 3–29.

attempt to reach a peaceful accommodation with his new dean, the belliger-
ent Rice built coalitions among her detractors. He particularly enjoyed the
company of one trustee who openly despised Dean Douglass and amused
him with the remark, "My idea of hell is to drive around in it and once every
10,000 years run into Mrs. Douglass."[41]

The only enjoyable part of New Jersey College for Rice was his association with the drama department. He loved to write and to act, and he had the
opportunity to do both. He wrote a play that was staged at the college, and he
took a part in a George Bernard Shaw drama. It was rumored that he had
formed a relationship with a female drama coach. The gossip circulated
widely enough to reach Rice's son eventually, but the relationship may have
been anything from a chimera to a serious extramarital affair.[42]

Rice viewed New Jersey College for Women as "a dispensary of information," and he freely shared that thought with others. His general unhappiness
at being in New Jersey, rather than in London on his Guggenheim Fellowship, heightened his usual tendency toward cynicism and his usual determination not only to join the fray, but also to instigate it. Furthermore, he may
have taken heart from the knowledge that John Martin Thomas, president of
Rutgers since 1925, did not have a harmonious relationship with Dean
Douglass and had only limited regard for New Jersey College. Rice, however,
decided that his problems with Dean Douglass stemmed not so much from his
words and actions as from her own deep-seated disdain for all professors. "I
learned, from the dean, that some colleges are founded out of hatred or contempt for professors," he later insisted. "She took me back to that day when
her professor of English had returned her theme penciled with disdain."[43]

By the middle of Rice's second year at the New Jersey College for
Women, Dean Douglass decided he had to leave. Rice reported that she
called him to her office to ask, "Mr. Rice, why did you ever leave Nebraska?"
Rice simply replied, "Dean Douglass, I've been asking myself that ever since
I got here." The dean insisted to members of the college board of managers
and to Rutgers president John Martin Thomas that Rice's teaching had not
met her expectations. Knowing the matter could not be concluded with a
simple request for Rice's resignation, however, she offered to continue his
salary until January 1, 1930, in exchange for his resignation and his departure
in June, 1929.[44]

---

41. Schmidt, *Douglass College,* 45; F. Rice, interview with the author, February 13, 1993.
42. F. Rice, interview with the author, November 24, 1995.
43. J. Rice, *Eighteenth Century,* 295–96; Schmidt, *Douglass College,* 73–74.
44. J. Rice, interview with Duberman, June 10, 1967; James B. Lipman to Frank Aydelotte,
March 14, 1929, in Aydelotte Papers, Swarthmore.

Members of the board of managers were uncertain as to whether they should support the dean's desire to request Rice's resignation, especially since he had the support of President Thomas. One member, James Neilson, invited Henry Allen Moe to make an appeal to the board by describing the Guggenheim foundation's estimation of his scholarly potential as a fellow. When Moe accepted the invitation and arrived at the meeting at the appointed time, however, Dean Douglass told him that he could not appear until she personally gave him permission. He waited an hour before he was summoned into the meeting to discuss Rice's scholarship, and he left with the impression that at least several board members wanted him to indicate that the Guggenheim research project was "silly."[45]

As Rice's brother-in-law and an interested college president, Frank Aydelotte decided to look into the matter. He initially defended Rice, claiming, "His success with his students has been so great everywhere else that I find it difficult to believe Dean Douglass' opinion is based on anything more than mere personal prejudice." Later, however, after he spoke with a variety of informed individuals, including President Thomas, Aydelotte became committed to helping the college ease out his brother-in-law in a way that would preserve Rice's status for accepting his Guggenheim scholarship and for someday returning to teaching. He acted as a go-between, convincing his brother-in-law that leaving was preferable to staying and convincing college administrators that granting a leave of absence, rather than requesting a resignation, did not mean they would ever have Rice back. Aydelotte personally promised President Thomas that he would assist Rice in finding work elsewhere when he finished his Guggenheim research. The agreement finally reached included a leave of absence for Rice, sweetened with $2,500 and undisturbed faculty status, and required from Rice and Aydelotte a gentlemen's agreement that the former did not intend to return to the New Jersey College for Women.[46]

With Nell, eight-year-old Mary, and twelve-year-old Frank, John Andrew Rice set out for England in June, 1929, at last activating the Guggenheim Fellowship he had twice postponed. Launching himself from the flat he had secured for his family in Hampstead Heath, he spent his time searching through manuscripts and letters in Oxford's Bodleian Library, the British Museum, the British Records Office, and private collections. Although he found little to confirm or discredit Jonathan Swift's authorship of *A Tale of a*

45. Henry Allen Moe to Adam Leroy Jones, May 14, 1931, in J. Rice File, Guggenheim.
46. Frank Aydelotte to James B. Lipman, March 27, 1929, John M. Thomas to Walter B. Gourley, May 4, 1929, John M. Thomas to Frank Aydelotte, May 13, 1929, Frank Aydelotte to John B. Thomas, May 14, 1929, all in Aydelotte Papers, Swarthmore.

Tub, his research took several other turns toward new information on the life of Swift, especially during his early manhood years as secretary to Sir William Temple. Rice also discovered the only known letter in the handwriting of Esther Johnson, the woman called "Stella" who was widely thought to be Swift's unacknowledged wife. Reported in the London *Times,* this find immediately enabled other scholars to identify additional manuscripts in Stella's hand.[47]

Rice enjoyed his detective work, especially since he began to identify closely with Swift's blunt wit and with the art and culture of the eighteenth century. However, he also decided that research entailed too much tedium for too little payoff to capture his energy beyond his stay in England. "Research is the report of what one has found out rather than of what one knows," he later explained. "The area of exploration is outside oneself. . . . I knew, at the end of my stay in England, I could not spend my life apart from life."[48]

Although Rice had at first hoped his research might lead to a dissertation in completion of his doctorate, a commercial book soon appealed more to him. He started outlining and working on a manuscript based on his Swift research during the spring of 1930. Although the Oxford University Press turned down his ideas for the volume as "too diffuse," another British publisher, Constable, Ltd., agreed to take it on speculation when it was complete. Unfortunately, however, Rice's one-year Guggenheim Fellowship was drawing to a close by the time he was able to determine his focus for a book. In glowing letters to his brother-in-law, Rice recounted the importance of his scholarship and the respect he had earned from British eighteenth-century scholars. He may have been hoping Aydelotte would use his influence to help secure additional Guggenheim funding when he suggested that with money for just one more year in England, he could make significant strides toward, not just one, but several books.[49]

Undoubtedly, one reason Rice would have liked to have stayed overseas was that his family seemed to have recovered from disagreeable times in New Jersey and was even thriving. Nell thoroughly enjoyed England, and Frank and Mary were happy in their new school. Rice would later claim that this was the only progressive school of which he ever thoroughly approved. His

47. John A. Rice to Frank Aydelotte, April 16, 1930, in Aydelotte Papers, Swarthmore; John A. Rice to Henry Allen Moe, February 19, 1930, in J. Rice File, Guggenheim; Frank A. Rice to Katherine Reynolds, December 4, 1994, in author's possession.
48. J. Rice, *Eighteenth Century,* 297.
49. J. Rice to Aydelotte, April 16, May 31, 1930, both in Aydelotte Papers, Swarthmore.

satisfaction may have been connected to his exchanges with the school's strong-willed headmaster, who forcefully acted on his beliefs. When Rice complained that something was wrong with a school where young Frank was struggling in all his subjects except art, the headmaster challenged him, "How do you know what's best for that boy?" Rice respected the man's candor.[50]

Subsequently, the father decided to let his son take his art seriously. Frank began spending much of his time sketching or just wandering through the Victoria and Albert Museum, where his father finally wrangled an assigned seat for him in the library. Much to Rice's surprise, he found that when his son was given free rein to pursue the area he enjoyed most, he began "developing into the best balanced youngster you can imagine."[51]

With no encouragement from Aydelotte about funding to remain in England a second year, and with the depression economy in America awaiting his return, John Andrew Rice began to worry again about employment. He fantasized about trying his hand at play writing, perhaps by starting part time while finding work with a New York foundation or publisher. "What I need," he explained to his brother-in-law while asking his help in making necessary employment contacts, "is some way to earn my bread and butter, with enough time of my own to write on the side."[52] When Aydelotte failed to respond positively to the play-writing notion, Rice knew he would return to teaching. He even toyed with the idea of returning to the New Jersey College for Women, from which he had never formally resigned. However, Aydelotte was as good as his word to the administrators there and insisted to Rice that he should not return to New Jersey. Instead, Aydelotte requested some time to consult his extensive network of contacts in higher education.

No unemployed academic could wish for more energetic efforts on his behalf than those of Frank Aydelotte at this time. During the spring of 1930 Aydelotte contacted Hamilton College president Frederick Ferry and Earlham College president William Dennis about Rice and sincerely recommended his brother-in-law with accolades like, "I consider Professor Rice one of the most brilliant and stimulating teachers of the classics that I have ever known; I think that is the opinion of his students everywhere." Both presidents, however, were trying to fill openings in their classics departments with lower-level, part-time faculty. Next, the Swarthmore president fol-

50. J. Rice, interview with Duberman, June 10, 1967.

51. J. Rice to Aydelotte, April 16, 1930, in Aydelotte Papers, Swarthmore; F. Rice to Reynolds, December 4, 1994, in author's possession.

52. J. Rice to Aydelotte, May 31, 1930, in Aydelotte Papers, Swarthmore.

lowed up on possibilities with several preparatory schools. He also enlisted the assistance of his friend Henry Allen Moe, who also had developed great respect for Rice. Moe extended the job hunt by exchanging letters with the presidents of Southwestern University (Memphis, Tennessee) and Phillips Academy (Andover, Massachusetts), as well as with faculty at the University of Chicago. Together, the two men carried out an impressive employment campaign for Rice during the late spring and early summer of 1930, writing several dozen letters on his behalf.[53]

Finally, Aydelotte heard that Hamilton Holt, president of Rollins College in Winter Park, Florida, would be spending the summer in England. He wrote to Holt extolling Rice's abilities and suggesting that Holt get in touch with Rice while in England. Holt contacted Rice when he arrived in England, arranging to meet him at a railroad station in the village of Stoke Poges, approximately thirty miles west of London. They struck up an immediate rapport and talked for several hours. By the end of the conversation, Holt told Rice, "Well, I haven't got a single liberal on my faculty. Maybe I'd better have you."[54]

On a train the next day, Holt drafted the terms of hire in a letter to Rice that would eventually become crucial to the outcome of a highly publicized debate about professorial tenure and academic freedom. Holt's letter noted, "I call you with the expectation that it will be permanent, but as I told you, I feel that either of us are at perfect liberty to sever the connection at the end of one or two years with or without any given reason and no hard feelings on either side." As soon as he received an affirmative reply from his new classics professor, a euphoric Hamilton Holt scribbled a quick note to Frank Aydelotte to thank him and to let him know he considered Rice "exactly the man I have been looking for, for he agrees with me (we always approve of those who agree with us!) that the classicists are the ones who have killed the classics—the most modern and human literature of the world; and the testimony I have already got from his students is that he makes them like it, as is just what professors are for, when you come to think of it."[55]

The confirmation of his new teaching appointment reached John An-

53. Frank Aydelotte to Frederick Ferry, May 23, June 4, 1930, to Lawrence Durborow, June 7, 1930, and to Henry Moe, June 7, 1930, *ibid.;* Henry A. Moe to W. C. Dennis, April 29, 1930, to C. H. Beeson, April 29, 1930, and to Alfred E. Stearns, June 19, 1930, all in J. Rice File, Guggenheim.

54. J. Rice, interview with Duberman, June 10, 1967.

55. Hamilton Holt to John A. Rice, July 13, 1930, and to Frank Aydelotte, July 16, 1930, both in Faculty Files, J. A. Rice, Department of College Archives and Special Collections, Rollins College, Winter Park, Fla.

drew Rice only two weeks after the news of his father's death in Tulsa, Oklahoma. His return to the United States had the aura of a fresh start. Somehow he was able to suppress the reality that he had failed to complete the scholarly project he had begun and instead embraced the idea that he had now achieved maturity of purpose. Although this attitude would eventually prove shortsighted and short-lived, it managed to launch him back into the arena he knew and enjoyed best. Somewhat to his surprise, John Andrew Rice found he did not regret putting aside fantasies about writing plays or extending his Guggenheim Fellowship in order to return to teaching. He later viewed his renewed enthusiasm for going back to the classroom as an important realization: "I had gone and left my girl, but when she crooked her finger, I came running."[56]

56. J. Rice, *Eighteenth Century*, 297.

4

The Rollins Years: A Gathering Storm

It was appropriate, and perhaps symbolic, that Rice returned to his beloved South to begin a new chapter in his career. He was once again delighted by night sounds of swamp frogs and locusts, by bountiful fishing lakes, by screened porches and bare feet. The small town of Winter Park, Florida, immediately surrounded by unpaved roads where goats and chickens emerged from various back yards, suited him just fine and probably brought back the best of his childhood memories.

Although the Depression weighed heavily on American minds, John Andrew Rice could not have returned to American education at a more exciting time. William James, whose ideas Rice had read and appreciated, had sown the seeds of popular pragmatic thought decades earlier when he decided that the finest expression of humanity was the individuality of diverse beliefs, hopes, and possibilities shaped and integrated by experience. James determined that the truth and meaning of an idea was in its function, not in its origin, and that experience was the essential test of an idea's value and validity.

Later, when John Dewey gave James's pragmatic philosophy its expression in education, his conviction that experience and individuality could be channeled toward learning that was more meaningful than the usual fare in American schools met with widespread agreement. By viewing education as an interactive process, Dewey included social behavior and individual capacities in his vision of both the means and the aims of education. He paved the way for reassessment by educators and scholars throughout the country when he asserted, "If democracy has a moral and ideal meaning, it is that a social return be demanded from all and that opportunity for development of distinctive capacities be afforded all."[1]

1. John Dewey, *Democracy and Education* (New York, 1916), 122.

Armed first with philosophies and ideas, the progressive movement inspired by Dewey and others soon moved on to classroom experimentation and professional networking. By the second decade of the twentieth century, Dewey's ideals of learning through discovery and educating through self-discipline also caught the imagination of college and university educators concerned with recent trends that put less emphasis on the development of students and more on the development of specialized knowledge. Critics of higher education, inside and outside the academy, had begun to rail against elective systems of great variety and little integration; disciplinary specialization that subdivided the curriculum into narrow and disconnected units; and teaching that was driven by lectures, assignments, tests, and rules.

During the 1920s and 1930s discontent with current practice and enthusiasm for progressive ideals combined to inspire a variety of new endeavors in higher education, especially in undergraduate liberal education. In the wave of this zeal for innovation, the honors program begun by Frank Aydelotte at Swarthmore College spread to ninety-three colleges and universities by 1927. Harvard, Dartmouth, the University of Chicago, and others experimented with independent examiners. New curricular strategies ranged from attempts to integrate specialized knowledge through survey courses at Dartmouth and Columbia to experiments with classic texts programs at the College of the University of Wisconsin and the College at the University of Chicago. At two new and experimental women's colleges—Bennington in Vermont and Sarah Lawrence in New York—highly individualized programs of study were supported by small classes and extensive use of faculty advisers. Both these colleges sought intellectual and emotional development and placed learning in the visual and performing arts on equal footing with education in the professions, natural sciences, and social sciences. Student participation outside the classroom, often including physical labor in the service of the college community, was part of experimental colleges such as Deep Springs, Berea, and Antioch.[2]

By September, 1930, when John Andrew Rice arrived at Rollins College, that small liberal arts school also had embraced the notions of experimentation and change. Founded in 1885 by a group of Congregational ministers and local citizens who were financially supported by Chicago businessman Alonzo Rollins, the college had struggled to remain financially viable. When Hamilton Holt assumed Rollins' presidency in 1925, he began a dramatic and single-handed revision of the school's traditional operations. Like

2. For discussions of the influence of progressive education on innovations in higher education during the 1920s and 1930s, see, for example, Cremin, *American Education,* 157–220, and Rudolph, *The American College and University,* 355–73.

John Andrew Rice, he viewed American higher education as a system gone awry, and he determined that Rollins would pioneer a better way. His 1925 inaugural address set the course when he announced his intention "to perfect and dignify the small college at a time when many of our foremost institutions are subordinating the college course, not only as a department of a university, but as a minor department at that, while devoting all their energies to specializing and emphasizing the development of graduate and professional work."[3]

Searching for a strategy to curb lectures and recitations in the classroom and to ensure more meaningful contact between students and teachers, Holt decided on a new format he dubbed "the conference plan of study." The plan required students to attend three two-hour class periods and one two-hour supervised extracurricular period each day. The two-hour class, or "conference period," was designed to include time for discussions of the full group, exercises in smaller groups, periods of individual study, and one-on-one meetings with professors while others in the classroom studied. Students had full election of the majority of their courses, each of which met three times a week. They were expected to accomplish all their work during the eight-hour days without further study. Once the conference plan was underway, Rollins offered an additional "concentration plan" of classes held for two hours each day but meeting five times a week.[4]

Rollins' new class format and its aims and implications prompted a great deal of initial enthusiasm among the faculty and created an atmosphere in which teaching and learning were subjects of vigorous attention and lengthy debate. Set in a lakeside town of only several thousand residents, Rollins was well positioned to acquire a sense of community less evident on larger or urban campuses. Most of its approximately fifty faculty members and three hundred students lived within walking distance of one another and shared the same recreational pastimes. Together they might boat or fish on Lake Osceola and Lake Virginia, picnic at the beach, or attend college functions. Even Winter Park natives and visitors interacted frequently with the college and its faculty. Barbara Dreier, wife of Rollins faculty member Ted Dreier, later recalled the stir generated by Holt's new plans for the college as "great excitement throughout Winter Park. We felt we were into something new

---

3. Presidential Inaugural Address, 1925, in Hamilton Holt Papers, Rollins.

4. Arthur Lovejoy and Austin Edwards, "Academic Freedom and Tenure: Rollins College Report," *Bulletin of the American Association of University Professors*, XIX (November, 1933), 420–21; Warren F. Kuehl, *Hamilton Holt: Journalist, Internationalist, Educator* (Gainesville, Fla., 1960), 179–90.

with all the talk about how to make learning really interesting. There were meetings about all this, and even the wives attended. It was really great fun and very active. Everybody was full of hope for the great college in the making."[5]

Educated at Yale and Columbia, Hamilton Holt had arrived at Rollins on the heels of a twenty-seven-year career in journalism, including editorship of the weekly magazine that he purchased from his uncle in 1912, the *Independent*. Well-schooled in schemes for increasing subscriptions and notions for attention-grabbing articles, Holt brought to Rollins a determined regard for the value of public relations. Everything new that happened at the college merited an identifying label and a press release. Faculty members were dubbed "golden personalities" and heralded as such in hiring announcements. The conference plan of study was announced as the "Rollins Plan" to the nation, with Holt submitting frequent articles about it to newspapers and magazines. He liked to mention his innovations as an "adventure in education" and to assert that Rollins had "put Socrates on the eight-hour day."[6]

Not surprisingly, some ideas that captured public attention were less well received by academic commentators. For example, Holt announced the appointment of interdisciplinary professorships with labels that included "professor of books," "professor of evil," and "professor of leisure." Abraham Flexner soon called attention to Rollins' professorship of books as "an absurdity" and an example of the "ad-hoc-ness" plaguing American colleges and universities. He fumed, "As if an educated boy could not through intelligence, initiative, and association find his way to a library, a bookshop."[7]

When Edwin Grover was appointed professor of books, Holt released the news to the wire services claiming it to be the first such academic position in the world. John Andrew Rice later asserted that Holt was temporarily set back when a librarian from a tiny midwestern college wrote to say that she had held that title for many years. Holt, according to Rice, recovered by clarifying that Rollins had appointed the first "Emersonian" professor of books.[8]

Five years into Holt's presidency, Rollins College had managed a growing public reputation as an innovative liberal arts college with a solid faculty. Holt moved quickly to parlay increased public recognition and community

5. Barbara L. Dreier, interview with the author, April 5, 1993.
6. J. A. Rice to Harold W. Tyler, April 24, 1933, in J. Rice File, Rollins; Ted Dreier, interview with the author, April 5, 1993; Kuehl, *Hamilton Holt*, 183.
7. Abraham Flexner, *Universities: American, English, German* (London, 1930), 72.
8. J. Rice, *Eighteenth Century*, 303.

interest into successful fund raising. Even before he was inaugurated as the college's president, Holt considered the physical appearance of the campus crucial to his vision for Rollins. The half dozen original square frame buildings scattered throughout the campus were no complement for the curving shoreline of Lake Virginia and the natural stands of palms and bamboo. Holt declared the appropriate architecture for a renewed campus to be Mediterranean style, with white stucco, orange tile roofs, arched curves at windows and doorways, and Moorish tile detailing. He took to the road, mostly up and down the East Coast, tirelessly seeking donations and bequests. By 1930 he had commitments for a large new chapel, a new theater, and a new dormitory.[9]

Confronting his Latin and Greek classes, John Andrew Rice was in his element. The conference plan format suited his expertise in Socratic dialogue, allowing him to ask a few questions that would generate discussions about anything from art to college policies. Teaching Greek and Latin language and culture generally took a back seat to educating students in how to criticize, analyze, and develop their own identities. His student Betty Young Williams later recalled that "his Greek civilization course basically had no content. It was Socratic dialogue all the time, and he was very stimulating. Then, I took Greek language, because that was the only other thing Mr. Rice taught that semester. We did learn some language of course, but the general classroom conversation was really much more interesting." Not all students were so intrigued. Emily Burks was disappointed to find so little Latin in Rice's Latin language course, having read only two pages of the language in one semester and deciding the class was, "more of an open forum where economics, religion, world literature, sex, love and everything else but Latin was discussed." Rice probably would not challenge this description too severely. He named his classes not Latin and Greek but Greek humanism and classical history. He later explained his teaching aims at Rollins: "While the conclusions about human life were the same in all ages, each generation had to find new premises, and I was looking for new premises."[10]

Though mentally vigorous, the sedentary Rice often ambled into the classroom late. One student who lived near Rice and his family, Dorothy Shepherd, later recalled the many times she passed his house at a fast walk to get to his class on time, only to notice her professor reading on his front porch with his feet up and his shoes off. In the classroom, Rice never left his seat,

---

9. *A Walker's Guide to Rollins College* (Winter Park, Fla., 1988).

10. Elizabeth Young Williams, interview with the author, May 10, 1993; Emily Burks, Student Affidavit, May 16, 1933, in Rice Case File, Rollins; J. Rice, *Eighteenth Century*, 305.

sucking and tamping his pipe, while probing the group of fifteen or twenty students around a conference table with questions such as, "What do you think of those calendar pictures on the wall? Are they art?" Often he would challenge a student or offer his own opinion. Sometimes he would let out a laugh that started deep in the belly and climbed to a higher pitch as it gurgled from his throat.[11]

During his first year, Rice was euphoric about his good fortune in landing a faculty position at an innovative college located in a warm southern climate with fishing and boating on Lake Virginia only steps from his back door. In a conversation with Hamilton Holt that ironically foreshadowed storms on the horizon, he mentioned that he and Nell kept waiting to discover something wrong with the college and the town, which couldn't possibly be as delightful as they seemed. He wrote enthusiastically to Henry Allen Moe, inviting him for a visit and noting, "During the day you may go around dressed as you are accustomed to on your farm for there is no one near us, with the exception of chickens and, across the road, several goats." To underscore the informality of his Florida life style, Rice added, "I will receive you in my underwear," although the comment was probably made tongue in cheek and possibly for the sport of giving the more staid Moe a bit of a shock.[12]

John Andrew and Nell frequently entertained students at the house they rented on Ollie Avenue. Animated groups clustered inside on the floor or gathered outside on the wide screened porch. If conversation lagged, Rice could be counted on to give it a jolt. One evening he posed to the group assembled a solution for ending time-consuming and distracting social relations between the sexes. Why not have a dean simply meet the students at the train station when they arrive in Winter Park and pair them off by some anonymous method, with the pairs staying together for the duration of their college careers? Student responses varied from silent indignation to raucous laughter.[13]

Rice also quickly made a few good friends among the faculty. Assistant professor of psychology John Malcolm ("Mac") Forbes of the wealthy Boston family (only distantly related to the wealthy Forbes family of New York) entertained Rice and others at sailing parties on Lake Osceola. In addition, Rice and his son Frank accompanied Forbes on some trips on the large, nautically unstable motorboat *Marlin* that Forbes himself had designed. Hamilton Holt, identifying his new classics professor as an intriguing and enter-

11. Dorothy Shepherd Smith, interview with the author, April 2, 1993.
12. J. A. Rice to Henry Moe, September 29, October 8, 1930, in J. Rice File, Guggenheim.
13. Affidavit of Bernard Bralove, May 15, 1933, in Rice Case File, Rollins.

taining conversationalist, often invited Nell and John Andrew Rice to the dinner parties where he entertained visiting dignitaries. Rice, likewise, enjoyed Holt's company in a social setting, and characterized the president later as "a very lovable man," if heavy-handed. Assistant professor of physics Ted Dreier, who had been Mac Forbes's roommate and best friend at Harvard, arrived on the faculty the same year as Rice, settling with his wife, Barbara, almost directly across the street from the Rice family. Dreier shared with Rice "an interest in life and in education," and they engaged in lengthy discussions about their ideas concerning higher education.[14]

Unfortunately for Rice, Mac Forbes resigned after Rice's first year at Rollins. Rice believed that Holt had asked for and obtained Forbes's resignation after some faculty members had decided Forbes was an inadequate teacher and lobbied for his removal. This interpretation, which reflected Rice's growing sense of Holt's heavy-handedness, seems questionable in light of Forbes's substantial contributions to Rollins. For example, he financed a national conference on liberal education curriculum held at Rollins in 1931, and he used his family connections to help encourage well-known educators to attend. The legacy of his three years at Rollins also included his donation (anonymous at the time) of funds to fully finance construction of the first of the buildings in the new Mediterranean style, Mayflower Dormitory. Additionally, Forbes had long planned to complete his Ph.D. in England, and he set about doing so upon leaving Rollins in 1932. A year into his studies at the University of London, he received letters from President Holt and Dean Winslow Anderson inquiring about the possibility of his return to Winter Park and indicating he was welcome to rejoin the faculty. Forbes, however, stayed in London to complete his degree.[15]

Upon his departure from Winter Park, Forbes gave his motorboat to Frank Rice, now a young teenager. Some of the best times for the Rice family were days at nearby Lake Osceola. Typically, Frank and his father would steer the boat to the middle of the lake and spend an afternoon gently rocking, casting their lines, and patiently waiting for a bite. Later, they might meet Nell and Mary for a fresh-catch meal at the lakeside cottage rented by the college for the faculty; but while they were fishing, Rice rarely uttered a

14. F. Rice to Reynolds, December 4, 1994, in author's possession; T. Dreier, interviews with the author, April 15, 1993, April 29, 1994; J. Rice, *Eighteenth Century*, 302.

15. T. Dreier, interview with the author, April 29, 1994; J. Rice, interview with Duberman, June 10, 1967; Winslow Anderson to Hamilton Holt, April 22, 1933, and Malcolm Forbes to Winslow Anderson, April 30, 1933, both in J. M. Forbes File, Rollins.

word. He had a remarkable capacity to sit completely still at great length, immersed in his thoughts.[16]

Rice's interpretation of the Forbes's departure reflected his growing observation that a great deal of power had accumulated in the presidency of Rollins. Holt, with a preference for quick and independent action, had overseen the forced departures of more than a dozen instructional staff during the depression years of the early 1930s. Official reasons listed in the personnel files included: "Holt wanted a man for the job," "immoral conduct," "unable to work with associates," "position abolished," "department abolished," "poor teacher," and "Holt wanted a man for debating."[17] Indeed, long before Rice's arrival at Rollins, Hamilton Holt had decided he would fully and personally run the college, often determining appointments and terminations on his own without faculty or trustee consultation. In those difficult economic times, many faculty who raised their eyebrows at Holt's suspension of collegial decision making or debate may have elected to do so only privately. After all, during a depression it was safest to keep a closed mouth and a steady paycheck.

But safe did not suit John Andrew Rice. Characteristically, he "determined to earn his hemlock."[18] He earned it at Rollins as he had before and would afterward: by venting large doses of candor that could be viewed accurately as insulting or honest, outrageous or courageous. Rice reserved his most cutting and cynical observations for fellow faculty members and for institutions, including the one that employed him. Everyone knew how Rice felt about people and events, and Rice undoubtedly knew how they felt about how he felt. He warmed to colleagues and students who appreciated his integrity and humor, and he cooled on those who bristled at his insensitivity and arrogance.

After his first year at Rollins, Rice began to give free rein to his natural bent for exasperated criticism. He discovered among the faculty a number he considered lesser thinkers and inadequate teachers. He discovered among the students many who still preferred lecture and recitation learning to long discussions that had little to do with Latin and Greek. Then he realized that the prescribed two-hour classes really did not suit his aim to pursue ideas at lengths determined more by the nature of discussion than by the clock; nor

16. F. Rice, interview with the author, February 13, 1993.

17. "Reasons for Faculty Changes," anonymous memo to files, [n.d.] 1933, in Rice Case File, Rollins.

18. David Jacques Way to Katherine Reynolds, May 4, 1993, in author's possession.

did twelve or eighteen hours a week in the classroom suit his ideas about faculty life. Rice continued to fume when he wrote a decade later, "The students complained that most of the teachers were no better than their high school instructors, and that two hours with bores was at least an hour too much. The teachers had grounds for complaint. Two hours on end with students, most of them there for a good time—had they not been offered freedom?—was a drudge."[19]

Rice also found the campus culture littered with elements ripe for objection. He directed his scorn at fraternities and sororities, debating teams, a physical education requirement, and alumni relations, among other targets. What had seemed inappropriate at the University of Nebraska he found preposterous at a liberal arts college of several hundred students. Rice's critical eye also began to rove beyond the campus to the Winter Park community, a haven for second-home owners from the Northeast and Midwest whose wealth caused them to merit significant deference from college administrators and local realtors. He later observed that "until November the houses along Interlaken [*sic*], the town's Park Avenue, had remained closed but now one over-length Lincoln and another rolled along at a solicitous pace, with their clear windows, like the windows of a hearse, giving one a full view of the untroubled calm within, white hair and white blank faces. How, I reflected, was a liberal college to live in the midst of this?" He determined that many of President Holt's more objectionable actions stemmed from his need to please "these second class rich folks in Winter Park."[20]

Rice's peevishness at Rollins surfaced first in intermittent potshots. When Laura Lee Hope, the author of the Bobbsey Twins series of children's books and sister of a Rollins faculty member, was invited to give a speech, her lecture was curiously titled, "The Bobbsey Twins and How They Came." Rice joked to students and faculty alike that he expected they would be hearing about an obstetrical case. When a popular and highly respected faculty member told her class that Eugene O'Neill's *Mourning Becomes Electra* was "the Greek spirit come to life," Rice countered with, "That's damn nonsense," to anyone interested. "I said this woman was talking nonsense because she was talking nonsense," he later asserted. "What are you going to say?" More generally provocative, when he attended a multifaith religious conference sponsored by Rollins for students, faculty, and community members, Rice could not resist the opportunity to shock the audience. He invited controversy by asking a panel of speakers what difference it would

19. J. Rice, *Eighteenth Century,* 299.
20. *Ibid.,* 300; J. Rice, interview with Duberman, June 10, 1967.

make if the citizens of Winter Park woke up one Sunday and found all the churches along Interlachen Avenue had disappeared, with stretches of green grass in their place.[21]

Beyond such displays of growing annoyance, John Andrew Rice still possessed substantial appeal. He had a brilliant mind and a capacity for good humor and charm. Many students gravitated to him as someone who treated them as adults and demonstrated a great deal of concern about what they thought and how they developed. During Rice's second year at Rollins, Hamilton Holt appointed him to the curriculum committee and to a task force to review the fraternity and sorority system. His fellow faculty members elected him to a committee to confer with the administration about an announced 30 percent cut in faculty salaries.[22]

Rollins also had not yet lost its appeal for Rice during his second year. Even as he poured out invective for the college's shortcomings, he recognized an atmosphere of vigor and experimentation. In 1931 Rollins hosted the week-long Conference on Curriculum for the College of Liberal Arts, a meeting that was, according to its chair John Dewey, "unique in devoting itself to the fundamental principles of college education as distinguished from those both of lower schools and of the university."[23] The conference, called to look at curricular content for Rollins and perhaps to develop a model for others, generated national publicity and renewed discussions about learning and teaching at Rollins.

Included in the impressive group of educators gathered to debate the ideal curriculum were Dewey, Antioch president Arthur Morgan, Sarah Lawrence College president Constance Warren, Lehigh University dean Max McConn, educational commentator John Palmer Gavit, and faculty members who had studied and written about education from a number of colleges and universities. Their deliberations were open to Rollins faculty and students, and the general public.

Dewey opened the conference with an appeal for a curriculum that recognized student interests and abilities, and he even asked a group of students who had been invited to represent their peers, "What do you students get spontaneously excited about?" The students responded with a short list: work, economic life, leisure, friendship, fame, and sex. Rather quickly, the

21. J. Rice, interview with Duberman, June 10, 1967; F. Rice to Reynolds, December 4, 1994; Affidavit of Edwin O. Grover, May 15, 1933, in Rice Case File, Rollins.
22. Lovejoy and Edwards, "Academic Freedom," 424–27; J. A. Rice to H. W. Tyler, April 24, 1933, in J. Rice File, Rollins.
23. John Dewey, "Closing Remarks," January 24, 1931 (Typescript in Curriculum Conference File, Rollins).

conference moved away from addressing specific subject areas, which had in-spired lively debate, to examining curricular philosophies. Dewey partici-pated little outside his opening and closing remarks.[24]

One of the signal problems that the conferees tackled was that of in–depth learning in an area of high interest versus required knowledge of prescribed information. Eventually, they proposed an upper division for immersion in the former and a lower division for imparting the latter. Gavit and Morgan had swum upstream in arguing for at least some formal course requirements, but their fellow conferees did not entirely close the door to their case. The final conference recommendation read: "There should be less emphasis on the acquisition of mere facts and more emphasis upon generalization, think-ing, application of knowledge and awareness of gaps in knowledge. . . . Pre-requisites for entrance and within the college have been too rigid, too formal and not fully justified."[25]

Hamilton Holt moved quickly to adopt the conference recommendations and by September, 1931, announced Rollins' "New Curriculum Plan." The plan used the device of upper and lower divisions and approximated two years of study in each to satisfy recommendations both of the curriculum conference and of professors disgruntled with teaching in preset two-hour blocks. Holt explained: "Courses in the Upper Division will be adjusted to the needs of the individual. Instead of limiting the teaching schedule of the instructor on the time basis alone, Rollins has assigned each instructor a given number of students only. . . . In the Lower Division the student will fill in the gaps in his preparation and lay a broad foundation for the specialized work he is to do later in the Upper Division."[26]

John Andrew Rice observed the conference deliberations with great in-terest and was delighted to meet men such as John Dewey and Arthur Mor-gan, both of whom he admired on contact. Typically, however, he also found reason for cynicism, as when, years later, he fumed that the conference was dominated by noted progressive educator Goodwin Watson of Columbia University. Referring to him as "this jackass from Columbia," Rice recalled that Watson "had a claque consisting of the president of Sarah Lawrence and her dean. So every time Watson said, 'I think it's raining outside,' the sun might be shining but they were applauding. So he took over the whole show,

24. "Rollins Institute Studies Liberal Arts Curricula," New York *Herald Tribune,* January 21, 1931, p. 5; "The Curriculum Conference," *Rollins College Bulletin,* XXVI (February, 1931), 2–8.
25. "The Curriculum Conference," 12.
26. "Individualization in Education," *Rollins College Bulletin,* XXVII (September, 1931), 5.

and John Dewey never said a word. He just sat and listened. He was a wonderful listener."[27]

Curriculum was not the only area showing Rollins' commitment to innovation. Particularly interesting to Rice was the college dramatics program, headed by a talented and indefatigable professor named Robert Wunsch. A native of Monroe, Louisiana, who also taught creative writing, Wunsch inspired students not only to take drama courses or write class papers, but also to work in summer stock theatre over summer vacation, try for publication of their stories, and consider careers in the creative arts. At Rollins he helped a group of students found a small, experimental community theater group that could produce plays at a facility they named the "Museum" in nearby Fern Park. Rice and Wunsch became close and supportive colleagues, both delighting in their students' development outside the classroom and in their own opportunities to collaborate on projects of mutual interest.

In the spring of 1932 one such collaborative project was the encouragement of a promising anthropologist working to preserve and dramatize African American folklore, Zora Neale Hurston. After studying with anthropologist Franz Boaz and conducting research under historian Carter G. Woodson, Hurston had managed to collect enough interesting folk tales and folk songs to mount "The Great Day," a one-performance musical production at the John Golden Theatre in New York. Authentic and earthy, the production focused on a day in the lives of black laborers at a sawmill camp and interwove rhythmic music with folklore tales. While it was a highly acclaimed artistic success and was repeated by invitation at the New School for Social Research, the production left Hurston financially bereft. She returned to her hometown, the small, all-black town of Eatonville, Florida, rich in the lore of American black life and only about four miles from Winter Park.[28]

Shortly after arriving back in Eatonville and beginning to craft some earlier folklore collections into stories, Hurston was in touch with Edwin Grover (Rollins' professor of books), Wunsch, and Rice. By August, 1932, she had met with Rice about the possibility of producing some version of her New York musical in Winter Park, and she characterized his response as "enthusiastic." Rice and Wunsch were soon helping Hurston plan performances

27. J. Rice, interview with Duberman, June 10, 1967.
28. Robert E. Hemenway, *Zora Neale Hurston: A Literary Biography* (Urbana, Ill., 1977), 177–85; Steve Glassman and Kathryn Lee Seidel, *Zora in Florida* (Orlando, 1991), 131–35; Zora Neale Hurston to Thomas Elsa Jones, October 12, 1934, in Thomas Elsa Jones Papers, Special Collections, Fisk University, Nashville.

at the Museum in Fern Park and at the larger Recreation Hall on campus, which would seat over one thousand; and they were even advising her about possible out-of-state performances. Hurston, excited about the possibilities for her work being batted about at Rollins, wrote to her New York patron, Mrs. Rufus Osgood Mason, that "the concert work is only the opening wedge. The Department is going in for creative negro art as it never has been done. We shall surpass by far what has been done by Paul Green et al at the University of North Carolina."[29]

Because Hamilton Holt was cautious about community response, he somewhat grudgingly gave permission for the production of Hurston's folklore musical, now retitled "From Sun to Sun." In a note to Wunsch, he gave his official approval for the use of the recreation hall, but warned that Wunsch should "go over the thing enough to know that there will be nothing vulgar in it." He also asked for only low-key advertising of the performance, mostly among Rollins students and faculty. In a comment sadly reflective of the time and place, he noted, "Of course we cannot have negroes in the audience unless there is a separate place segregated for them and I think that would be unwise." Nevertheless, Holt managed to soften, if somewhat confuse, his lukewarm acceptance with a closing comment that he considered Wunsch's work on the production "one of the best steps in the right direction." Hurston was disappointed with the parameters for the production, but apparently her spirits were only slightly dampened. She wrote Mrs. Mason, "Tickets [go] to the general public—except Negroes. I tried to have a space set aside, but find that there I come up against solid rock. So early in February we sing at Hungerford, the Negro school, so that our own people may hear us. The interest here is tremendous among whites and blacks."[30]

The two performances at the Museum in January, 1933, and the performance at the recreation hall in February met with standing ovations, numerous encores, and rave reviews from the Orlando *Morning Sentinel* and the Winter Park *Herald*. Shortly afterward, Robert Wunsch played a highly influential role in Hurston's career by recognizing the potential in one of her unpublished short stories, "The Gilded Six-Bits." He read the piece to one of his creative writing classes and then sent it to *Story* magazine. After it was

29. Zora Neale Hurston to Edwin O. Grover, August 7, 1932, in Zora Neale Hurston Papers, Special Collections, University of Florida, Gainesville; Zora Neale Hurston to Mrs. Rufus O. Mason, January 6, 1933, in Alain Locke Papers, Moorland-Spingarn Research Center, Howard University, Washington, D.C.

30. Hamilton Holt to William Robert Wunsch, November 1, 1932, in Faculty Files, W. R. Wunsch, Rollins; Hurston to Mason, January 6, 1933, in Locke Papers.

published in August, 1933, Hurston was approached by Bertram Lippincott about whether she might be working on a book that the J. B. Lippincott Company could consider for publication. Rarely known to blink twice at opportunity, Hurston replied—somewhat precipitately—that she did have such a manuscript underway, and she immediately began to craft her first novel, *Jonah's Gourd Vine,* published by Lippincott in 1934.[31]

In her 1942 autobiography, *Dust Tracks on a Road,* Hurston graciously acknowledged the support and encouragement she received from Rice, Wunsch, Grover, and Holt. The dedication to her first novel, however, indicates her summary estimation of who ignited her acceptance as a serious writer: "To Bob Wunsch who is one of the long-wingded [*sic*] angels right round the throne. Go gator and muddy the water."[32]

During the year of Zora Neale Hurston's success with her Rollins connections, the "New Curriculum Plan" of upper and lower divisions was beginning to prove less than successful. In the aftermath of initial trials, difficulties began to surface in reconciling the eight-hour day of the original "conference plan" with the individualized learning of the new plan. Hamilton Holt, reluctant to abolish the conference plan that had just a few years earlier garnered so much attention for the college, submitted the problem of reconciling the two plans to the curriculum committee. John Andrew Rice, as a member of that committee, pushed for the termination of the eight-hour day instituted by the conference plan. Others on the committee agreed that it was incompatible with a new plan that purported to emphasize individual achievement rather than time in seat. Ultimately, in January, 1933, the faculty committee voted to abolish the eight-hour day in order to allow for a system that could accommodate fewer or more hours in class or, in some cases, independent study without attendance in class.[33]

Hamilton Holt was outraged by the curriculum committee's findings, and he decided that Rollins would not adopt the recommendations of its report. He also called a meeting with committee members to vent his personal anger at them. In fact, the curriculum committee had become a thorn in Holt's side on a number of counts, as it ranged well beyond its charge and passed resolutions about day-to-day college operations. One of these that particularly in-

31. Orlando *Morning Sentinel,* January 25, 1933, p. 5; Winter Park *Herald,* January 26, 1933, p. 5; Zora Neale Hurston, *Dust Tracks on a Road* (Philadelphia, 1942), 217; Hemenway, *Zora Neale Hurston,* 180–90.

32. Hurston, *Dust Tracks,* 209; Zora Neale Hurston, *Jonah's Gourd Vine* (Philadelphia, 1934), dedication page.

33. "Resolution Presented by the Curriculum Committee," January 26, 1933 (Typescript in J. Rice File, Rollins); Lovejoy and Edwards, "Academic Freedom," 420–23.

furiated Holt was a terse resolution protesting an address by tennis professional Bill Tilden, arranged by the administration, that required attendance during the prescribed class period of the eight-hour day. Using a back-door method to demonstrate that anything of an extracurricular nature would interrupt the schedule of Holt's favored conference plan, the committee forwarded to him a resolution labeling Tilden's appearance "a meeting on the bleachers whose purpose was to advertise an exhibition of tennis professionals."[34]

Holt was no more pleased with the results of the committee on fraternities. Chaired by Rice, that committee reported in March, 1932, its particularly negative findings about the campus Greek system. The committee report pointed out that the expense involved in membership in a fraternity or sorority effectively precluded participation of middle- or lower-income students and fostered class distinctions and petty cliques. The document also charged that their undemocratic processes "discriminate against the socially undesirable rough diamond and against certain races." Rice later characterized Holt's angry reaction as somewhat surprising, since he felt that the president had understood his negative position on the fraternity system when he appointed him to chair the committee. Rice explained, "He knew how I felt about this, and he knew damn well what I was going to say. And then what I said made him furious. And made other people furious, naturally. I didn't blame them, because I said they [fraternities and sororities] had no business there."[35]

The report of the faculty committee looking into the 30 percent faculty pay cuts must have been equally infuriating to Holt. He afterwards labeled the cuts a "retain," perhaps to soften the blow by suggesting the possibility of impermanence. But the committee's findings, reported in January, 1933, probably struck him as insubordinate: "We are, of course, all aware that the present financial situation of the college is the result of capital outlays made during past years, and not the result of paying large salaries. In other words an underpaid faculty now faces the prospect of paying for capital improvements made in past years by accepting a salary scale below their present living costs."[36]

34. Kuehl, *Hamilton Holt,* 225–26; Lovejoy and Edwards, "Academic Freedom," 421; Curriculum Committee to Hamilton Holt, January 18, 1933, and Hamilton Holt to Curriculum Committee, January 23, 1933, both memos in J. Rice File, Rollins.

35. Committee on Fraternities to Hamilton Holt, March 14, 1932, memo in J. Rice File, Rollins; J. Rice, interview with Duberman, June 10, 1967.

36. Curriculum Committee to Hamilton Holt, January 11, 1933, memo in J. Rice file, Rollins.

Rice's presence on faculty committees that disagreed with administration policies was only one source of growing dissatisfaction with him shared by President Holt and Dean Winslow Anderson. Some students had complained to Holt or to Anderson that Rice was insensitive to their needs and uninterested in their work. Others had objected that he spent too little time teaching Latin and Greek language. Some faculty members charged that he had insulted them and their work.

Particularly disturbing to Holt was Rice's outspoken objection to the architecture and services of the new Knowles Memorial Chapel, the monumental centerpiece in Holt's fund-raising and building campaign. Constructed with a $250,000 gift from Mrs. Frances Warren in memory of her father Francis Knowles, the building was dedicated in 1932, much to the delight and pride of the entire Winter Park community. This first new public building of the Holt era at Rollins had a lot of Holt ego residing in the eaves. He had visualized the chapel as a new and essential focus for community and college activity, a "great showplace." Holt had personally overseen the planning of the elaborate chapel services. Rice quickly let it be known that he found the edifice and the services more concerned with worship of people than with worship of God. Word raced through the community that the classics professor called the Christmas service there "obscene."[37]

According to Ted Dreier, Holt's patience with Rice wore thinnest when donors or potential donors were among those stung by his outspokenness. "Holt was dependent on many of the wealthy residents of Winter Park for funds," explained Dreier. "And when Mr. Rice didn't hesitate to say exactly what he thought about things, it raised great hackles and anger among some of the donors."[38]

Ultimately, Holt decided that Rice possessed "the most intelligence and the least wisdom of any man on the faculty." He also decided that Rice had to go. On Monday, February 27, 1933, the president called his classics professor to his office and asked him to resign, explaining that he had no single charge but an accumulation of issues and charges. In a written report a month later, Holt explained that Rice's "indiscretions, intolerances and insulting speeches to his colleagues, students and people of the town," were the basis of his dismissal. He summarized: "There is no doubt that he has been very, very indiscreet, and worse than that, quite intolerant, and worse than that, insulting. . . . He has been lax in keeping class hours; has not hesitated

37. Harold Sproul to Hamilton Holt, [n.d.] 1933, in J. Rice file, Rollins; Lovejoy and Edwards, "Academic Freedom," 424–25.

38. T. Dreier, interview with the author, April 5, 1993.

to attack other professors in class and out of it, before students and other faculty members; does not probably teach very much of the old-fashioned Latin or Greek and is apparently hostile to students who are not in his group but very friendly to those who are. . . . In faculty meetings he has shown temper and sarcasm against those who disagreed with him."[39]

Rice refused to offer his resignation, launching into a discussion with President Holt on his recent thinking about a philosophy for living and for teaching. Socrates had for some time been his ideal, but Rice now recognized that Socrates was not a sufficient single role model. Jesus, the other great teacher, must be embraced in equal measure to add the affection so essential to teaching and to life. "Too much Socrates, not enough Jesus," became a frequent lament afterwards voiced by Rice, who generally employed the observation as a sweeping philosophical statement but undoubtedly knew it applied to himself as well. Holt was intrigued enough to offer Rice a second meeting a week later, but he would not go so far as to retract his request for resignation. On March 4, at the second meeting, he reaffirmed the dismissal.[40]

In the weeks and months that followed, a nationally publicized drama unfolded that embroiled faculty, students, parents, trustees, spouses, and others in relentless verbal warfare about academic freedom and presidential power. Rice's students, colleagues, and former colleagues—even a former landlord—were called upon to submit testimony in his dismissal case. A furor erupted that would mark a low point in the conduct of personnel affairs in higher education.

Hamilton Holt probably had no idea that his decision to dismiss Rice would generate such volatile consequences. Not surprisingly, Holt's closest friends on the faculty generally agreed with his ideas and encouraged his actions. They were men such as Professor Willard Wattles, who referred to Holt as "my captain" and to himself and other supporters as "your loyal faculty." Furthermore, Holt understood that students felt comfortable with him. He was amiable and accessible, inviting students to his home or joining them at their dormitory dining halls. Students called him "prexy" and rarely voiced to him any objections about his ideas or plans. Comments that reached Holt generally were circumspect and loyal. The candor of John Andrew Rice and the opposition of faculty committees must have seemed anomalous, and

39. Hamilton Holt, "Memo in Regard to Professor John A. Rice," March 28, 1933, in Rice Case File, Rollins.

40. *Ibid.*

Holt may have imagined a barrel with a bad apple or two that simply needed to be discarded.[41]

However, when John Andrew Rice was dismissed in the midst of the Depression, faculty, students, and even trustees found their voices. The opening salvos in the Rollins fracas were letters and visits to Holt from Rice supporters. These were followed by letters and visits from Rice detractors. Several board of trustee members even joined in the fray. Aging actress Annie Russell, in whose name a new theater recently had been built on campus, wrote to Holt that she had always found Rice "affectionate and loyal to you in all things," and commended his "brilliant intellect and sensitive understanding of the arts." However, another trustee, John Goss of Connecticut, characterized Rice's conduct as "distinctly licentious and very bad."[42]

Nell Rice firmly backed her husband in conversations with other faculty spouses, becoming one of his most outspoken advocates. She was the first to inform her brother, Frank Aydelotte, of the dismissal and to place him once again in the role of consultant and negotiator on behalf of his brother-in-law. Nell's first letter about the matter to her brother explained: "There has been a big quarrel at Rollins and Holt wants John to resign—in fact will fire him if he does not. The faculty, except four, stand up for John and most of the student body. I feel I need a detached point of view. Could you come down? Or would it be easier to send someone, or should John call in the University Professors' union? Holt will make no charges—says in fact they are trivial. Some people think that money is back of it." Aydelotte, with a great well of professional self-restraint and a fair knowledge of his brother-in-law's capacity to alienate employers, had no intention of jumping into the fray merely on the strength of Nell's appeal. Within a month, however, a cautious Aydelotte had made some inquiries on his own and decided that Holt's action toward his brother-in-law was indeed "a grave injustice." He wrote from Swarthmore to advise Rice to contact the American Association of University Professors (AAUP) with details of the case. Then he himself wrote to the AAUP's executive director informing him of a possible request for an AAUP investigation.[43]

41. Willard Wattles to Hamilton Holt, March 10, 1933, in Holt Papers, Rollins; Kuehl, *Hamilton Holt,* 219–21; Rice, interview with Duberman, June 10, 1967.
42. Annie Russell to Hamilton Holt, March 7, 1933, and John Goss to Margaret R. Dreier, May 15, 1933, both in Rice Case File, Rollins.
43. Wattles to Holt, March 10, 1933, in Holt Papers, Rollins; Nell A. Rice to Frank Aydelotte, March 5, 1933, Frank Aydelotte to John A. Rice, April 6, 1933, and Frank Aydelotte to H. W. Tyler, April 6, 1933, all in Aydelotte Papers, Swarthmore.

The AAUP drafted a letter of inquiry to Hamilton Holt on the day that Aydelotte's letter arrived at that organization's Washington, D.C., headquarters. Upon receipt of it, however, Holt was not particularly worried. In its eighteen years the AAUP had already compiled an impressive record in the defense of academic freedom, and did not scruple to publicly embarrass institutions that ignored it. But Holt undoubtedly knew that the AAUP generally launched an investigation only in those dismissal cases that involved tenure issues. He explained to AAUP officers that John Andrew Rice, was still several months short of the three years that Rollins required for permanent tenure. Not cognizant of Frank Aydelotte's initiative, Holt then met with faculty members to ask which of them had contacted the AAUP and to warn them that he considered it an act of great disloyalty.[44]

The AAUP, even after several additional inquiries from Frank Aydelotte, was reluctant to investigate. That stance changed, however, with the arrival of a formal investigation request to AAUP director H. W. Tyler from Rice, dated April 24, 1933, which included a sixteen-page statement about his dismissal. In his statement, Rice traced his troubles with Holt to others on the faculty, notably Dean Winslow Anderson, whom he felt had frequently complained about him to Holt. He admitted that Holt had spoken to him several times about his insensitive manner with colleagues, but he considered these friendly chats rather than official warnings. Frequently out of town, Holt did in fact get much of his information about campus activities and issues from his dean. Rice's statement to the AAUP also depicted Holt's increasing tendency to centralize academic control within his own office, rather than allow for collegial decision making shared by faculty. Rice charged that problems with this system at Rollins typically came to a head when faculty committees made recommendations that Holt would not accept, including those committees on which Rice served, such as the committee on curriculum, the committee on sororities and fraternities, and the committee concerned with the 30 percent faculty pay cut.[45]

The quotation from his July 13, 1930, letter of appointment that Rice included in his request for an investigation undoubtedly convinced AAUP officials. There Hamilton Holt had stipulated, "I call you with the expectation that it will be permanent, but as I told you, I feel that either of us are at perfect liberty to sever the connection at the end of one or two years with or

44. Hamilton Holt to H. W. Tyler, April 19, 1933, in Holt Papers, Rollins; Lovejoy and Edwards, "Academic Freedom," 428–29.

45. H. W. Tyler to Frank Aydelotte, April 27, 1933, in Aydelotte Papers, Swarthmore; John A. Rice to H. W. Tyler, April 24, 1933, in J. Rice File, Rollins.

without any given reason and no hard feelings on either side." Now it appeared to the AAUP that Rice had passed into tenured status when he was reappointed at the end of his second year. Holt may have forgotten about the details in his appointment letter when he asked Rice to resign. After all, the letter had been hastily drafted by Holt when he was traveling in England, and it did not carry the tone of an official document. However, at least one other appointment letter that Holt wrote during the summer of 1930, his letter appointing Ted Dreier, used almost the same wording: "If at the end of the first or second year either of us for any or no reason wish to sever the connection, it can be done without any hard feeling."[46]

When Holt was faced with the problem of the appointment letter, he took the position with the AAUP that the wording was not binding. Instead, he insisted, it had been superseded by a 1932 resolution of the Rollins board of trustees that only faculty with three or more years of service could continue without annual notification. He noted to the AAUP that the terms stated in his appointment letter to Rice had not been authorized by the school's trustees. Therefore, Holt felt he and the trustees could safely circumvent the appointment agreement, and on April 26 they took final action. In a hand-carried letter, Holt informed Rice that the board of trustees had passed a resolution that his services were terminated effective that date, and he requested that Rice remove all his personal effects from campus by noon, April 28. Perhaps to send a message about his full control, perhaps to take the offensive before public debate began, or possibly to continue the habits of a journalist, Holt sent copies of the resolution to the Florida press.[47]

With Rice finally dispensed, Holt called the remaining faculty into his office, read them the resolution of the board of trustees dismissing Rice, and informed them that any further involvement on their part to encourage the reinstatement of Professor Rice "would be considered an act of disloyalty to the College and dealt with summarily." At a meeting with ten professors the following week, Holt generated a fairly friendly discussion of how to return to business as usual and even to improve conditions for faculty. However, that meeting took a dark turn as it drew to a close. Holt presented each professor with a typed promise, ready for signature, to abide by the authority of the president in all college matters. Amid general protest against signing these pledges, Ralph Lounsbury, professor of political science and senior faculty

46. H. Holt to J. A. Rice, July 13, 1930, in J. Rice File, and Hamilton Holt to Ted Dreier, June 19, 1930, in Dreier file, Rollins.

47. Lovejoy and Edwards, "Academic Freedom," 423; Hamilton Holt to John A. Rice, April 26, 1933, in J. Rice File, Rollins.

member present, took the floor. A white-haired, gentle sort seldom given to loud or lengthy speech, Lounsbury displayed a calm wisdom as he protested that ultimately the college would suffer from publicity about the pledge incident. "In order to avoid that possibility," he offered, "I'll pass my copy back." When all the professors followed suit, the meeting ended at an impasse.[48]

Only one strategy was left for Holt to pursue that might put the Rice issue behind him in a way that quieted the campus and upheld his authority: to undergo an AAUP investigation, keep it narrowly focused on the circumstances of Rice's dismissal, and demonstrate that overwhelming cause existed for firing Rice. To that end, Holt wrote the executive secretary of the AAUP that its representatives were welcome to come to Rollins "for the purpose of permitting me to place before your Association all the material at my disposal on which we based our decision."[49]

Arthur O. Lovejoy, professor of philosophy at Johns Hopkins University, and Austin S. Edwards, professor of psychology at University of Georgia, assigned as an AAUP investigating committee of two, arrived in Winter Park on May 17, 1933. Holt, who had spent several busy weeks of telephoning, telegramming, and letter writing, was armed with more than sixty letters and affidavits solicited about John Andrew Rice from students, community residents, parents, former Rice colleagues, and faculty members. He also was willing to provide the committee with documents concerning official Rollins policy, although he held back at least some of the items requested.

Much of the week-long AAUP inquiry took place at a long table set up in the vestry room of the Knowles Chapel, with Holt reading affidavits for hours on end and Rice responding. Holt insisted on including Rollins treasurer Ervin T. Brown and Dean Winslow Anderson. Thus, Lovejoy and Edwards maintained that Rice should be allowed two individuals of his choice to accompany him. Although they were not Rice's close friends, professor of political science Ralph Lounsbury and professor of chemistry Frederick Georgia volunteered. Both had served with Rice on the committee that examined the 30 percent faculty pay cuts, and both were becoming increasingly alarmed about the status of academic freedom at Rollins. Georgia, a professor at Rollins for seven years, headed the Rollins branch of AAUP. Lounsbury, a former lawyer and one of Holt's undergraduate classmates at Yale, had come to Rollins three years earlier and had received notice of his reappointment in March for the 1933–1934 academic year. Of the eight men present for the detailing of events and the reading of letters and affidavits,

---

48. Lovejoy and Edwards, "Academic Freedom," 428–29.
49. Hamilton Holt to H. W. Tyler, May 4, 1933, in Rice Case File, Rollins.

Rice, Holt, and Lovejoy engaged in the majority of the conversation by far. The other four participants from Rollins intruded only when they had specific involvement with or special knowledge of an issue that surfaced.[50]

In casting about for affidavits, letters, and memos, Hamilton Holt had netted a collection that included statements both in support of and in objection to Rice. Those used by Holt to bolster his case for Rice's dismissal displayed a spectrum of feelings from petty irritations to serious contentions. Among them were charges that Rice had left fish scales in the sink at the beach cottage rented by the college, that he had whispered in chapel, that he had failed to turn in student absence slips each day to the college registrar, that he had appeared at the beach clad only in a jock strap, and that he had failed to pay rent to a former landlord.

Rice responded vigorously to the charges. For example, he countered the last mentioned accusation by observing that the information about stiffing a landlord had come not from the landlord but from a student whose father was acquainted with the landlord. And on the subject of Rice's beach attire, witnesses were brought in who testified that he was actually wearing white bathing trunks, conforming with Rice's insistence, "I never wore a jock strap in my life." Even when a student passed along the rumor that Rice had hung obscene pictures on the walls of his classroom, the dismissed professor offered a ready explanation. The crudely executed calendar pictures he had hung, none even remotely suggestive, had incited approximately two weeks of discussion between him and his students about the definition and meaning of art. When, near the end of that time, students had asked Rice what he thought of the pictures, he charged, "I think they're obscene." Rice explained to the AAUP committee that he meant strongly objectionable in form and execution, not pornographic in substance.[51]

Those charges that were most devastating and difficult to refute detailed the experiences of students who believed Rice had mistreated them. Some students portrayed a side of Rice that was bullying and insensitive with those who were unprepared to withstand his verbal blows. One student, for example, wrote of his experience: "He [Rice] was chosen last year to be my advisor, and in that capacity he was an absolute failure in every way. I received no advice whatsoever except frequent caustic remarks such as, 'If you are too

50. Lovejoy and Edwards, "Academic Freedom," 433–35; Kuehl, *Hamilton Holt,* 228–31; J. Rice, *Eighteenth Century,* 309–11.

51. "Meeting of May 18, 1933," and "Meeting of May 19, 1933" (Typescripts of meetings with Arthur Lovejoy and Austin Edwards in Rice Case File, Rollins); J. Rice, interview with Duberman, June 10, 1967; J. Rice, *Eighteenth Century,* 309–11; Ervin T. Brown, "Notes," May 19, 1933, in Rice Case File, Rollins.

damn dumb to make out a schedule, why did you come here?' . . . He made me appear before him once a week for the rest of the year during which time he entertained the students who were in the room by making wise cracks at my 'damned dumbness.' I stood for his bullying and insults for the remainder of the year." Another student verified that Rice's in-class interactions could be severe: "Picking some point he'd hold to it and argue for half a class period. It might be on what good was art to the world in general. [My friend] Lib was a favorite prey upon which to pounce, for she would work herself into a perfect frenzy after he had harried her about her interest in painting and finally leave the class in tears."[52]

In general, students who offered statements against Rice recounted one or more of a number of objections. They cited, among other transgressions, his limited adherence to teaching standard Latin and Greek languages, his verbal attacks on students and even on other faculty in class, his intolerance of students who did not appreciate or enjoy his distinctive style, his early dismissal of classes, his encouragement of wide-ranging discussions in which students did most of the talking, and his preference for counseling students about their personal lives rather than about their academic endeavors. One student who took exception to Rice's negative view of fraternities wrote his father (who, like Rice, was a member of Sigma Alpha Epsilon fraternity) asking him to use his connections to determine whether Rice might have had a troubled personal experience with his own fraternity. In his statement to the AAUP committee, the student charged:

> My father never got a reply to his inquiry but Professor Rice some way heard of it and in one of his mixed classes in which I know there was one or more girls present, Professor Rice proceeded to attack me. After raking me back and forth over the coals and saying that I was the kind of a man he would like to put out of Rollins College, I understood Professor Rice to make the following statement: "If you had knocked up a girl in Georgia and then had come down here to Rollins and I had written up there to find out all about it so as to tell the authorities here and get you put out of Rollins, that would have been exactly the same as you have tried to do to me."[53]

On the other hand, many students agreed with student body president Nat French, who wrote to Hamilton Holt:

> During the past year and a half I have been almost consistently in the company of adults because of my physical condition, but among all those men and

52. Student Affidavit, May 16, 1933, and Phyrne Squier to Hamilton Holt, April 25, 1933, both in Rice Case File, Rollins.
53. Student Affidavit, May 17, 1933, in Rice Case File, Rollins.

women there has been only one or two who have stimulated and helped me as Mr. Rice has. It is impossible to talk with him without continually harking back to fundamentals. Perhaps the most valuable part of my character that has developed under him has been the moral side. Background and tradition had prompted most of my good behavior, but now I feel that it is more prompted by a working philosophy and therefore more secure. . . . Viewing Professor Rice impersonally he seems to me to do an excellent job of giving to students those fundamentals for which a college education should stand. He helps them to develop fine moral character, to form intelligent philosophies of life which will motivate these moral beliefs, to appreciate wisdom and to understand art.

In sum, student testimony supporting Rice's personal and professional behavior about equaled that which condemned it. It appears that Professor Rice could be characterized accurately as "the first person who started me really using my mind at all," as well as someone who "gave me no chance and didn't help me at all."[54]

Information gathered by Lovejoy and Edwards about the status of faculty retention and tenure at Rollins was nearly as equivocal. Holt was much less forthcoming with documentation that did not bear directly on his reasons for dismissing Rice, and what he did provide was often contradictory. In the 1933 report of their findings, Lovejoy and Edwards described to AAUP members conflicting information, charging: "He [President Holt] has, on different occasions, ascribed the power of dismissal (a) to himself, (b) to the Executive Committee [of the board of trustees], (c) exclusively to the Board of Trustees; he has informed representatives of the Association that professors and associate professors who have had three years of service are thereafter 'automatically reappointed,' and also that no professor has more than one year's tenure; he has described as probationary the status of a teacher in his third year of service who had at appointment been notified that his probationary period would be two years."[55]

Still, the two committee members completed their investigation uncertain whether the AAUP should file a full report to its membership on the matter and remove Rollins from its approved list of colleges. Any doubt about doing so was erased, however, shortly after they left Winter Park. At the end of the first week of June, just after graduation and as students and faculty were scattering from campus, Holt dismissed Professors Frederick Geor-

54. Nathaniel French to Hamilton Holt, March 8, 1933, Blanche Fishbach to Hamilton Holt, n.d., and Student Affidavit, May 16, 1933, all in Rice Case File, Rollins.
55. Lovejoy and Edwards, "Academic Freedom," 437.

gia and Ralph Lounsbury and Assistant Professor of Philosophy Alan Tory, citing in each instance "pernicious activity in Rice case." He asked for and received the resignations of Assistant Professor Sylvester Bingham and Associate Professor Cecil Oldham. Along with Bingham went his wife, Dean of Women Virginia Bingham.[56]

Ted Dreier believed he would have been fired at the same time had it not been for the presence of his aunt, the wealthy and well-known Margaret Dreier Robins (Mrs. Raymond Robins), on the board of trustees. Mrs. Robins was, like her nephew, entirely sympathetic to the Rice camp. Dreier had served with Rice on the curriculum committee and had written to Holt that he agreed with the committee on fraternities in opposing Holt's enthusiasm for the Greek system. He also stated his objections to Holt's handling of the committee process: "Your mind was made up ahead of time and your asking us to consider the matter was a mere gesture." While his memos and meetings with Holt always included some polite and politic wording about something of which he approved, Dreier generally found himself at odds with many of Holt's actions. On June 2, 1933, Holt and Dean Anderson met with Dreier to inform him that he could return for the following academic year, but that they intended that to be his last year. Holt claimed in a memo, "We did not think he had the rare and genuine gift of imparting knowledge, which is the essential ideal of every professor at Rollins College." Given the disheartening situation with regard to academic freedom and knowing that he and President Holt had lost any basis for friendship or respect, Dreier decided to not to accept the offer of one last year teaching at Rollins. He resigned on June 27, 1933.[57]

Drama professor Robert Wunsch, whose respect for Rice held fast after attending his Greek class as a student for two semesters, did little to align himself publicly with one side or the other of the conflict during the spring. His sympathies were with Rice and his supporters, but he was concerned to keep his employment because he was financially responsible for an ailing mother. However, as summer began and Wunsch retreated to Asheville, North Carolina, to conduct some summer workshops for the Asheville city schools, he began to reflect on instances when Dean Anderson and President Holt had failed to support his work with drama groups and had criticized

---

56. "Reasons for Faculty Changes," memo to files, [n.d.] 1933, in Rice Case File, Rollins; Lovejoy and Edwards, "Academic Freedom," 416; "Rollins Fires Prof. A. P. Tory," Orlando *Morning Sentinel,* June 4, 1933, p. 2.

57. Ted Dreier to Hamilton Holt, April 4, May 5, 1933, and Hamilton Holt, memo to files, June 2, 1933, all in Rice Case File, Rollins; T. Dreier, interview with the author, April 5, 1993.

him for failing to adhere strictly to the classroom hours required by the conference plan. He considered the crowning insult to be Holt's indecisiveness in providing a reference letter necessary for him to obtain a fellowship for summer study in drama. Holt may have hesitated out of knowledge, even without any overt acts of support, that Wunsch was friendly with Rice. On May 30, when Holt finally did provide a lukewarm reference about Wunsch's work at Rollins, it was far too late to meet the application deadline. By August, even though he had no other offer of employment for the fall, Wunsch made up his mind and, with words voicing more sadness than anger, penned his resignation letter to President Holt. Although Holt tried to dissuade him from his decision, Wunsch held firm and eventually accepted instead a teaching position at Louisville Male High School in Louisville, Kentucky.[58]

Although he could not reasonably have expected much less, Hamilton Holt was furious with the AAUP decision to publish a full report that exonerated John Andrew Rice and sanctioned Rollins. For months after the AAUP's official Rollins report was published, Holt carried on a campaign of letter writing to university and college colleagues throughout the country, explaining his case, charging AAUP bias, and encouraging a cooperative effort to urge the Association of American Colleges to investigate the practices of the AAUP. Ever the consummate publicist, he published a special edition of the *Rollins College Bulletin* in December, 1933, devoted entirely to explaining Rollins' side of the story. It was mailed to hundreds of university, business, and government leaders throughout the country.[59]

Many of those who received Holt's correspondence replied in sympathy to his cause, shocked at Holt's description of the unfair treatment Rollins received from the AAUP. For instance, Berea College president William J. Hutchins wrote, "I had not realized before the almost unlimited authority given to a committee whose actions apparently have not adequate supervision whatever. . . . If I had before me such testimony as that which you have brought forward in your discussion, I should either have to have that testimony disproved or I should insist on [Rice's] retirement on the ground that he had voided his contract by his words and deeds."[60]

However, at least some others who did not respond to Holt may have been

58. Hamilton Holt to William R. Wunsch, May 30, 1933, William R. Wunsch to Thomas P. Bailey, August 7, 1933, Hamilton Holt to William R. Wunsch, August 14, 1933, William R. Wunsch to Hamilton Holt, August 15, 1933, William R. Wunsch to Hamilton Holt, October 30, 1934, all in Wunsch File, Rollins; T. Dreier, interview with the author, April 5, 1993.

59. "Rollins College Versus the American Association of University Professors," *Rollins College Bulletin*, XXIX (December, 1933), 3–28.

60. William J. Hutchins to Hamilton Holt, December 27, 1933, in Rice Case File, Rollins.

more disposed to the view expressed ironically to him by Allan Gilbert of Duke University: "I believe you deserve the thanks of all Americans interested in education for so clearly demonstrating the great value of the AAUP as an upholder of right standards in academic life."[61]

The report authored by professors Lovejoy and Edwards and published in the *AAUP Bulletin* portrayed a stubborn and controlling side of Hamilton Holt. It noted, for example, "The authority thus asserted and on occasion exercised by the President appears to the Committee to have exceeded the custom of academic institutions, to have been in violation of the By-Laws, to have been used at times in a manner humiliating to the faculty, to have been incongruous with the spirit of cooperation in an educational experiment ostensibly characteristic of the College and to have worked badly in practice."[62]

The AAUP committee members also attempted to capture the extremes of John Andrew Rice's complex persona. On the positive side, the report asserted, "It is clear that Mr. Rice gave generously of his time and energy outside the classroom to efforts to help individual students find themselves. In the Committee's judgment his dismissal eliminated from the faculty a teacher who appears on the one hand to have done more than any other to provoke questioning, discussion, and the spirit of critical inquiry among his students, and on the other hand, to have aimed, with exceptional success, at constructive results both in thought and character." However, Lovejoy and Edwards also declared, "Professor Rice had unquestionably much disturbed the harmony of the local community and had seriously offended a number of his colleagues and other persons. . . . This effect was, however, much intensified by the frequently vehement, sometimes intemperate, and in several instances discourteous language in which his criticisms were couched, and by a sometimes inopportune humor."[63]

Although the official AAUP report was not published in that organization's monthly bulletin until November, 1933, Lovejoy and Edwards publicly released their preliminary report by the end of May. During the following months, Hamilton Holt got his news coverage, but a liberal press was inclined toward the liberal professor. *Time* magazine, for example, reported, "Hamilton Holt seemed doggedly intent on having his own way even if it meant decimating his faculty and losing leading students." The Orlando *Morning Sentinel,* summing up the number of removed or resigned faculty that Holt had once dubbed "golden personalities," titled its article, "Rollins

61. Allan Gilbert to Hamilton Holt, December 10, 1933, in Rice Case File, Rollins.
62. Lovejoy and Edwards, "Academic Freedom," 419.
63. *Ibid.,* 427, 424–25.

off the Gold Standard: Personality Professors Removed." Editorials searched out the larger implications of the conflict, generally in the direction taken by the *New Republic,* which charged, "Loyalty to Dr. Holt is clearly put above loyalty to the individual's educational ideals. The tragic thing about this situation is that it is not exceptional, but to a large degree typical of American college life today. There are hundreds of other small institutions whose presidents or boards of trustees act quite as ruthlessly as do those at Rollins."[64]

The *New Republic* editorial was a fairly accurate portrayal of the problems often encountered in higher education during the early years of the AAUP. Holt's heavy-handed treatment of his faculty had precedent on numerous campuses where the organization had conducted investigations into the status of academic freedom and tenure since its founding in 1915. While it was reluctant to commit its scarce resources to full on-site investigations and generally resolved issues with more distant mediation strategies, the organization found that the majority of the cases it took on did not concern ideological conflicts or free expression problems. Instead, challenges to academic freedom were usually driven by personality clashes between dictatorial presidents and their professors or by the vindictiveness of high-level officials in removing faculty members. The Rice case was one of many that helped to demonstrate the need for the AAUP. Later, with the development of widespread recognition for its defense of academic freedom, its investigatory competence, and its thoughtful decisions about censure, the AAUP was able to ameliorate these circumstances.[65]

The curtain closed on the drama that was the Rice fracas without a winner among the players. A furious Hamilton Holt fired off a confidential memo to his trustees insisting that the AAUP had acted badly by putting him on trial rather than Rice. With his classes assigned to another professor since April, John Andrew Rice packed in a dark personal rage heightened by the uncertainty of what to do next; he stomped about and threw family items into boxes and suitcases. Only Arthur Lovejoy had ventured to offer any positive advice to Rice about his future, suggesting perhaps he should consider employment in a larger institution, "where you'd spread a little thinner."[66]

---

64. "Rumpus at Rollins," *Time,* June 19, 1933, p. 33; "Rollins off the Gold Standard: Personality Professors Removed," Orlando *Morning Sentinel,* June 9, 1933, p. 2; "Rollins College," *New Republic,* January 17, 1934, p. 265.

65. Walter P. Metzger, *Academic Freedom in the Age of the University* (New York, 1955).

66. Hamilton Holt to Board of Trustees, May 25, 1933, memo in Rice Case File, Rollins; F. Rice, interview with the author, February 13, 1993; Rice, interview with Duberman, June 10, 1967.

5

Black Mountain College:
Socrates and Serendipity

The beginnings of Black Mountain College—punctuated by a series of lucky accidents and occasional flashes of audacity and wisdom—foretold much about its early years. For example, if Richard Feuerstein, a professor of French and German at Rollins College, had been more decisive about his intention to remain or resign, Black Mountain College never would have gotten off the ground. After spending the summer of 1933 scrambling to attract teachers, students, and money to a proposed new college in North Carolina, a group of dissident Rollins faculty members willing to plunge into an underfunded educational experiment had dwindled to five: John Andrew Rice, Ted Dreier, Frederick Georgia, Ralph Lounsbury, and Richard Feuerstein.

By mid-August, the five from Rollins decided they had the bare minimum of cash and faculty resources to start a college; any less of either and they would scrap the idea. On August 25, Feuerstein telegraphed Rice news of his change of heart, explaining, "I am afraid to subject my family and others dependent on me to such a chance." To Rice, temporarily lodging at Frank Aydelotte's home in Swarthmore, the Feuerstein announcement signaled the end of the idea. He soon discovered otherwise.[1]

Ted Dreier, driving from Swarthmore to his family home at Lake George, New York, had decided to stop unannounced at the New York *Herald Tribune* to promote press coverage of the new Black Mountain College scheduled to open its doors on September 25. He located an eager young reporter who found the story fascinating and thought he might be able to write an article

---

1. Richard Feuerstein to John A. Rice, telegram, August 25, 1933, and letter, August 28, 1933, both in Faculty Files, BMCP, N.C. Archives.

just in time for the next morning's edition. Dreier then drove on to Lake George in time for a few hours of sleep. He awoke to a phone call from Rice informing him they would have to scuttle the plans for a new college. However, when they realized the announcement of the opening was already on the newsstands, they agreed it was too late to squash the fledgling venture. On August 26, less than a full day after Rice received Feuerstein's decision, the *Herald Tribune* broke the story under the headline, "Rollins Group, Ousted in Row, Founds College." As the news traveled through the Associated Press wires to other papers, the four faculty remaining committed to the plan knew for certain there would be no turning back.[2]

The timing of Feuerstein's decision was just one of many factors and events that combined rapidly and serendipitously during the summer of 1933 to shape some inchoate ideas about higher education—more what it should *not* be than what it should be—into a maverick college that would become one of the most renowned and vital experiments ever to occur in American higher education.

In the wake of the faculty terminations and resignations from Rollins, not only did other faculty resign, but many students who had been vocal in their support of Rice quit as well. At first Rice thought he might go off and become the writer he had always wanted to be. On second thought, however, how could he turn his back on the courageous Rollins students and faculty who supported him? And how would he support a family while waiting for publication of his plays or books? Nell encouraged him to give up teaching altogether, as for Rice it seemed a vocation prone to agitation at best and family uprooting at worst. The marriage suffered growing strain, and was especially troubled when Rice found himself under fire at work. Rice also had an idea about taking a group of students to Europe and forming a "traveling college." Again, however, the issues of funding and abandoning friends weighed heavily against any such scheme.[3]

Rice had talked often about educational ideals and ideal educational settings, especially with Ted Dreier. It was natural that he and Dreier, with support from other Rollins faculty and enthusiasm from disaffected students, would dream out loud about the possibility of starting a new college. Dreier's own background and experience, very different from Rice's, had afforded

2. T. Dreier, interviews with the author, April 5, 1993, April 28, 1994; Ted Dreier to Mervin Lane, August 31, 1988, in Faculty Files, BMCP, N.C. Archives.
3. Frank Aydelotte to John A. Rice, April 29, 1933, in Aydelotte Papers, Swarthmore; F. Rice, interview with the author, February 13, 1993; F. Rice to Reynolds, December 8, 1994, in author's possession.

him a broad range of thought and activity that could readily contribute insight to discussions of the aims and means of education.

Headquartered in New York and endowed with a fortune accumulated in the mid–nineteenth-century iron trade, Dreier's family was active and energetic in the arts, social reform movements, and business. Ted Dreier's mother, Ethel Eyre Dreier, was head of the Women's Suffrage Party of Brooklyn. His aunt, Margaret Dreier Robins, was for fifteen years the president of the National Women's Trade Union League and was the wife of notable social reformer and Bull Moose party politician Raymond Robins. As a Rollins College trustee, Mrs. Robins had been outspoken in her objection to Hamilton Holt's handling of the Rice affair. Another aunt, Katherine S. Dreier, was a painter who joined with Marcel Duchamp and Man Ray in founding the Société Anonyme, an extensive and celebrated collection of modern art that was the precursor of the Museum of Modern Art.

On the surface, Ted Dreier appeared to veer away from family interests when he majored in physics and engineering at Harvard and then worked as an electrical engineer at General Electric for five years before moving to Winter Park to teach physics at Rollins. However, Dreier and his wife, Barbara, maintained extensive interest in social reform, the arts, and education. Barbara Dreier, born Barbara Loines to a wealthy Staten Island family, was at home with the upper crust and socially conscious Dreier clan. Her grandmother was a founding patron of the women's suffrage movement; and her parents, aunts, and uncles were active in urban improvement causes. Ted and Barbara shared an interest in art and music, and they enjoyed the company of many artists and art patrons. For several summers they attended the Concord Summer School of Music founded and administered by famed music educator Thomas Whitney Surette. Through their close friendship with Malcolm Forbes and his family, they became acquainted with John Dewey and were inspired by his progressive ideas in education.[4]

When Rice and Dreier discussed higher education, their conversations typically touched on their mutual beliefs about the role of building on individual interest and experience and the purpose of acquiring responsibility for life in a democratic society. They agreed that too much of what passed as education was recitation and too little was preparation, and both had been enthusiastic that Rollins seemed committed to departing from the norm.[5] When Rollins disappointed them, the possibility of starting an alternative

---

4. B. Dreier and T. Dreier, interviews with the author, April 5, 1993; Mary Emma Harris, *The Arts at Black Mountain College* (Cambridge, Mass., 1987), 13–14.
5. T. Dreier, interview with the author, April 5, 1993.

college naturally occurred to them, as did the idea's highly speculative and idealistic nature.

Increasingly, however, in May and June, that possibility seemed at least less than fantastic in light of a ready-made nuclear faculty and student body composed of those leaving Rollins. Fired Rollins faculty members Cecil Oldham and Alan Tory expressed some interest in teaching history and philosophy, respectively, at a new school. Robert Wunsch badly wanted to join a new venture if it became solvent enough to meet his need to support his mother. Ousted professors Lounsbury (government and political science) and Georgia (chemistry) were just desperate enough about their futures to consider seriously trying even an unlikely new venture. Prominent retired geologist Josiah E. Spurr, a member of the board of overseers at Harvard University and visiting faculty at Rollins, also expressed outrage at the Rollins incidents and supported, at least in principle, the idea of a new college.[6]

Aside from Dreier and Wunsch, few on the faculty dissident roster could be counted as friends or admirers of Rice, but they were steadfast in their distaste for how his case had been handled. Rice knew that Ralph Lounsbury, at sixty years old, was devastated by his termination in the midst of economic depression. Lounsbury had been a successful New York lawyer until his health started to deteriorate and he could no longer withstand the rigors of New York. His friend "Hammy" Holt had offered him a position at Rollins, and Lounsbury frequently expressed to Holt his gratitude and esteem in return. Three years later, he was fired. Rice felt Lounsbury had more to offer the new venture than he thought but was held back by his conservative nature and his distress about his current circumstances. However, Rice was skeptical of Georgia, whom he viewed as having little interest in the ends and means of education but great eagerness to be influential—perhaps even as president—in a new venture. He recalled Georgia as "amiable, but anti-intellectual."[7]

The students who hoped for a new college to attend were much more ardent Rice supporters than the faculty members poised for a new place to teach. Nathaniel French, son of prominent progressive educator John French who headed the Cambridge School in Massachusetts, led the charge as student body president. He was joined by George R. Barber of Swarthmore,

6. Winslow Anderson to Hamilton Holt, August 12, 1933, in Holt Papers, Rollins; John A. Rice to John Applegate, July 13, 1933, in Faculty Files, BMCP, N.C. Archives; John A. Rice to Frank Aydelotte, September 11, 1933, in Aydelotte Papers, Swarthmore; Martin Duberman, *Black Mountain: An Exploration in Community* (New York, 1972), 13.

7. Ralph Lounsbury to H. Holt, May 7, 1933, in Faculty File, R. Lounsbury, Rollins; J. Rice, interview with Duberman, June 10, 1967.

Pennsylvania, who had been editor of Rollins' student newspaper. Both publicly resigned from the Rollins student body in protest of Rice's dismissal. They were followed by more than a dozen other students. These students frequently joined faculty in the ensuing discussions about the possibility of a new school.[8]

Some of the students who left Rollins, however, knew little about Rice or the other departed faculty. Norman Weston, for example, categorized himself as one of "many, many students who weren't particularly interested in Rice and didn't know much about the uproar going on." Weston's girlfriend, however, Anne ("Nan") Chapin, was vocal in her support of Rice and determined to leave Rollins for a new college venture headed by him. Weston was able to join her when Rice offered him a full scholarship to Black Mountain after finding that Weston's family had no money to continue his college education. Long after his experience at Black Mountain Norman Weston recalled that when he got to know Rice at Black Mountain, he discovered him to be, "a wonderful teacher both in the classroom and in his daily contacts with people. . . . When I got there, he then fully supported my academic efforts. . . . Make no mistake; he was the moving force."[9]

Anne Chapin grew up in Connecticut, the youngest child of a poor widow struggling to support her six children. That changed in 1928, however, when Anne was fifteen years old and her mother married a distant cousin of substantial wealth, Arthur S. Dwight. In the summer of 1933 the Dwight family became the first to offer financial support to the former Rollins faculty members planning a new venture. Mrs. Dwight loaned the Rice family use of a house in Stafford Springs, Connecticut, where her family had lived prior to her second marriage. Colonel Arthur Dwight provided one thousand dollars to assist through the summer's planning for a new venture. He then persuaded a friend, William Barstow, to contribute the same amount. With actual seed money, the new college venture that began as a vague dream suddenly took root.[10]

Frank Aydelotte encouraged Rice to attempt a new college, perhaps because he had exhausted his patience for job hunting on behalf of his brother-in-law or perhaps because he felt genuine curiosity about how some of the experimental ideas might fare. Most influential, however, in cementing the

8. "Rollins Students Will Quit College," Winter Park (Fla.) *Reporter-Star,* June 7, 1933, p. 3; Williams, interview with the author, May 10, 1993; Norman Weston, interview with the author, April 13, 1993.

9. Norman Weston to Katherine Reynolds, April 14, 1994, in author's possession.

10. Norman Weston to Katherine Reynolds, April 25, 1993, in author's possession; M. Harris, *The Arts at Black Mountain,* 4.

commitment of Rice and others to start the venture was identifying a location that seemed like a perfect site for their college. Bob Wunsch, a graduate of the University of North Carolina, had taught high school in Asheville, North Carolina, and was residing at the Asheville YMCA during the summer of 1933. He knew of a campuslike area eighteen miles east of Asheville, just south of the town of Black Mountain, known as Blue Ridge Assembly. A collection of buildings on 1,619 acres, constructed in 1906 by the Blue Ridge Association, the site was used as summer conference and camp facilities for the YMCA and various Christian religious groups and for the summer educational program of the YMCA Graduate School. Frederick Georgia, who had a summer home to the southwest in Highlands, North Carolina, agreed with Wunsch that Blue Ridge Assembly might wonderfully serve to house a new college during the academic year.[11]

The YMCA complex Wunsch and Georgia had in mind was located near the bluntly serrated southern slopes of the Blue Ridge Mountains, where the state of North Carolina achieves the summit of its slow westward tilt from sea level at the Atlantic Ocean to mountain level at the eastern continental divide. The valley town of Black Mountain is shadowed to the north by Mt. Mitchell, at 6,684 feet the highest peak east of the Mississippi River. Just a few miles south of town, where tree-covered foothills converge into gentle ridges, Blue Ridge Assembly had claimed a slope that yielded spectacular views across a wooded valley to the mountain ridges beyond. The sight inspired Henry Miller, an early visitor to Black Mountain College, to write in *The Air-Conditioned Nightmare,* "From the steps of Black Mountain College in North Carolina one has a view of mountains and forests which makes one dream of Asia."[12]

The natural beauty of the area was strikingly complemented by the location and architecture of the Blue Ridge Assembly buildings. A long and narrow drive, sometimes tunneling through arches formed by dogwoods, rhododendrons, and poplars, ended in a circle spanning the open meadow that provided an enormous front lawn for the main building, Robert E. Lee Hall. Immense in its proportions, including a central portico supported by eight columns, each three stories high and four feet in diameter, the white shingle and stone structure appeared built as a gigantic and lasting monument to southern plantation architecture. Another large building, just a few steps behind Lee Hall and connected by a walkway, housed dining and gymnasium

11. J. Rice, interview with Duberman, June 10, 1967; T. Dreier, interview with the author, April 5, 1993; F. Rice, interview with the author, November 24, 1995.

12. Henry Miller, *The Air-Conditioned Nightmare* (New York, 1945), 286.

facilities. Smaller Abbott Hall, also with pillared portico, flanked Lee Hall to the east and adjoined it with a covered walkway. Tucked into the woods that sprawled over most of the Blue Ridge Assembly property were fifty additional buildings, mostly providing cottage-type housing, as well as tennis courts and a swimming pool. Azaleas and mountain laurel were profuse throughout the property, especially along the streams that toppled through the woods. The perfume that hung in the air on a warm day was the unmistakable scent of the South.

After Wunsch made calls to ascertain that Blue Ridge Association would consider leasing the grounds from late September to early June, Frederick Georgia drove John Andrew Rice to the town of Black Mountain, across the railroad tracks bordering it to the south, and up the long drive to Lee Hall. Rice knew immediately that if there was to be a new college, it would be located here. He later described his unforgettable first impressions: "Blue Ridge was perfect. . . . Here was peace. Here was also central heating against the cold of winter, blankets, sheets, dishes, flatware, enough for a dozen colleges, all at a moderate rental, and besides these the one guarantee of civilization, a perfect chef, Jack, a Negro, and the only authentic gentleman on the staff of Black Mountain College—still a notion—and a perfect assistant chef, his wife Ruby[e]."[13]

The site spoke to the great affection Rice had since boyhood for all things of the South—especially the "Old South" of his grandmother Smith. He was at home with the plantation architecture, the humidity, the flowering trees, and the front porches waiting for rocking chairs and conversation. This was his emotional home in a way that Nebraska, New Jersey, or even Florida, had never become.

Before the visit to the Blue Ridge site, when talk about starting a new venture became serious enough to conjecture about a name, Rice and others among the faculty and students departed from Rollins agreed upon "New College." However, Rice later recalled that on the drive to inspect the Blue Ridge Assembly site, Georgia stopped the car twenty miles west of Asheville and showed Rice a turn sign announcing "New College." The name had been taken by a Columbia University extension site near Canton, North Carolina.[14]

Location dictated the next name selected, "Black Mountain College." On August 19, 1933, the state of North Carolina issued the college a certificate

13. J. Rice, *Eighteenth Century,* 318.
14. *Ibid.,* 317–18; Katherine Schlesinger to Frederick Mangold, September 3, 1936, in Faculty Files, BMCP, N.C. Archives.

of incorporation, signed by incorporators Frederick R. Georgia, Nell A. Rice, and Helen B. Lounsbury. The document established Black Mountain as a coeducational school that could grant degrees or certificates and would be governed by a faculty committee called the "board of fellows." "In six weeks we made a college," Barbara Dreier later exclaimed about the frantic weeks of late summer, 1933. "From scratch, without any money, in the middle of a depression," added Ted Dreier. The founding of Black Mountain College was to become one of the most remarkable start-up sagas in American higher education, punctuated by a series of small victories and substantial setbacks in the race to develop programs, policies, and financial and human resources.[15]

John Andrew Rice traveled through thirteen states by car that summer, with his teenage son Frank serving as chauffeur. Frank Rice had become well accustomed to weeks at a time alone with his father, since Nell regularly took off with daughter Mary for her home town of Sullivan, Indiana—sometimes encouraged (and provided with train fare) by her busy brother Frank, who liked to know someone was checking on their aging parents, and sometimes prompted by growing marital problems. Nell and Mary had left Winter Park for Sullivan well in advance of Rice's final departure, leaving Rice to fume alone about his termination and leaving Frank to help him pack. Frank knew his father's habits well, right down to a preference for the clean socks that Frank washed for him. He was not surprised that his father retreated deep into thought and rarely spoke a word as they drove throughout the eastern United States.[16]

Lounsbury and Georgia stayed in North Carolina most of the summer to negotiate a lease, correspond with prospective students and faculty, and draft official college documents, while Rice and Dreier headed north to attract money, recruit students, and seek support among their most influential academic friends. Henry Allen Moe at the Guggenheim Foundation lent them some of his New York office space and some advice about potential faculty and funding sources. Not surprisingly, the president's mansion at Swarthmore College also was a regular stop. There, on Aydelotte's front porch, Dreier and Rice, sometimes joined by Georgia, gave greater definition to their thoughts on higher education. As the academic and administrative

---

15. "Certificate of Incorporation of Black Mountain College," August 19, 1933, in Official Documents, BMCP, N.C. Archives; B. Dreier and T. Dreier, interviews with the author, April 5, 1993.

16. F. Rice, interview with the author, February 13, 1993; Frank A. Rice to Lewis Shelly, August 1, 1966, in the private collection of Frank A. Rice.

structure of Black Mountain College began to take shape, Frank Aydelotte joined enthusiastically in the discussions, some of which also were attended by his summer visitor from England, F. J. Wylie, Oxford secretary to the Rhodes trust. Other planning sessions and philosophical discussions occurred throughout the summer, notably one that lasted nearly a week and included former Rollins students and faculty at the summer home of Josiah Spurr in Alstead, New Hampshire.[17]

Rice's experiences and reflection in a variety of higher education settings already had provided him with a clear philosophy about purposes. "Education for democracy" was how he broadly characterized the end for which Black Mountain would be a means, later elaborating that education should address the capacity of citizens to act responsibly in a democratic setting. Now, with an opportunity to shape the means, he began to articulate that it needed to closely match the end. If responsible democratic action was the goal of education, then responsible democratic action also should be experienced within the educational setting.[18]

Rice could look back to Thomas Jefferson, whom he referred to as a "coeval," for early inspiration concerning higher education as a setting for practice in democracy.[19] When he started planning for the University of Virginia in 1818, Jefferson committed himself to the ideal that each student's interest should guide his choice of study, with students allowed to range freely around courses offered in a variety of fields and disciplines. His plan, experimental in its time and abandoned by 1831, included elimination of labels for prescribed levels (freshman, sophomore, junior, and senior) and elimination of degrees in favor of diplomas of completion. Jefferson was determined to elevate the goal of learning. He was convinced that a way to accomplish this elevation was to give students liberty to make choices in pursuit of personal preferences, some of which might be strictly vocational.

The ideal of an educated individual as a responsible actor, in addition to thinker or truth knower, was not unanimously espoused by American educators, but neither was it considered a new concept. Ralph Waldo Emerson, in 1837, had intimated an action end for education when he insisted, "Character is higher than intellect." He also had promoted action as an educational means when he asserted, "The true scholar grudges every opportunity of ac-

---

17. Frank Aydelotte to Ralph Lounsbury, August 15, 1933, in Aydelotte Papers, Swarthmore; Francis J. Wylie to J. A. Rice, n.d., in Faculty Files, BMCP, N.C. Archives; F. Rice, interview with the author, February 13, 1993; Duberman, *Black Mountain,* 13.

18. J. Rice, *Eighteenth Century,* 327.

19. *Ibid.,* 324.

tion past by as a loss of power. It is the raw material out of which the intellect molds her splendid products."[20]

Rice defined the education end—the responsible actor in a democracy—as an individual of both "intellectual and emotional maturity" whose actions would be informed by feelings as well as knowledge. He railed against the German university system—and, by implication, its widespread adaptation in American research universities—for its emphasis on knowledge acquisition and ignorance of human emotion, and he scoffed at the emphasis on book learning still preferred by many American liberal arts colleges. Instead, he insisted that students must be guided to seek their own truths and their own meanings through experience, observation, and criticism. With mature and meaningful action as his pragmatic educational objective, Rice frequently insisted that, "What you do with what you know is the important thing. To know is not enough."[21]

The means of higher education to be embodied in Black Mountain College were perhaps more difficult to explicate than the end. It was relatively easy to determine that students preparing for responsible action in a democracy needed experience in responsible democratic action. It was more difficult to set forth plans and policies embodying that thought. Issues in the area of means attracted hours of discussion among the students and faculty planning the new college during the summer of 1933. The remote location and small size of the college came to condition their understanding of the two arenas in which Black Mountain students would pursue their educational aims: community and curriculum. Both arenas needed to be fashioned to contribute to the education being sought.

Rice and his colleagues decided that the community could best contribute to its members' educational aims by becoming a social unit that would involve everyone's extensive participation and interaction. Students would have a voice in academic and administrative affairs, even representation on the governing faculty committee. Students and faculty would live together in Lee Hall (except for married faculty with small children, who lived in nearby cottages); eat meals together in the dining hall; and participate together in Saturday evening dances, concerts, and theater productions. They would join together in at least some work around the college such as clearing dining tables and unloading coal for the furnace. The first official catalog

---

20. Ralph Waldo Emerson, "The American Scholar," in *Ralph Waldo Emerson: Selected Essays,* ed. Larzer Ziff (New York, 1982), 92–94.

21. Adamic, "Education on a Mountain," 518; J. Rice, "Fundamentalism and the Higher Learning," 595.

noted early in its foreword that "the distinction is broken down between work done in the class room and work done outside, and the relation is not so much of teacher to student as of one member of the community to another. This ease of communication restores one of the time-tested necessities of education." Ted Dreier would prove particularly enthusiastic about and adept at organizing student work efforts, but Rice felt the sense of community did not necessarily require organized labor or full participation. He decided that those who liked to work with their hands in service of the college should do so, but "if somebody would rather walk around the woods, or sit and listen to a record, or read a book or talk to somebody, then that's the thing to do." Rice, given more to indolence than industry, was not partial to the idea of physical labor for himself.[22]

The issue of coeducation was accepted without discussion among the Black Mountain College founders, although they often felt the mix of men and women in a small college contributed to their difficulties in securing funds, especially from large foundations. Nevertheless, they viewed the mix of men and women as essential to the contribution that community could make to education in and for democracy, noting in the first Black Mountain catalog that male and female students should establish a relationship "not of opposites, but of those who live upon the common ground of humanity." Interestingly, the two colleges most closely resembling Black Mountain during the 1930s were single-sex (female) schools: Sarah Lawrence, which began with some similar curricular aims in 1930; and Bennington, which opened its doors in 1932. Rice later explained his belief that coeducation was "essential" where equality and democracy were aims of society, "not in the sense merely of having men and women in the same classroom, but in the sense of education in relation to each other. American civilization has been an experiment in co-education from the beginning. To separate men and women in colleges is to be guilty once more of stupidly copying Europe." The decision in favor of coeducation was noteworthy enough to prompt the New York *Times* to headline its article announcing the college's founding: "Coeducation in A New College."[23]

Rice's experiences at Oxford and at Webb School had set the stage for his ideas about how decisions concerning curriculum could help to realize his

22. *Black Mountain College, 1933–1934* (N.p., 1933), 1; J. Rice, interview with Duberman, June 10, 1967.

23. *Black Mountain College, 1933–1934*, 2; Adamic, "Education on a Mountain," 518; "Co-education in a New College," New York *Times,* September 17, 1933, p. 3.

ideal of education in and for responsible action in democracy. A commitment to a variety of individual interests and freedom to pursue those interests, reflecting the entreaties of John Dewey and other progressive educators, led readily to course offerings aimed at liberal learning, lower and upper divisions of study, elimination of course requirements, faculty advisors for ongoing guidance, interdisciplinary seminars, candidacy for graduation based on a student's readiness rather than on accumulation of course units, and final evaluation by outside examiners.

Rice's strong methodological bias for the role of experience in and out of the college classroom was summarized in his later statement of example: "To read a play is good, to see a play is better, but to act in a play however awkwardly is to realize a subtle relationship between sound and movement." It was only natural that he would begin to ponder about the place in education of forms of experiential expression like drama, music, and fine arts. With Ted Dreier he often had mulled over ideas about how artistic training could contribute to a nonartist's general education. "It was such a natural concern to me, being the only one in my family who ever went into the sciences," recalled Dreier. "And the art issue was one of the things that drew John Rice and me together."[24]

Eventually Rice's thinking and talking about art led him to the conviction that the arts—especially drawing, painting, sculpture, music, and dramatics—should be central to a college curriculum. This idea would eventually become the most distinguishing feature of Black Mountain College. Dreier and Wunsch, as well, had experienced the influence of the arts and were readily drawn to the same conviction. Rice, however, had only a distant fondness for the arts and generated the idea more from thought, a favorite pastime, and intuition. Later, he insisted he had no exact idea how he concluded art should be central, claiming, "I just knew that I knew it, that this [art] was the core of the thing."[25]

Undoubtedly, Rice also identified with artists, whom he felt were seeking to expand understanding through creativity and experience, rather than to ascertain knowledge through control and experimentation. Rice himself reveled in the ambiguity he defined as artistry for its possibilities and uncertainties, later explaining, "The artist is never quite sure what is happening, and is quite incapable of knowing what will happen. . . . For every human

24. J. Rice, "Fundamentalism and the Higher Learning," 588; T. Dreier, interview with the author, April 5, 1993.
25. J. Rice, interview with Duberman, June 10, 1967.

action there are alternative explanations. No single one is absolutely sure: better keep in mind the other, the unknown. Determinism, however refined, is too easy."[26]

The importance of the arts in education was not an entirely new thought. Bennington and Sarah Lawrence, for example, had begun to incorporate similar notions into their educational plans. John Dewey, the icon of progressive schooling, insisted, "Every art communicates because it expresses. It enables us to share vividly and deeply in meanings to which we had been dumb. Art breaks through barriers that divide human beings, which are impermeable in ordinary association." Although Dewey reflected more on the roles of aesthetic emotion and expressive communication than on the disciplined process of artistic creation, he had, through the progressive education movement, begun to lend respectability to art as a serious academic endeavor.[27]

What would eventually distinguish the Black Mountain commitment to the arts was the level to which the practice of art was elevated and the idea of using creative experience to enhance any area of professional or academic interest. As the centerpiece of the curriculum, the arts were experienced by every student, whether aspiring artist or budding biologist. To John Andrew Rice the practice of art, especially by those with limited natural talent, was the best way for students to internalize the importance of method and process over substance and results. Although he thought much about the idea, he put little into words and less into print on the subject. Author Louis Adamic, during a 1936 visit to Black Mountain, captured the following explanation from Rice:

> Nearly every man is a bit of an artist, at least potentially a person of imagination, which can be developed; and, so far as I know at this moment, there is but one way to train and develop him—the way discovered, not by me but by Black Mountain College as a whole. Here our central and consistent effort now is to teach method, not content; to emphasize process, not results; to invite the student to the realization that the way of handling facts and himself amid the facts is more important than facts themselves. For facts change, while the method of handling them—provided it is life's own free, dynamic method—remains the same. . . .
> The common expression "to get" an education is significant. It lights up the whole fallacy of the prevailing system, for education can only be *experienced;* one "gets" only information or "facts." . . . There are some stubborn

26. J. Rice, "Black Mountain College Memoirs," 575.
27. John Dewey, *Art as Experience* (New York, 1934), 244.

facts in the early stages of the physical sciences, in mathematics and biology, that must be learned. But once those stages are passed, one is in the realm of imagination, where often even professional scientists get lost because of too much education in facts and scant training in imagination. I am especially opposed to mere head-stuffing in philosophy, literature, art, music, and dramatics; for these subjects are the best training grounds for imagination, the chief distinction of man.[28]

Rice's idea of art in education went beyond what creative expression could accomplish in the classroom. William Rice, his grandson, later recognized that "for him, the point of art in education was to take it out of the classroom, to *use* the artistic point of view. . . . Art was not seen only as self-expression, but as a source of *discipline* that helped each person to see, to learn, to listen, and to make choices about their lives." Certainly, Rice and his founding colleagues never conceived of Black Mountain College as an "art school." Instead, they sought a place for arts in the curriculum that might or might not attract students who seriously wanted to pursue careers as artists but that would assuredly inspire all students to use artistry—its discipline and awareness—in every area of personal life and in every type of professional pursuit.[29]

One of the most challenging assignments for Rice and his colleagues during the summer of 1933 was to recruit the right individual to teach art at Black Mountain College. Rice was adamant that whereas the instruction of music, dramatics, and writing would be important at the college, the greatest need was for someone who could guide drawing and painting "because that's the simplest thing. It's between you and the pencil and the piece of paper and your ability to see." With Dreier's family connections in the art world, it was fairly easy to find people who could recommend potential recruits. Typically, however, they would suggest somebody who sounded ideal for teaching in a new art school but not so likely to want involvement in art education as it was defined at the outset of Black Mountain College. Rice was insistent that an art school was "the last thing I want. They're the worst places on earth." Rice and Dreier also realized that art in college often had been regarded as, according to Dreier, "a sissy subject." Thus, Dreier later explained, they decided from the outset that in addition to finding someone who would teach art with a regard for its importance as a method and process, they wanted "somebody with a strong, virile approach to art as an important part of life,

28. Adamic, "Education on a Mountain," 518–19.
29. W. Rice, interview with the author, January 6, 1993.

so there would be no underlying negative attitudes about it among male students."[30]

One of Dreier's contacts in the art world was a friend of his mother's, Margaret Lewisohn, wife of the secretary to the board of trustees of the Museum of Modern Art, Samuel Lewisohn. Mrs. Lewisohn suggested that Dreier and Rice take their inquiry about a possible art instructor to Edward M. M. Warburg, then a twenty-five-year-old trustee of the museum who had taken an interest in helping Jewish scholars and artists in Germany. Warburg, in turn, included his good friend and associate, architect Philip C. Johnson, in fielding the inquiry about an art teacher. Johnson, curator of architecture and industrial design at the Museum of Modern Art, was an avid admirer and supporter of the teaching and work of the Bauhaus, the highly regarded German design institute, which in September, 1932, had been closed by Adolf Hitler for representing thinking and artistry that appeared too Marxist, too anti-German, and too Jewish. Mies van der Rohe had then tried valiantly to reorganize the Bauhaus as a private institution and move it from Dessau to Berlin. Soon after, however, Hitler became chancellor. In April, 1933, his Nazi police arrived in trucks at the Berlin facility to remove the last vestiges of the fourteen-year Bauhaus legacy.

Rice visited Warburg and Johnson in New York in early August, 1933, to describe the type of individual needed to direct the art program at Black Mountain College and to solicit suggestions. Johnson understood immediately and claimed, "I can guarantee you a perfect person for what you want, if you can just get the money to bring him over." Warburg had thought of Bauhaus master teacher and assistant director Josef Albers at almost the same instant. In Germany Johnson had visited Josef Albers and his wife Anni, an impressive artist herself in weaving and textile design. Although he had not actually observed any of Albers' classes, he was convinced Albers would be perfect when Rice explained he wanted someone who could work with all students, not just aspiring artists. "I knew him, knew his work, knew his personality, knew the feeling at the Bauhaus, and knew how his students felt," Johnson later recalled of his certainty about Albers. He then showed Rice photographs of some work by Albers and his students, including wire sculptures and material studies using folded paper. Without a minute's hesitation, Rice announced, "This is just the kind of thing we want."[31]

30. J. Rice, interview with Duberman, June 10, 1967; T. Dreier, interview with the author, April 5, 1993.

31. Philip Johnson, interview with the author, January 16, 1996; Edward M. M. Warburg to Alfred Barr, August 31, 1933, in Alfred H. Barr Papers, Museum of Modern Art Archives, New York; T. Dreier, interview with the author, April 5, 1933.

Johnson thought Albers might be willing to join a new venture, although no other Bauhaus artist had yet left Germany and many were still hoping their situation might improve. Albers, however, was early to see the handwriting on the wall, and he was growing concerned for Anni, who was from a prominent and wealthy Jewish family in Berlin. The one difficulty in hiring Albers, Johnson was quick to caution Rice about: "He doesn't speak a word of English." Rice did not count language as a barrier. Among the students and faculty coming to Black Mountain there were some, including Rice himself, with a fair working knowledge of German. Surely they could get someone to act as an interpreter in the classroom. Rice agreed with Johnson's belief that "the language of art is in the hand and the mind."[32]

Both Warburg and Johnson were enthusiastic about the prospects of having the Albers couple in the United States, enough so that they took active roles in the arrangements to bring them over. The U.S. Immigration Bureau wanted proof of employment and a guaranteed salary, neither of which the shaky new college had been able to extend to other faculty being hired. Warburg wrote to noted art critic and scholar Alfred Barr and communicated with Abby Aldrich (Mrs. John D.) Rockefeller about a contribution. Eventually, Warburg himself matched Mrs. Rockefeller's five-hundred-dollar contribution for the Albers' travel expenses and added another five hundred as a donation to the college. Johnson made the first contact with Albers on behalf of the college, and Albers replied with scrupulous honesty, warning, "Dass ich anfanger im englischen bin" ("I am a beginner in English"). Ted Dreier was equally scrupulous in his reply, drafted with assistance from Emmy Zastrow, who later would teach German at Black Mountain College. He explained to Albers the philosophy of the new college and warned it was a pioneering venture.[33]

In fact, the idea of an experimental college with a pioneering philosophy heartened Josef and Anni Albers. The Bauhaus itself had been such a venture, with its astonishing accomplishments drawn from excellence in teaching, community in learning, and experimentation in forging a meaning for the arts that went beyond expert artisanship. Under the founding vision of Walter Gropius in 1919, that unique design institute had turned its back on the signature traits of German higher education: professorial preeminence and reverence for research. At the Bauhaus, teachers were masters and stu-

---

32. J. Rice, interview with Duberman, June 10, 1967; Nicholas Fox Weber, *Patron Saints: Five Rebels Who Opened America to a New Art, 1928–1943* (New York, 1992), 197–98; Warburg to Barr, August 31, 1933, in Barr Papers.

33. Josef Albers to Philip Johnson, August 30, 1933, in Josef Albers Papers, Sterling Memorial Library, Yale University, New Haven, Conn.; M. Harris, *The Arts at Black Mountain,* 9; T. Dreier, interview with the author, April 5, 1993.

dents apprentices in a guildlike workshop system where learning and experience were indistinguishable from one another. The community of artists, architects, printers, graphic designers, stage decorators, and others shared interdisciplinary learning in art theory and design principles. They also shared a heady schedule of extracurricular concerts, plays, dances, costume balls, lectures, and art exhibits.[34]

However, the Bauhaus had its share of eccentric personalities and professional tensions. John Andrew Rice, who admired Albers' desire to build something that did not replicate the German art institute, later estimated that "the Bauhaus had evidently not been paradise and Albers showed no inclination to building another on the foundation of memory. Nor, whatever may have been a secret desire, did he so much as suggest, while I was there, that the college become an art school."[35]

Josef Albers had been noted at the Bauhaus for connecting learning about art to learning to question and criticize. He explained that the connection between art and education could best be understood by considering the tension among opposing aspects of an artist's work. He posited, "on the one hand, the intuitive search for and discovery of form; on the other hand, the knowledge and application of the fundamental laws of form. Thus all rendering of form, in fact all creative work, moves between the two polarities: intuition and intellect, or possibly between subjectivity and objectivity. Their relative importance continually varies and they always more or less overlap."[36]

When Albers arrived at Black Mountain College, Rice was immediately certain that the decision about him had been correct, later explaining with his characteristic dash of sarcasm, "You know, every now and then you meet a gracious German, and it's wonderful; and he was it. We took to each other at once. I was a little leery about Anni, but she was tagging on behind." Upon his arrival Albers had managed to learn just enough English to define perfectly his mission as the first Bauhaus transplant to the United States. When asked what he hoped to accomplish in his new country, he replied, "To open eyes."[37]

34. For discussions of the origins and closing of the Bauhaus, see, for example, Frank Whitford, *Bauhaus* (London, 1984), and Hans Maria Wingler, *The Bauhaus: Weimar, Dessau, Berlin, Chicago* (Cambridge, Mass., 1969).

35. J. Rice, "Black Mountain College Memoirs," 578.

36. Josef Albers, "Concerning Art Education," *Black Mountain College Bulletin*, II (June, 1934), 1–2.

37. J. Rice, interview with Duberman, June 10, 1967; M. Harris, *The Arts at Black Mountain*, 17.

Rice and Dreier had been just in time in their approach to Albers. Only weeks after Albers agreed to come to Black Mountain, he received an offer from artist and architect Edwin Park, chair of the art program being developed at Bennington College, asking him to consider joining that faculty. Albers may have been just as happy to be committed elsewhere, however, as Bennington wanted him to transplant the Bauhaus philosophy, rather than teach as he would or try new approaches.[38]

Other faculty recruitment efforts during the summer of 1933 centered on filling in gaps that existed in the lineup of Rollins faculty willing to join Black Mountain. The roster shrank as July and August wore on. Robert Wunsch could not afford to join the venture, as it would only pay his living expenses. That left an opening in English and drama. Cecil Oldham and Alan Tory had demonstrated more curiosity than real interest in the experimental college. Both found more stable work elsewhere, leaving history and philosophy positions unfilled. The group had intended to name Josiah Spurr head of the college, capitalizing on the respect he commanded in academic circles but allowing him as much time as he desired to continue the semiretired status he had enjoyed during his visiting professorship at Rollins. In midsummer, however, Spurr had a heart attack and withdrew from involvement in the college.

Frederick Georgia, headquartered at his summer cabin in Highlands, North Carolina, fielded inquiries from potential faculty and students, and locating Rice in New York, Connecticut, or Pennsylvania, forwarded ideas or resumes to him. Many suggestions for faculty came from Frank Aydelotte, who responded quickly whenever one of the originally interested faculty dropped out. Some applicants simply heard news of the planned college and were willing to take a chance there; perhaps some of them were desperate for any work during the depression. For a young scholar fresh from graduate school, the prospect of teaching amidst beautiful mountain scenery, and earning free room and board beside interesting colleagues, was not bad at all.

Hilda Margaret ("Peggy") Loram was one of the original faculty recruits, taking over in English and dramatics when Wunsch dropped out. Her experience was fairly typical of how faculty members were located and hired. Her father, Charles Templeman Loram, was a professor at Yale University and founder of its Department of Race Relations. She attended Swarthmore College, where she graduated in the honors division in three years and where she got to know the Aydelotte family well. In 1932, at the height of the depression, she found no job market for a new young graduate in English, so she

---

38. Thomas P. Brockway, *Bennington College: In the Beginning* (Bennington, Vt., 1981), 116.

John Andrew Rice, Sr., *ca.* 1912
Courtesy Frank A. Rice

Anna Belle Smith Rice, *ca.* 1885
Courtesy Frank A. Rice

Tanglewood, Grandmother Smith's plantation
Courtesy Sam Holland, photographer

John Andrew Rice at Oxford, 1913
Courtesy Frank A. Rice

Nell Aydelotte Rice, 1913
Courtesy Frank A. Rice

John Andrew and Nell Rice with Frank and Mary
in Winter Park, Florida, *ca.* 1932
Courtesy William C. Rice

John Andrew Rice with Ted Dreier (right rear) and
Cecil Oldham (left rear) in the *Marlin* on the Indian
River near New Smyrna Beach, Florida, 1932
Courtesy Frank A. Rice

Robert E. Lee Hall, Black Mountain College, 1935
Courtesy North Carolina Division of Archives and History

The front portico of Robert E. Lee Hall
Courtesy North Carolina Division of Archives and History

Rice with students in an outdoor seminar, Black Mountain College
Courtesy North Carolina Division of Archives and History

Josef Albers with students at Black Mountain College
Courtesy North Carolina Division of Archives and History

Remembering Black Mountain College
Courtesy author

went on to graduate school. When she received her master of arts degree from Columbia University in spring, 1933, she again entered the job market. Not surprisingly, Frank Aydelotte connected her with Rice, who soon interviewed her in New York. The interview was uneventful, with Loram deciding, "He [Rice] was quite interesting, although I don't think either of us had a great deal to say to each other in the interview. He showed me some pictures of the site for the college, and I made some comments on them. It was very brief, very neutral, just polite conversation. A few days later, I got a call from Ted Dreier offering me the job, and I was quite surprised. I accepted as more of an adventure than anything else. I was tired of studying and didn't want to get a Ph.D. This just sounded new and interesting." Since Bob Wunsch could not join the venture, Loram was asked at least temporarily to teach not only English, but also dramatics, a subject about which she confessed to have nearly no knowledge.[39]

Joe Martin, also hired to teach English, applied for the job at the urging of his sister, one of Rice's student supporters at Rollins. After graduating from Haverford College and Oxford University, he had just begun work on a doctorate at Columbia University. Beginning to tire of student life, however, he also opted for the adventure beginning at Black Mountain. He met twice with Rice and was hired.[40]

John Evarts, music critic for the Brooklyn *Daily Eagle,* was hired to teach music on the basis of his gift for piano improvisation. A twenty-five-year-old musician educated at Yale University, the Concord Summer School of Music, and abroad, Evarts wrote to Rice when he heard of the opening of a new college. Undoubtedly, Rice was attracted by the candor and creativity evident when Evarts confessed his bent for improvisation and for limited use of the written score.[41]

Several weeks before the college opened in late September, a skeleton faculty could be introduced in official literature—a six-page mimeographed announcement that later grew into a small catalog—with the caveat, "Additions to this list will be announced later." The initial teaching staff of seven men and two women was announced as: Rice, classics and philosophy; Dreier, physics and mathematics; Georgia, chemistry; Lounsbury, government, public law, and history; Loram, English and dramatics; Martin, En-

39. Margaret Loram Bailey, interview with the author, May 10, 1993; Margaret Loram Bailey to Katherine Reynolds, April 9, 1994, in author's possession.

40. Duberman, *Black Mountain,* 6; Joseph W. Martin, "Black Mountain College: Personal Memoir" (MS in Faculty Files, BMCP, N.C. Archives).

41. John Evart to John A. Rice, September 7, 1933, in Faculty Files, BMCP, N.C. Archives.

glish; Evarts, music; Helen Elizabeth Boyden, economics; and William W. Hinckley, psychology. Josef Albers and several other faculty members arrived after the fall term was underway.[42]

Fortunately for those on the faculty and staff, Ted Dreier had worked out a lean budget for the college's first year. While it could not accommodate actual salaries for the faculty, this plan could provide for living quarters, meals, and a fund to be tapped for incidental expenses according to individual need. During the summer of planning, Dreier proved himself to be a guardian of philosophical optimism and financial pragmatism. At one of the midsummer sessions at Frank Aydelotte's house, Rice insisted that if they wanted to start a new college, they should just announce it and let the students and donors flock to them. Dreier was appalled, charging that with no budget or financial plan for getting through at least the first year, it would be irresponsible to announce the new venture. "We went to bed still debating this question," recalled Dreier. "So I stayed up all night developing a budget." The document unveiled at the Aydelottes' breakfast table the next morning was spare and sensible, appropriate for a time when, as Dreier knew, "Money was almost impossible to find." The bottom line for the first year was $30,000 on the operating expense side. Income was estimated at $15,000 from fifteen students who would pay $1,000 tuition each (although several others would be offered scholarships) and $15,000 from donors. Frank Aydelotte reviewed the budget calculations and told Rice, "Looks to me like you'd better make Ted your treasurer." It was a post Dreier would hold for the next sixteen years.[43]

Neither development nor student recruitment work were particularly favored by either Rice or Dreier, but they gamely split up and set off for various parts of Pennsylvania, New York, and New England to probe contacts and follow up on leads. Rice claimed he was no good at raising money because he exhibited skepticism toward the wealthy and lacked the diplomacy required to tap their fortunes. As he sat before potential donors in their paneled offices or columned mansions, he wanted badly to give voice to his uppermost thought: "You've got no business with all that money. Now shell out." Rice did not fare any better with the big foundations, although he knocked on some doors at the Rockefeller, Carnegie, and Marshall Field foundations. In Rice's estimation, their executives appeared disturbed by the absence of a

42. "Black Mountain College," preliminary catalog (Typescript in Official Documents, BMCP, N.C. Archives).

43. T. Dreier, interview with the author, April 5, 1993; Ted Dreier to M. Lane, August 31, 1988, in Faculty Files, BMCP, N.C. Archives.

clear plan with requisite objectives and timetables and by the faculty's commitment to coeducation.[44]

Rice did, however, meet resounding success when he made a trip to the Forbes estate on Naushon Island, Massachusetts, to discuss the financial needs of the new college. He knew that Malcolm Forbes, his colleague at Rollins, admired him only "in a grudging way," finding him "too abrupt, arrogant." Nevertheless, Rice had been friendly with Forbes, even defending him when there was a movement among faculty to push Forbes out of Rollins. He spent an afternoon on Naushon explaining the idea of Black Mountain College to Forbes, and Forbes offered five thousand dollars. As Rice was leaving, Forbes's wife, Ethel, decided to match that contribution. Later in the summer, Forbes nearly lost his resolve to contribute to the unsteady effort, but his good friend Ted Dreier managed to persuade him and his wife to activate their pledges. Ted Dreier recalled that one of his most important activities that summer was keeping Forbes on track. In addition to meeting with Forbes during the summer, Dreier and his wife, Barbara, socialized whenever possible with Malcolm and Ethel Forbes. It is likely that without Dreier's friendly persistence, the Forbeses might well have retracted their pledges. Until Malcolm Forbes's death in 1941, only Rice and Dreier knew the identity of these anonymous donors who were most responsible for making the creation of Black Mountain College financially possible. They headed the list of underwriters that year, who included Arthur S. Dwight, William Barstow, and Dreier's parents, Edward and Ethel Dreier. The Dreiers' contribution was two thousand dollars.[45]

Student recruitment presented the founders of Black Mountain College with another problem. Potential students often had skeptical parents who were hesitant to put their resources toward the risky college their offspring had chosen. By late summer it was clear that former Rollins students would make up the majority of the Black Mountain student body, but it was uncertain exactly how many would come. As word of mouth about the college passed among college-age students, requests for information dribbled in to Frederick Georgia, who was installed at the college by late August. He sent out his mimeographed sheets and begged Rice to provide information for a printed catalog. By the time the college opened on September 25, thirteen students who had abandoned Rollins to enter Black Mountain were joined

44. J. Rice, interview with Duberman, June 10, 1967; J. Rice, *Eighteenth Century,* 326.
45. T. Dreier, interviews with the author, April 5, 1993, April 29, 1994; Dreier to Lane, August 31, 1988, in Faculty Files, BMCP, N.C. Archives; Duberman, *Black Mountain,* 14; M. Harris, *The Arts at Black Mountain,* 4.

by eight who had not attended Rollins. Some were siblings or friends of the Rollins group, such as Margaret Dwight of Summit, New Jersey, sister of Ellsworth E. Dwight, who had attended Rollins for three years. Others bravely jumped in on the strength of early recommendations of the new school. Doughten I. Cramer came from Morristown, New Jersey, after hearing about the new college from his older brother, Maurice, who counted as his closest friend William Aydelotte, son of the Swarthmore president. Two students arrived from Massachusetts without Rollins histories, but they were acquainted with three others from the same state who had transferred from Rollins. Frank A. Rice, who skipped his senior year of high school, was enrolled as another student from outside the Rollins group, as was John G. McGraw—the only nonresident student ever accepted—who commuted to campus from the town of Black Mountain. Of the twenty-one pioneering youths, most were from East Coast states. Former Rollins student Alice Lee Swan of Oshkosh, Wisconsin, could boast having traveled farthest from her hometown to attend.[46]

Official Black Mountain College literature explained a bit of the school's philosophy and a bit of its administration. Although the college could be readily categorized as "experimental," that aspect was played down—perhaps to alleviate the worst fears of paying parents. The first printed catalog conservatively emphasized building on proven educational methods, stating:

Black Mountain College was founded in order to provide a place where free use might be made of tested and proved methods of education and new methods tried out in a purely experimental spirit. There is full realization, however, of the fact that experiment is, for the individual, also experience; hence, no experiment is being tried which is not submitted beforehand to the test of reasonable likelihood of good results. It is for this reason that the College is for the present content to place emphasis upon combining those experiments and the results of those experiences which have already shown their value in educational institutions of the western world, but which are often isolated and hampered from giving their full value because of their existence side by side with thoughtless tradition.

The first official catalog also explained the importance of the arts, especially fine arts, dramatics, and music, noting that these were areas considered "least subject to direction from without and yet have within them a severe discipline of their own." It elaborated that the faculty held the conviction that, "through some kind of art experience, which is not necessarily the same as

46. Frederick Georgia to John A. Rice, August 28, 1933, in Faculty Files, BMCP, N.C. Archives; *Black Mountain College, 1933–1934,* 12; Blanshard, *Frank Aydelotte,* 203.

self-expression, the student can come to the realization of order in the world; and by being sensitized to movement, form, sound, and the other media of the arts, [he] gets a firmer control of himself and his environment than is possible through purely intellectual effort."[47]

Curricular choice at Black Mountain would be exercised by students with the advice and assistance of faculty and with some latitude for experimentation. Students would attend classes on a trial basis free from any formalities of registering, adding, or dropping. As in the system that John Andrew Rice had encountered at Oxford, students were welcome to attend classes in a variety of areas and expected eventually to home in on what would be most valuable to them given their interests and needs. However, while in the junior division, students would undergo a "period of discovery and of exploration," attending a broad range of courses in science, social science, the arts, and literature in order to make an informed choice about a specialized field of knowledge in the senior division. While working in each division, every student was to develop an individualized plan of work with faculty consultation and approval.

The curriculum was to include not only classes by the announced faculty and those yet to be appointed but also interdisciplinary seminars organized by four or more faculty members around periods of history, trends, or issues. These seminars would meet after dinner, with other classes meeting in the morning and late afternoon. Faculty were to select their own methods of instruction, which might include "recitations, lectures, tutorials, and seminars."[48]

Approved plans of work, along with oral and written comprehensive examinations, were required for advancement from junior to senior division. The senior division work, with faculty approval, included courses or independent study in a specialized area and related fields. In order to complete his or her studies or "graduate," a student would be required to submit a lengthy statement of accomplishments and to pass oral and written examinations, several days in length, administered by outside examiners from other colleges and universities. The use of outside examiners was explained as a way "to change the relationship of teacher and student, to put their work on a more agreeable footing, and [to] increase the student's willingness to work hard." Both advancement to the senior division and graduation would be based on individual readiness rather than on terms or units completed.[49]

47. *Black Mountain College, 1933–1934,* 2, 4.
48. *Ibid.,* 3.
49. *Ibid.,* 6–8.

A notable innovation for Black Mountain College was the absence of a board of trustees. Aydelotte, eager to see how some unusual ideas (perhaps too unusual for Swarthmore) would work, encouraged the decision to obviate trustees and by-laws. The notion fit Rice's conviction that higher education in the hands of trustees was in the hands of people who knew little about education. Black Mountain did have an advisory council to formalize its network of interested individuals such as Thomas Whitney Surette, J. Malcolm Forbes, Mrs. H. Edward (Ethel) Dreier, and, later, John Dewey. According to a system similar to those used at Oxford and Cambridge, the faculty elected from among them a board of fellows as the governing body of the college. Its four to six members, with staggered three-year terms, initially did not include student representation, although a student representative was scheduled to be added by the second year of college operations.[50]

With the notoriety brought about by the events at Rollins and with the formal AAUP report still pending, the college founders agreed that John Andrew Rice should not be named the formal head of Black Mountain College. When Josiah Spurr became too ill to participate in the venture, the stewardship title fell to Frederick Georgia. Rice was appalled, however, that by mid-September Georgia had installed himself in the largest first floor office in Lee Hall and posted a large "president" sign on the door. Rice and Dreier eventually convinced Georgia that the label they had in mind indicated more an educator among equals than a leader. They believed the title "chairman" appropriate, but Georgia held out for "president." Eventually, Rice suggested the compromise designation "rector," the title that would remain throughout the college's history. The position of "registrar," including the functions of general administrative assistant, was filled by 1932 Rollins graduate Elizabeth Vogler.[51]

Rice intended that all the founding faculty automatically have lifetime tenure. He later recalled, "I got that from Oxford. There you could be the biggest damn fool on earth, but short of murdering your mother-in-law you were safe." However, at Black Mountain it was left up to the board of fellows to determine the rules of faculty tenure and to revise them as they saw fit, within the general guideline of quality and "without prejudice to the incumbents."[52]

50. Frank Aydelotte to John A. Rice, October 5, 1933, in Aydelotte Papers, Swarthmore; *Black Mountain College, 1933–1934,* 10.
51. John A. Rice to Frank Aydelotte, November 6, 1933, in Aydelotte Papers, Swarthmore.
52. J. Rice, interview with Duberman, June 10, 1967; "By-Laws of the Corporation of Black Mountain College, Adopted October 28, 1933" (Typescript in Official Documents, BMCP, N.C. Archives).

Rollins president Hamilton Holt had eagerly kept himself informed about the activities of his former Rollins faculty members. Throughout the summer, Dean Winslow Anderson and others sent Holt newspaper clippings and reports of conversations, as well as rumors, about the founding of Black Mountain College. Professor Edwin Grover, still an avid supporter of Holt, asked a young woman he knew to pose as a potential student and write to the "registrar" of the new college for information. When she received an informative letter from Mrs. Georgia, acting as temporary registrar, Grover immediately sent copies to Holt, to other Rollins officials, and to some of the Rollins trustees. Ever the journalist, Holt decided to release his own statement to the press in early September. He extended best wishes to the founders with the backhanded compliment, "I have every reason to believe that Black Mountain College will be a success. I hold this belief because of the logical reason that the college, apparently, will be organized on the Conference Plan of Study, adopted at Rollins seven years ago, and the upper and lower division system, which was inaugurated at Rollins two years ago. . . . We at Rollins are proud of the compliment that Black Mountain pays by organizing its educational plan along lines similar to those which have proved satisfactory at Rollins."[53]

Most of the students and at least some of the faculty arrived in time for the official opening day of Black Mountain College on September 25, 1933. Students and unmarried faculty settled into bedrooms on the second and third floors of Lee Hall. Married faculty, including the Rice family, took suites in the wings that angled back from Lee Hall's main corridor. Married faculty with small children moved into some of the small cabins on the property. As students and faculty arrived, they rummaged about Lee Hall, collecting furniture to install in their rooms and quizzing one another about when classes might start and what might be required. Faculty pooled their books into a small library and discussed possible class meeting times and places. The first semblance of a schedule was defined by meals.

The first community meeting, held on the portico of Lee Hall on opening day, September 25, 1933, was marked by understatement. No invocation or procession took place. The only speech was the nomination of Nat French to preside over the student body in the office of "student moderator." There also was some debate about the rates to be charged by the college-

53. Lolita (Mrs. F. R.) Georgia to Evelyn G. Haynes, August 7, 1933, Edwin O. Grover to Ervin Brown, August 8, 1933, Winslow Anderson to Hamilton Holt, August 12, 1933, all in Rice File, Rollins; "Dr. Holt Congratulates New College Venture," Winter Park (Fla.) *Reporter-Star,* September 7, 1933, p. 1.

operated laundry. Frederick Georgia, in his official capacity as rector, then took the floor and did what John Andrew Rice later characterized as the "right and appropriate thing." He called on the Blue Ridge Assembly's permanent caretaker to explain fire precautions. The meeting then adjourned, launching the college with greater simplicity and ease than it would experience throughout most of its future.[54]

54. Martin, "Black Mountain College," in Faculty Files, BMCP, N.C. Archives; J. Rice, *Eighteenth Century,* 321.

6

Provocative Patriarch

Shortly after Doughten Cramer arrived at Black Mountain College in late September, 1933, he scheduled a meeting with his faculty adviser, John Andrew Rice. The portly, pipe-smoking Rice held the interview from one of the many large green rocking chairs on the front portico of Lee Hall. There he and the eighteen-year-old Cramer could gaze out on wisps of clouds floating toward distant mountaintops. All was serene, except for young Cramer's nerves.

Rice began, as he often did, with a statement launching into a question. "You are now entering college for the first time; you have a whole new world before you. What are you interested in studying?"

Cramer was taken aback. Interest had never been the salient question as he plowed through the high school courses required of a student preparing for college. Determined to show no ambiguity of purpose, however, he searched his mind, shifted his weight, and ventured, "W-well, history is sort of fun." Rice, unwilling to spare Cramer with small talk or suggestions, bored in with, "What phase of history do you like?"

Again, Cramer was stumped. But he was unwilling to expose any ignorance or lack of direction. He instead mentally fumbled upon the obvious, stating, "I want to know what caused the Depression." With that, he launched his academic major as recent American economic history. Rice chuckled appreciatively and admitted, "Well, you have given the college a large order!" He then guided Cramer to courses in economics and history, and, much to the surprise of the successful high school athlete with little academic focus, secured his decision to try English composition and music.[1]

---

1. Doughten Cramer, "I Went to Black Mountain College," 1940 (Typescript in private collection of William C. Rice, Boston).

Doughten Cramer, at least for the time being, had done just the right thing for a nervous eighteen-year-old. By acknowledging a personal preference, he avoided the darker side of John Andrew Rice that poked holes in arguments too imperfect, language too vague, or ideas too uncertain. By simply stating his own interest outright, he invoked the side of John Andrew Rice that gave freely of conversation, humor, and guidance. Only later would Cramer come to know his adviser's willingness to push intellectual sparring and candid observation to the point at which a student was belittled or a colleague was insulted.

The two personae of John Andrew Rice were manifested during his six years at Black Mountain College. Their opposition made it possible for various students and faculty to have very different experiences with the maverick and mercurial professor. "He was always brilliant and could have the tongue of angels," decided faculty member John Evarts. Yet Evarts conceded that Rice was an ambivalent figure at Black Mountain, concluding, "He was loved, feared, and sometimes hated. A real father figure."[2]

Rice was a large and constant presence in a small community in which interaction among all participants was continual and close. While other faculty might teach in a more distant manner, Rice held class as a conversation. While some might sneak off after dinner to be with their families, Rice lingered with a table of students. Later, he might appear at a student's study door and say, "Let's have a chat." Often, Rice pulled up a chair in front of the massive stone fireplace centered on the back wall of Lee Hall's barnlike main room, which served as foyer and meeting hall. There, or out on the portico if the weather was mild, he peaceably smoked his pipe and drew anyone who walked by into conversation. He might gather a group and raise a curious proposition, as he did the night he challenged, "Let's invent a religion. How about one where you get your better nature up into your body and push your worst elements down into the surface of the world?" He might intercept a passing student in the foyer to proffer unsolicited advice, as he did when Hope Stephens was on her way out to meet a male student whom Rice thought unsuitable for her. He pulled her aside to ask, "Hope, would you want him to be the father of your children?"[3]

Rice believed that education happened all the time—in and out of the classroom, in serious or silly moments—especially for those who observed and analyzed what was taking place. He later described Black Mountain as a

2. Lily Byrd McKee, "They Made Their Mark . . . Balance at Black Mountain," *Mountain Living*, II (Summer, 1971), 16.

3. Robert Sunley, interview with the author, April 22, 1993; Richard Andrews, interview with the author, May 11, 1993; Hope Stephens Foote, interview with the author, May 13, 1993.

place where there was "no escape" from education and where "a man taught
by the way he walked, the sound of his voice, by every movement. That was
what it was intended to be, the fulfillment of an old idea, the education of the
whole man: by a whole man." By Rice's estimate, two thirds of the value of
Black Mountain College for its students derived from what happened outside the classes. Of course, Rice's convictions about education perfectly reflected his own style. He favored unstructured conversation and interaction
well above formatted classes or sustained, scholarly exposition; and he ex-
celled at creating teaching moments at unexpected times. On his first visit to
Black Mountain, Louis Adamic was impressed to find Rice "right in the
mob, laughing, asking questions, stopping to argue, discussing the 'mess of
things,' showing by his demeanor there is nothing to fear, going into the deep
murk off the road, wherein his voice explodes angrily as he tries to get people
to stop grubbing in the muck and to look starward."[4]

Nell Rice made two trips home to Sullivan, Indiana, that fall; but John
Andrew Rice was content to preside over the beginning of the new college,
to conduct his Socratic classes, and to partake in the small faculty and student dramas that unfolded in the front room of Lee Hall. Even without the
official "rector" title, he was evidently the central figure. Students, and more
than a few faculty members—even frequently his closest colleague, Ted
Dreier—referred to him as Mr. Rice.[5]

Students quickly found they enjoyed the opportunity for education at
every turn. "You could just sit down with Albers or Rice and talk," recalled
Norman Weston many years later. "Or you could watch Fritz Moellenhoff
[who arrived from Germany in 1935 to teach psychology] carry eight full
cups of coffee to the dining room table. It was a wonderful setting for learning." Robert Sunley, who transferred from Oberlin, also remarked on the
ease of interchange, noting, "At Oberlin, the faculty taught their courses
and that was it. They were gone, and students were herded into a separate
world. Black Mountain was so different and exactly what I wanted."[6]

Within a few weeks of the Black Mountain College opening, a place of
higher education began to shape itself out of the initial confusion about
learning and teaching responsibilities. The students had moved in and had
quickly adopted an attitude of interpersonal informality and intellectual en-

4. J. Rice, *Eighteenth Century,* 322; General Meeting, minutes, February 16, 1937, in Official
Documents, BMCP, N.C. Archives; Adamic, *My America,* 621.
5. John A. Rice to Frank Aydelotte, October 25, November 25, 1933, both in Aydelotte Papers, Swarthmore.
6. Weston, interview with the author, April 13, 1993; Sunley interview, April 22, 1993.

thusiasm. The faculty roster was becoming respectable. The initial chaos of deciding who should teach what and who should learn what had subsided for the moment. John Keith, recommended by Frank Aydelotte, arrived in October to teach romance languages. Emmy Zastrow was appointed to instruct in elementary German. Josef and Anni Albers were expected to arrive in late November. Rooming and housing issues were settled. Faculty members began to warm to one another and find ways to collaborate. And young, first-time teachers quickly overcame any initial intimidation. Joseph Martin loosened up after early meetings with colleagues, when he was "inclined to take every silence to mean profound scholarly contempt of my last remark." Meal times were set. Class meeting times were scheduled for morning and late afternoon, each to be an hour in length. Similar to the schedule Rice had encountered at Oxford, the midday was left free for outdoor exercise. Any purely experimental courses, such as the interdisciplinary seminars, were scheduled to meet after dinner, so they could continue as long as participants desired. The library, organized from faculty contributions, quickly grew to more than five thousand volumes. Rice himself loaned several thousand books, which he later tried unsuccessfully to retrieve. It was expected that students and faculty would pitch in with the necessary work of daily living—clearing tables, sweeping floors, cutting firewood, shoveling furnace coal. Perhaps out of heady enthusiasm, Rice, who was not generally in favor of organized outdoor labor, made the uncharacteristic suggestion that the college should look into the possibility of farming on some nearby lands.[7]

Bylaws were debated by the faculty, but the discussions were more reasoned than resentful. Eventually, they resulted in provisions for students to attend faculty meetings and for the student moderator to serve on the board of fellows. The growing faculty group stuck by the early vision barring trustees and mandating governance strictly by the community of faculty and students. They maintained their commitment to educate students for life in a democracy; thus they developed a small, democratic model of society, which included students and faculty in making decisions, rather than preempting them with decisions made by outside boards with greater power.

As life in the small community took hold, the founders also became convinced of the efficacy of their commitment to coeducation. Rice concluded that coeducation at Black Mountain created the opportunity "to know what we are talking about when we speak of the equality of men and women. It

7. Black Mountain College Bulletin, I (Fall, 1933), 2; Board of Fellows, October 2, 1933, in Board of Fellows Meeting Minutes, in BMCP, N.C. Archives; "Black Mountain College," preliminary catalog.

doesn't exist of course, but [we need to] find out whether it can be put into practice. My personal opinion is that coeducation is good for a number of reasons. It is easy enough for the world, for the world in general, to fall in love, but only in a coeducational institution small enough can one learn how to fall gracefully out of it."[8]

Progress in organizing the college took a sad turn when Ralph Lounsbury unexpectedly suffered a stroke and died on October 16. Rice had come to believe that Lounsbury joined the new venture only out of desperation and with a deep sense of personal failure after experiences as a New York lawyer and a Rollins professor. Nevertheless, he recalled the loss felt by faculty and students at Lounsbury's death, explaining, "We were all quite shaken because without being aware of it, we had all become quite fond of him." At a memorial service held at the college, eulogies by Dreier, Rice, and Georgia all noted their regrets that they had not gotten to know better this man who possessed apparently great intellectual honesty, a commitment to justice, and a sense of humanity.[9]

True to the school's democratic underpinnings, the course selection process at Black Mountain meant that faculty needed to recruit their students. There were no devices, such as core requirements, to protect the faculty member who taught subjects of no interest or who earned a reputation as a poor teacher. Depending on student interest, Rice offered to teach classes in Greek language, Plato, Virgil, Latin lyric poetry, and Latin comedy. Greek language and Plato, however, became his course offerings that first academic year. He was also part of a faculty team teaching an interdisciplinary seminar on the eighteenth century. Eventually, Rice would teach Plato in a two-course sequence, as well as a writing seminar. At Black Mountain, Rice's approach in class veered dramatically away from the classical language and thought courses he had taught at the University of Nebraska and even to some extent at Rollins. Now he gave free rein to his desire to question and converse about whatever was on someone's mind. "All his classes were the same," recalled Morton Steinau. "They were all Rice. He taught Rice." Steinau found that class discussions were unpredictable, with Rice "holding forth on whatever, following the scent wherever it led. So if somebody wondered how the Romans compared to the Greeks, we might follow that for about two weeks. You learned a lot in those classes, but not necessarily in the

8. General Meeting Minutes, February 16, 1937, in Official Documents, BMCP, N.C. Archives.

9. J. Rice, interview with Duberman, June 10, 1967; "In Memorim: Ralph Reed Lounsbury," October 20, 1933 (Typescript in Faculty Files, BMCP, N.C. Archives).

area the class was supposed to cover. We might have a discussion about why the people in the town of Black Mountain resented our being there. Or we might discuss the derivation of a word. I learned one phrase in Greek the year I took that language course. I never did learn the Greek alphabet."[10]

All students, whatever their interests, were encouraged to take Rice's Plato course and Albers' first-level art course, both considered key curricular contributions to the aims of the college. That guidance positioned Rice and Albers differently, at least in the view of students, than other faculty, who might find their own courses dwindling to just one or two participants by midsemester. Attendance in Rice's classes was difficult to gauge, since many students, and often some faculty, just dropped by when they heard a good conversation in progress in the lobby of Lee Hall where he taught. Weather permitting, the group might gather on the lawn or on a second-story rooftop that covered a rear portion of Lee Hall and could be accessed through large windows.

Although there was some exposition of Greek philosophy and some reading aloud in Greek and in translation by Rice in his "rich voice that made all others sound thin," he generally opened a Plato class with a question. What is sentimentality? What is your view of time? Why shouldn't the world end? Rice liked candid and assertive answers, but he challenged respondents who were uncertain or vague. Why do you say that? What do you mean when you use that word? Typical of Rice's approach was the time when he placed a number of small objects on a table and pointed to them at the beginning of class, asking, "Is this order?" Johanna Jalowetz, a faculty wife attending the class, stated without reservation that the objects did represent order. When Rice asked her why, she replied, "Because you put them there." Partial to any response so simple and assured, Rice quickly admitted, "You're probably right."[11]

After the first few years that Black Mountain College was operational, any pretense of a Greek language course was dropped. When Robert Sunley arrived in the fall of 1936, he had some knowledge of Greek and wanted to continue. Rice put him off with, "Well, I don't know about that for you. It may not be the best route to take." Later, Sunley realized that there never really had been a course that taught the Greek language. Rice continued to teach Plato I and Plato II, although the classes evolved more and more into conversations among whoever gathered in their general vicinity at the time.

---

10. "By-Laws of the Corporation of Black Mountain College; Steinau, interview with the author, May 3, 1993.

11. Page, interview with the author, June 14, 1993.

Both classes and conversations often went on well into the night or over-flowed into table talk in the dining hall. Students debated at length ideas and concepts like moderation, justice, and tolerance, with the Socratic Rice probing their assumptions and meanings. Student David Way later decided that Rice's Plato I and Plato II were not simply casual conversations; rather, they were opportunities for cultivating community awareness of the need to observe and understand oneself in relation to others, to stamp out personal pretenses and prejudices, and to develop mature values and emotions. "By means of Plato I, Rice tried to give the community a common vocabulary and community of values," Way decided. "His intention in Plato II was to engage the community in dialogue about the larger philosophical issues."[12]

As at Rollins, students often disagreed about the effectiveness and impact of Rice and his teaching. In fact, their interpretations of their experiences with him varied widely. Sue Spayth Riley found him to be "an understand-ing and empathetic human being with genuine respect for the student. He was a listener, one of the few teachers anywhere who I felt reached, touched, inspired, and challenged my thinking." Betty Young Williams agreed, insist-ing, "Mr. Rice had such a powerful influence without being in any sense au-thoritarian or presenting his own points of view, so what we learned was to question everything. For many years after, I found myself silently having conversations with Mr. Rice. If I was puzzled or troubled or trying to decide something, I'd silently address the arguments one way and another to him." However, Morton Steinau represented another view, when he recalled of Rice, "He was quite direct, often demeaning of other faculty or students. He was not at all restrained about what he thought, and he was opinionated. . . . He might go as far as to tell someone, 'I never heard such a dumb idea.' Sup-posedly he was trying to get some sort of response, and some students would come back at him. He admired those."[13]

Doughten Cramer characterized himself as one of those students who felt belittled and demeaned by Rice. His father and two brothers had attended Princeton, where he could not hope to be accepted with his low entrance examination scores. His father had died when he was twelve years old, and he may have been looking for a father substitute in the brilliant college patri-arch. Although he became close friends with Frank Rice and received

12. Sunley, interview with the author, April 22, 1993; David Jacques Way to Mervin Lane, March 1, 1988, in Student Files, BMCP, N.C. Archives.
13. Sue Spayth Riley, "John Andrew Rice at Black Mountain College," 1992 (MS in posses-sion of Sue Spayth Riley), Charlotte, N.C.; Williams, interview with the author, May 10, 1993; Steinau, interview with the author, May 3, 1993.

affection and encouragement from Nell Rice, he found no parental sensitivity in John Andrew Rice. In its place, he encountered in Rice a combination of intolerance and hopefulness. Cramer perceived that Rice enjoyed students who, like the mythical phoenix, arose fully formed out of the ashes. In class and out, Rice confronted him bluntly about his academic inadequacies, prompting Cramer to later maintain, "Mr. Rice succeeded in beating me down until I was pulp. He was an inspiration to me, and everything he said was the gospel truth. Once, when I went to him for advice, my chances of graduating came up. Mr. Rice baldly said, 'Of course, you are not bright. I don't expect you to be able to graduate. You can't hope to amount to very much in this life—a mechanic or a conscientious office worker.' When you are eighteen and the wisest person you've met says this sort of thing, it is a major blow." Cramer eventually became the first student to graduate from Black Mountain College after heading there directly from high school rather than transferring from another college. He later believed that Rice's treatment of him actually may have strengthened his resolve to complete college and graduate school.[14]

Students knew their experiences and perceptions concerning John Andrew Rice were decidedly different from one another. Some believed he altered his approach depending on whether a student was male or female, and apparently meek or aggressive. Marian Nacke Teeter believed Rice was "more attuned to women" and seemed "to have a very tender feeling toward women and girls." With male students and faculty, in contrast, she observed that he was "more challenging and hostile at times." John R. P. French, Jr., on the other hand, recalled being appalled in a class when Rice unleashed "harsh criticism" on a female student. Others sensed that Rice formed a rapport with students who enjoyed his Socratic approach and appreciated his sardonic humor and keen intellect, but a distaste for students who were less at ease with free-flowing conversation in the classroom. Barbara Dreier, for example, believed that an intuitive rapport was the key to Rice's reactions, noting, "He wasn't a good teacher of those he couldn't get a caring feeling for."[15]

Still others conjectured that Rice's personal style was simply contrary and that he needed to bait people when things were going too smoothly. He enjoyed debate and dissent, and he would create the context for it by provoking

14. Cramer, "I Went to Black Mountain College," and Doughten Cramer to William C. Rice, August 24, 1988, both in possession of William C. Rice.
15. Marian Nacke Teeter, interview with the author, May 12, 1933; John R. P. French, Jr., interview with the author, July 27, 1993; B. Dreier, interview with the author, April 5, 1993.

those he found most easy or enjoyable to challenge. David Jacques Way was a student who found himself profoundly and favorably influenced by Rice, but he recognized later why Rice's style did not universally delight others. His mentor seemed "the enemy of all who wanted to 'know' something securely. That is a hell of an uncomfortable condition for young or old. You can't 'love' such a person, even though he may be completely without malice (as Rice was). People like Rice are meant to be suffered, not loved. For me the yoke was easy, but there were those, I know, who found him profoundly unsettling."[16]

Many students and faculty found Rice to be a great teacher, but nearly all described Josef Albers in these terms, including Rice himself. Albers was as disciplined as Rice was undisciplined, and yet the two somehow managed to share "top teacher" appellations in a small community without demonstrating undue rivalry. It was perhaps fortunate that only one of them—Rice—was demonstrative in nature.

Albers' fellow faculty member Peggy Loram shared with many students and faculty a love for Albers' artistry and style. She later exclaimed, "The course I took with him was the best course I ever had in my life"; nothing she had experienced in her student days at Swarthmore or Columbia was comparable. True to his words on arriving in the United States, Albers wanted only to open eyes. He was not interested in developing disciples or in discovering budding artists who would become famous (although two later students at Black Mountain, Robert Rauschenberg and Kenneth Noland, did just that). Thirty-five years later, when an elderly John Andrew Rice penned fragments of memoirs, he applauded Albers' self-effacing qualities, noting that he never pushed a visitor to view his art and never pushed the faculty at Black Mountain to do more in the arts. In fact, Rice recalled that in 1935, when well-known art collector Albert Barnes of Merion, Pennsylvania, visited Black Mountain, Albers did not organize an exhibit of his work and even provoked Barnes into a public dispute. Several years later, however, Josef and Anni Albers joined the very few who were occasionally invited to view Barnes's very extensive and very private collection.[17]

Although some similarities in educational philosophy connected the men, Rice was not wholly uncritical of Albers. Both men placed a much higher premium on process than on product, and both believed that students were best brought to understanding through their own experiences rather

16. David Jacques Way to Katherine Reynolds, April 27, 1993, in author's possession.

17. Bailey, interview with the author, May 10, 1993; J. Rice, "Black Mountain College Memoirs," 576–80.

than through outside information. Yet Rice was certain that Albers had a blind spot in refusing to recognize any influence from the past and in turning away from any art he could not classify as modern. Rice, who drew from ancient cultures and philosophers in all his teaching, could not comprehend why Albers seemed to ignore the history and past accomplishments of his discipline. However, having regularly attended Albers' classes, Rice also characterized Albers as a great teacher and an individual of great charm. He later claimed that Black Mountain College could not have succeeded without Albers.[18]

Albers demonstrated his greater interest in the process, rather than product, of a student's artwork with much attention to individual problem solving. He required that assignments be completed as a ticket to a next class. Precision in process was important even if precision in the final work may or may not have been achieved. In class, he was encouraging and gracious, willing to work at length on the smallest problem a student was having with getting one line or one space correct. He talked sparingly and addressed his remarks to individuals. Hours were spent arranging found objects on boards to demonstrate relationships between objects as well as the forms taken by the spaces between the objects. Students began to see what they had never seen before.

Albers believed students needed to learn early the boundaries of materials. He brought this conviction from the Bauhaus, where he was noted for material studies. A single piece of paper could be folded and turned into a spiral reminiscent of a conch shell but not into a perfect sphere. The boundaries of each sort of material were noteworthy. "He didn't like clay because it had no boundaries," remarked Hope Stephens Foote, who one day took to Albers a clay foot she had sculpted. "Ja," he remarked, "but make one in paper." After she managed to stretch and fold the paper into something akin to a foot, Albers nodded approval but said, "Ja, now make one in wire."[19]

Fond students referred to Albers as "Juppi," and many who had no previous interest in art became architects, graphic designers, or creative artists after Albers opened their eyes. Some students, however, never caught the enthusiasm, finding Albers' Teutonic tendencies too formal and impersonal. Dick Andrews, a student from Bronxville, New York, found Albers personally "warm," but he qualified this perception: "Albers was a reductionist who believed in absolutes. He thought art should be cerebral. That's why he did not like the French art or German expressionism." Students who tended to

---

18. J. Rice, "Black Mountain College Memoirs," 578–79.

19. Sunley, interview with the author, April 22, 1993; Foote, interview with the author, May 13, 1993.

be great admirers of Rice and his loosely structured ways often found too much distance and constraint in Albers. Robert Sunley remarked of the artist, "Even when he was being warm, he was remote. He'd say, 'wunderbar, schon,' like it was carved in crystal." While Rice viewed Albers as a superb teacher, he also realized that the German master could never understand his own very unstructured and informal style of teaching and leadership.[20]

By the autumn of 1933 Arthur Lovejoy and Austin Edwards had issued a public report that exonerated Rice and blasted Hamilton Holt's actions at Rollins. On December 31, 1933, the AAUP voted to remove Rollins from its eligible list of voting membership (along with the U.S. Naval Academy and Brenau College, which were put on ineligible status the same day). The AAUP action cleared the way for Rice to be elected rector of the college in its second year, with Georgia placed in the position of secretary. During this year Albers became dismayed with the lack of formality and format in faculty and board of fellows meetings. What Albers preferred, Rice explained, was "a strict agenda so everybody would know ahead of time what we were going to talk about." Instead, Rice described his approach as one where the faculty "would just go in and sit down; and if anyone had anything they wanted to talk about, they did." Ted and Barbara Dreier became close friends of the Alberses, and Barbara later confirmed that Albers saw Rice as "totally undisciplined. Albers couldn't understand why he was just sitting around talking instead of doing anything. But, of course, for Rice, his doing was talking."[21]

Conversation was not only Rice's favored mode of teaching but also his preferred route to building the community into a social unit. He left it to others to experiment with communing around physical labor and cooperative work projects. Ted Dreier's energy and enthusiasm guided student interest in farming, which was further fanned by the nearly college-wide reading of *Flight from the City: The Story of a New Way to Family Security,* by Ralph Borsodi. This guide to self-sufficiency was coincidentally published the same year that Black Mountain College was founded. Students intrigued by the idea of farming called general meetings on agricultural possibilities at the college. According to Joseph Martin, farming became a "full-fledged cause," and its proponents created an "atmosphere tense with proselytizing." A number of students decided milk cows would be just the right thing to raise at the college; and a group of them called upon Asheville Farm School, a nearby labor community and school for workers, to get information. Several students

20. Andrews, interview with the author, May 11, 1993; Sunley, interview with the author, April 22, 1993.

21. J. Rice, interview with Duberman, June 10, 1967; B. Dreier, interview with the author, April 5, 1993.

took additional early morning trips to the farm school for lessons in milking. Others toyed with the idea of raising beef cattle and slaughtering cattle on the property.[22]

While not all the enthusiasm translated into sustained activity, subsistence farming occurred for a time at the college with a hired farmer helping to produce approximately 50 percent of the vegetables consumed in the dining hall. A few students tried raising pigeons, and some attempted to harvest apples. Many pitched in to haul coal in the college pickup truck from the Black Mountain train station and to unload it at the college. Others tried running a campus store. A cottage school, staffed by students, for several years provided alternative schooling for faculty and staff children, as well as for some children living in the town of Black Mountain.[23]

Even John Andrew Rice enjoyed planning and planting a healthy vegetable garden and strawberry patch, but not overly much. He claimed, "The gospel of work has always made me tired." He also gently mocked Ted Dreier's enthusiastic efforts and organizational abilities concerning outdoor work activities. "Ted," he later recalled, "had this notion, having been born in Brooklyn Heights, and never having seen more than a few blades of grass, that there was some kind of mystical experience in touching the soil."[24]

At Black Mountain, "community" happened because people were living together and therefore talking and planning activities together. However, the college had almost nothing in common with earlier experimental utopian communities such as Brook Farm or New Harmony. The satisfaction of its participants was not the end or goal that Black Mountain College set for itself, but rather their education. At a general meeting attended by some visiting students, Rice elaborated: "One of the difficulties we have here is that the students and faculty come here with the idea that this is going to be an ideal community. And when this idea goes haywire, as it always does, they get disturbed on that score. . . . Here, our job is to have people do what they came to do and then leave. That is why we don't stress graduation."[25]

There was, however, at Black Mountain a good deal of group influence.

22. F. Rice, interview with the author, February 13, 1993; Martin, "Black Mountain College," Faculty Files, and Soren K. Ostergaard to James G. Sallade, October 27, 1934, Student Files, both in BMCP, N.C. Archives. The Asheville Farm School eventually became Warren Wilson College, a liberal arts college affiliated with the Presbyterian Church. It is now noted for experimentation in required work programs and service learning and offers a full range of academic subjects.

23. Duberman, *Black Mountain,* 72; T. Dreier, interview with the author, April 5, 1993.

24. Sunley, interview with the author, April 22, 1993; J. Rice, interview with Duberman, June 10, 1967.

25. General Meeting Minutes, February 16, 1937, in Official Documents, BMCP, N.C. Archives.

Without rules or prudery, students and faculty seemed to set some acceptable boundaries of behavior. They knew that openness and informality were good but that anything shocking to the residents of the town of Black Mountain (who generated an active rumor mill about life at the college) could risk the college's continued existence. "Be intelligent" was the frequent watchword among students, who nevertheless exercised ample latitude individually in interpreting it.

The students also respected privacy, a necessity in such close quarters, and quickly agreed to the sacrosanct meaning of a "do not disturb" sign on a door. When one of the early weekly community meetings became a discussion of whether men and women should be in each other's bedrooms, it was as much a meeting about responsibility and privacy as about sex. It ended in a consensus to terminate single rooms and to give everyone a roommate (same sex) and a private study. However, ample time was spent debating whether the bed in each study could be made up with sheets and blankets. That lengthy discussion may have been exceeded by a four-hour community debate to determine whether there should be two or three meals on Sunday. The resulting compromise agreed on two hot meals with prescribed seating times and one informal, optional meal of buffet cold cuts. "It sounds laughable, but these were serious issues," recalled Norman Weston.[26]

While John Andrew Rice opposed any emphasis on the college as an experiment in community, he thoroughly enjoyed the unpredictability and volatility of total community interaction. From the perspective of student Betty Young Williams, he was "an expert at conducting community meetings without saying much." To Rice, everyone on the property was an important part of the whole. He revered the cooks, Jack and Rubye Lipsey, claiming that you could tell what Jack thought of someone by the way he handed that person a plate of food. He loved faculty wife Mary Barnes, who arrived in 1938 with history professor Walter Barnes, for her wisdom and compassion. Rice even decided she was "the most important woman in the place, by far," and occasionally assigned her student tutoring duties. One of his favorite activities was his daily walk after lunch with the half dozen or so dogs owned by various faculty members. He instituted a tradition of afternoon tea in Lee Hall and of Saturday evening dances. At the latter, everyone left their usual blue jeans and work shirts in their closets and dressed up— some men even in tuxedos—to enjoy dancing and singing to music played by John Evarts at the piano. In 1935 Evarts was joined on the music faculty

26. Duberman, *Black Mountain*, 22, 28, 82–83; Cramer, "I Went to Black Mountain College," 10–11; Weston, interview with the author, April 13, 1993.

by two composers: Allan Sly and Dante Fiorillo. Fiorillo was appointed composer-in-residence while supported by a Guggenheim Fellowship.[27]

The curriculum at Black Mountain was full and time-consuming by any standards. In addition to the classes held in morning and late afternoon, interdisciplinary seminars were conducted after dinner. During the first year, the team-taught interdisciplinary topics were the eighteenth century, writing (in any subject), and contemporary philosophies. Rice played the leading part of the country squire in William Congreve's *The Way of the World*, a comedy of manners produced as part of the seminar on the eighteenth century. Young faculty member Margaret Loram, directing her first play, was perplexed when Rice consistently flubbed his lines in rehearsal. Finally, when time and patience ran short, Loram lashed out at the cast, "None of you are yet perfect in your lines; and you, Mr. Rice, are one of the worst. You set a very bad example." Although she expected from Rice a note of reprisal, or even termination, she later found he had only gained greater respect for her. Rice was a humorous hit in the play, although he needed to refer to printed lines he carried on narrow lengths of paper rolled around a toilet paper tube.[28]

Much of the faculty work during the first year the college was in operation was aimed at determining academic policies and procedures, which often seemed to follow somewhat behind actual practice. Entrance requirements were adopted halfway through the year, with a decision to waive the use of college entrance examinations and to rely instead on high school grades, recommendations, and, as necessary, interviews or essays. Application forms were adopted early in 1934, and graduation requirements and fees were set a year later. By the end of the first academic year, the faculty was still hammering out standards guiding students' invitation at year's end to return as well as rigorous requirements governing their advancement from junior to senior division and for graduation.[29]

The studies of Nancy Farrell, who transferred from Bennington College to Black Mountain in 1935, were typical of the course load carried at the latter. Aiming at an emphasis in art for her senior division plan of study, Farrell registered for about half her courses in drawing, color, and other art studies. Among the other half were courses in German language, French literature,

27. Williams, interview with the author, May 10, 1933; J. Rice, interview with Duberman, June 10, 1967; Rice to Aydelotte, November 25, 1933, in Aydelotte Papers, Swarthmore.
28. Bailey, interview with the author, May 10, 1993; Rice to Aydelotte, November 6, 1993, in Aydelotte Papers, Swarthmore.
29. Faculty Meeting Minutes, December 7, 12, 1933, May 14, 1935, in Official Documents, BMCP, N.C. Archives.

music appreciation, world economy, and Plato (with Rice). After advancing to the senior division, Farrell reduced her courses from six to five each semester in order to spend more time in independent work on her senior division final project and her examination studies.[30]

In addition to producing scholarly materials in keeping with the senior division studies, the candidate for graduation submitted to one or two days of written examinations and to a day of oral examinations. The written questions were determined by outside examiners, generally from other universities, who also appeared for the oral examinations. Undoubtedly, the use of outside examiners helped word get around about Black Mountain College, although the school never met requirements for regional or national accreditation. However, even without grades to reflect their successes, Black Mountain College students were accepted for transfer or graduate study at Harvard, Columbia, Swarthmore, Radcliffe, Stanford, the University of Chicago, and many other top schools.

Because the Black Mountain experiment favored democracy and artistry and boasted a beautiful retreatlike setting, almost immediately it attracted the curiosity of artists, educators, and general observers of the American scene. Authors Thornton Wilder, Clifford Odets, Aldous Huxley, and Henry Miller were among the notables who showed up at the college. These renowned visitors generally spent their time hiking in the mountains, enjoying the excellent food and conversation, meeting informally with students, and perhaps giving public lectures.

When art collector Albert Barnes arrived, he brought with him, according to Rice, "the most divine whiskey I've ever drunk—a whole case full of it." Concert musician Yella Pessl brought her harpsichord by train and then pickup truck to spend a week playing duets, trios, and quartets with any students playing instruments who would gather about her. Rice promoted complete informality between students and visitors, and the distinguished guests were integrated into whatever was happening in the community at the time. Robert Sunley recalled, "You'd get a knock on your study door and there would be Rice saying, 'Come on, Aldous Huxley's here. Let's go talk with him.'" Every visitor was welcomed as a possible resource, adding his or her viewpoint to the unstructured learning that occurred around the clock.[31]

One august educator whose status at the college evolved from visitor to

30. Mervin Lane, ed., *Black Mountain College, Sprouted Seeds: An Anthology of Personal Accounts* (Knoxville, Tenn., 1990), 64–65.

31. J. Rice, interview with Duberman, June 10, 1967; Weston, interview with the author, April 13, 1993; Sunley, interview with the author, April 22, 1993.

faculty member was Thomas Whitney Surette, nationally known for his progressive ideas about the role of music in the schools and for his Concord (Massachusetts) Summer School of Music. Surette came often enough at first to be considered visiting faculty and to have a lasting impact on expanding the role of music education in the curriculum. By 1937 Surette was able to accept a faculty postion, although Rice later felt that his music influence at the college was eclipsed by his literary interests. "He sure put [William] Blake on the map," observed Rice. "He read Blake aloud all the time. Everybody started reading Blake." Another multigifted adjunct to the community was William Morse Cole, a finance professor at Harvard, who arrived each spring to audit the college books. While he was there, he stayed long enough to teach some accounting principles and some Shakespeare plays. Ted Dreier, who as college treasurer worked closely with Cole, remembered, "He was wonderful with Shakespeare, had everyone reading the plays."[32]

Most prominent among the many notable visitors to the college was John Dewey, who made two visits during the 1934–1935 academic year, each lasting a week or more. He attended classes and said very little; but in the evenings he was a jolly companion for the students whom he accompanied to Roy's, their favorite beer joint in the town of Black Mountain. When Rice took John Dewey and a group of students to a regional meeting of the Progressive Education Association in Atlanta, the students were surprised at the flurry of attention Dewey caused. However, they saw that the royal treatment did not change the open and human side of John Dewey when he cut an official luncheon to join them at a beer parlor.

Dewey attended Rice's Plato class each day during a two-week visit but said little and offered teaching suggestions or observations only when pressed. Rice concluded that Dewey was "the only man I have ever known who was completely fit and fitted to live in a democracy. He sat and said nothing; but something happened when he was there. . . . He had respect for the process of learning. He had it because he had respect for people. John Webb and John Dewey are the only men I have known who never questioned the individual's right to be alive. They took that for granted, and began from there." When Rice expressed to Dewey his fear that all the excitement and experimentation at Black Mountain might eventually become pedestrian, Dewey, true to progressive ideals, reassured him, "As long as you keep your eye on the individual, that won't happen."[33]

32. Harris, *The Arts at Black Mountain*, 31–32; J. Rice, interview with Duberman, June 10, 1967; T. Dreier, interview with the author, April 5, 1993.

33. J. Rice, *Eighteenth Century*, 331, 324–25.

Students and faculty from other educational experiments also dropped by to visit their counterparts at Black Mountain. Sarah Lawrence College president Constance Warren traded with the faculty ideas about administration and curriculum. Former student Emil Willimetz recalled a visit from a St. John's College delegation during which the methods and curricula of the two colleges were debated for several days. Willimetz maintained, "Rice was never more impressive than in that setting." Students and faculty from the Chicago School of Design came to investigate the art program. When several students from Antioch visited, one, Will Hamlin, decided on the spot to transfer to Black Mountain after three years at the Ohio school.[34]

Visits from those at Black Mountain to the world outside also were fairly frequent, and John Andrew Rice sometimes took students along when he traveled to speaking engagements or conferences. He especially enjoyed travel that included his native South Carolina. Richard Andrews accompanied him on a car trip to Charleston, South Carolina, and recalled that at some point along the way, Rice asked him to please take off his hat. A few minutes later, however, Rice encouraged Andrews to put the hat back on if he wanted. Andrews recalled that when he asked his professor what the request and its withdrawal were about, Rice smiled reverently and replied, "We were passing into South Carolina." Andrews later explained, "Mr. Rice was a very playful person. It was wonderful fun to be around someone like that."[35]

Indeed, Rice was as generous with his laughter as he was with his intellectual sparring and personal baiting. What perhaps distinguished him most was his full and constant participation in every aspect of the college community. He took the lead not only in acting in a college play, but also in drafting the college catalog, communicating with parents, dealing with faculty committees, speaking at conferences and to the press, and hosting visitors. He was, in the early years of the college, true to his dictum that learning occurred twenty-four hours a day. His methods indeed reflected innovation concerning both the ends and means of education. He took seriously his frequent admonition, "Black Mountain College is not just another college; it is a new college," and he did his part to break with traditional patterns of higher education. According to Sue Spayth Riley, the unconventional college was not always home to unconventional practices, since "many of the faculty, while talking experimental, actually used the old tired yardsticks to teach, to mea-

34. Faculty Meeting Minutes, December 7, 1936, in Official Documents, BMCP, N.C. Archives; Emil Willimetz, interview with the author, July 1, 1993; Duberman, *Black Mountain,* 99.
35. Richard Andrews, interview with the author, April 3, 1994.

sure, to judge, and to relate to the student. John Andrew Rice, however, had *really* thrown those old yardsticks out."[36]

Rice regularly attended regional and national conferences of the Progressive Education Association and visited other colleges to give speeches or seminars or just to see what was happening. He frequently accepted invitations to speak throughout North Carolina and in New England, addressing chambers of commerce, chapters of the American Association of University Women, college clubs, and others. Removed from his familiar Black Mountain setting, he rarely deviated from his usual pattern of seeking opportunities to shock. At a symposium at Harvard, for example, one of the speakers struck a comparison between Sarah Lawrence and Black Mountain Colleges. Although Rice believed the two were nothing alike, he sought out the participant from Sarah Lawrence afterwards and heartily congratulated her for her school's comparison to Black Mountain College. Closer to home, Rice rankled Central High School Parent-Teacher Association members in Charlotte, North Carolina, when he delivered a speech that referred to children as "general nuisances," and insisted that humans were closer to apes than one might think in their limited ability to reason. After telling his audience they would be better off learning from their children than attempting to teach them, Rice drew fire from the Business Men's Evangelical Clubs of North Carolina for being "radical and communistic," and inspired a week of angry outbursts in letters to the editors and in editorials printed in the Charlotte *News,* that city's daily afternoon newspaper.[37]

After visiting a number of progressive schools, Rice decided that most were too doctrinaire for his taste. "They've got the thing figured out: This is the way to do it; and by God if you don't do it that way, you're just not 'it,' " he decided. He wrote his friend Elmer Davis, after making discouraging visits to a number of progressive schools in 1934, that he had become convinced, "Progressive education, when it is stupid, is much more stupid than the other kind." He did, however, maintain a great deal of respect for John R. P. French, Jr., headmaster of the progressive Cambridge School, Kendal Green, Massachusetts, who sent two sons to Black Mountain College; and for Hans Froelicher, an early influence in the Progressive Education Association and founder of the Park School in Baltimore.[38]

36. Riley, "John Andrew Rice"; Martin, "Black Mountain College," in Faculty Files, BMCP, N.C. Archives.

37. "Rice's Talk Draws Fiery Censure," Charlotte *News,* October 26, 1937, pp. 1, 8; "Hold up Your Hands," Charlotte *News,* October 27, 1937, p. 6; "Dave Believes Everything," Charlotte *News,* October 24, 1937, p. 8.

38. J. Rice, interview with Duberman, June 10, 1967; F. Rice, interview with the author, February 13, 1993; John A. Rice to Elmer Davis, May 1, 1934, in Faculty Files, BMCP, N.C. Archives.

Rice was particularly rankled to hear Black Mountain College referred to as progressive education, although he could not convince reporters or editors to eliminate the comparisons in print. The New York *Evening Post* set the tune when it announced the college's opening under the headline "Progressive Education Becomes Collegiate." Although Rice might admit to some points of philosophical similarity that informed his own practices and those of many progressive educators, he also believed that the teaching and learning process at Black Mountain College was far too diverse and complex to fit the constraints of the "progressive" label. In the general public's mind, he surmised, progressive education was quickly evolving from instruction drawing on student interests to laissez-faire teaching that allowed students free rein in the classroom without the burden of educational objectives.[39]

Rice was rather impressed with other experimental—or at least distinctive—colleges, although he was disappointed that they seemed to have difficulty adhering to their initial visions. For example, he greatly admired Antioch president Arthur Morgan, as well as some of the ideas tried at Antioch concerning the close connection between in-class learning and off-campus work experience. However, he noted an unhappy consequence of the idea in action, observing, "The administrative portion required to get jobs for the Antioch students became so top heavy and expensive that Morgan had to spend all his time on the road begging money." Visiting Berea College, Rice was initially eager to view firsthand the student craft industries that led to self-sufficiency. Then he was disappointed when he was told that the college was far from self-sufficient and, in fact, could not survive without subvention from local churches.[40]

Rice's responses to experimental St. John's College in Annapolis, Maryland, demonstrate his characteristic blend of admiration and disdain. He could not resist labeling its great books curriculum "a gimmick" that created "a vocational school without a vocation." Yet Rice admitted the school might be appropriate for students who needed a "stiff course in philosophy." He also had high regard for the energies and ideals of the two widely respected educators who initiated St. John's great books program, Scott Buchanan and Stringfellow Barr. After meeting them, he claimed, "I greatly admired Scott Buchanan. . . . He believed passionately in what he was doing, and he was coming out fine. And Stringfellow Barr was a nice fellow." However, on one visit to the Annapolis campus, he paid this backhanded compli-

39. David Gow, "Progressive Education Becomes Collegiate," New York *Evening Post,* September 30, 1933, p. 3.
40. J. Rice, interview with Duberman, June 10, 1967.

ment to Buchanan: "You people should get all the money you want. This is really right down the conservative lane, and they [foundations and private donors] should really come across."[41]

In contrast, Rice had no patience with Robert Maynard Hutchins' experiment with a classic texts curriculum at the University of Chicago. A prolific writer of articles and books, even while serving as president of the University of Chicago, Hutchins summarized his thoughts about education in his 1936 book *The Higher Learning in America*. The framework from which Hutchins' notions about education took shape, and which struck Rice as both ill conceived and ill delivered, was summarized in that volume as follows: "Education implies teaching. Teaching implies knowledge. Knowledge is truth. The truth is everywhere the same. Hence education should be everywhere the same. . . . The heart of any course of study designed for the whole people will be, if education is rightly understood, the same at any time, in any place, under any political, social, or economic conditions." Hutchins fleshed out his ideas with journal and magazine articles that attacked two of Rice's most passionate convictions: the overarching importance of the teacher and the need for education to concern itself primarily with thought processes and human emotion, rather than only with knowledge acquisition. Hutchins labeled the first of these convictions "the great man theory" and the second "the character-building theory." He scoffed at the "nauseating anecdote about Mark Hopkins on one end of the log and the student on the other," and he promoted "the single-minded pursuit of the intellectual virtues" through a program based on reading classic Greek and Latin texts.[42]

A furious Rice lashed back at Hutchins in a 1937 article in *Harper's* magazine titled "Fundamentalism and the Higher Learning." He charged that Hutchins' proposed education, "universal and everlasting, is explicitly to be removed from experience," and asked, "Why exclude from a general education all but one means of getting experience? Why include what can be printed and leave out what must be seen or heard? To some, Aeschylus and the sculpture of Chichen-Itza are in quality very near together. But we are to exclude one because it cannot be got from a book?" Rice continued with his most cogent statement of the philosophy that had brought him to Black Mountain: "Education, instead of being the acquisition of a common stock of fundamental ideas, may well be a learning of a common way of doing

41. J. Rice, *Eighteenth Century,* 265; J. Rice, interview with Duberman, June 10, 1967.
42. Robert Maynard Hutchins, *The Higher Learning,* 66; Hutchins, "Confusion in Higher Education," 457–58.

things, a way of approach, a method of dealing with ideas or anything else. What you do with what you know is the important thing. To know is not enough."[43]

Interestingly, Rice and Hutchins perceived the same roots beneath their deepest concerns about higher education; they only parted toward divergent branches of educational philosophy when promoting methods of addressing these concerns. Both mistrusted the reliance on scientific method in truth seeking, expressing mutual distaste for its anti-intellectualism and its reverence for facts and utility. Both particularly disparaged attempts by the social sciences to gain status among academicians by embracing scientific methods to count and measure toward truths in areas like sociology, political science, and anthropology. For Rice, however, Hutchins' proposal for an education that schooled all students in the same disciplines through the same great texts was as dogmatic as the indiscriminate use of scientific methods to advance knowledge in all disciplines. The selection of truths and texts presupposed a substantial dose of authoritarianism. He agreed with his friend John Dewey, who frequently debated Hutchins in print and insisted: "I would not intimate that the author [Hutchins] has any sympathy with fascism. But basically his idea as to the proper course to be taken is akin to the distrust of freedom and the consequent appeal to some fixed authority. . . . Much may be said for selecting Aristotle and Saint Thomas as promulgators of first truths. Others may prefer Hegel, or Karl Marx, or even Mussolini as the seers of first truths; and there are those who prefer Nazism. As far as I can see President Hutchins has completely evaded the problem of who is to determine the definite truths that constitute the hierarchy."[44]

Rice may have frequently found fault with other endeavors in higher education and with the ideas of other educators. But he also freely admitted a great debt to the educational, social, and philosophical currents and institutions that initiated some ideas he put into play at Black Mountain College. Several decades after he left the college, while examining his thoughts for a possible memoir, he jotted down on a yellow legal tablet these notes about ideas he borrowed for Black Mountain: "from Communists, 'From each, etc.'; from the Quakers, consensus; from Oxford, teachers not taskmasters, outside examiners; from New England, the town meeting, everybody having his say; from Greece, Socratic following of the argument; from Webb

43. J. Rice, "Fundamentalism and the Higher Learning," 587–88, 595.

44. Harry S. Ashmore, *Unseasonable Truths: The Life of Robert Maynard Hutchins* (Boston, 1989), 153–63; John Dewey, "President Hutchins' Proposals to Remake Higher Education," *Social Frontier,* III (January, 1937), 103–104.

School, another chance; from Harvard, hospitality in ideas, however strange; from the South, its inheritance; from New College, 'Manners Maketh Man.' "[45]

The college may have succeeded better in adapting several of these elements than did Rice himself. Certainly he was more hostile than hospitable toward at least some ideas posed in the classroom, and his approach toward colleagues was notable for ill-mannered outbursts. Paradoxically, attributes Rice admired in Black Mountain and its students included those he could not—or perhaps would not—champion as a role model. His impressive mind and forceful personality held no place for the compromise and care necessary to hold back opinions or allow others their small victories. However, any satisfaction he gained by molding interactions to conform with his own preferences and impulses would eventually prove short-lived.

45. Lane, ed., *Black Mountain College,* 24.

7

Strident Voices and Stormy Exits

Three years into Black Mountain College's precocious, if still financially precarious, existence, one of the notable visitors was John Andrew Rice's good friend Walter Locke. Locke had been a voice for liberalism on the editorial staff of the *State Journal* in Lincoln, Nebraska, during Rice's years at the University of Nebraska. Since then he had become the fiercely independent editor of the Dayton *Daily News* and a wise and widely read purveyor of social justice. Rice referred to him as "one of the few real believers in democracy I have ever known."[1]

Locke arrived at Black Mountain College to view a growing community of approximately fifty students and sixteen faculty members. Turmoil in Europe had brought several more immigrant German teachers, including Albers' former student Xanti Schawinsky (art and stage), Anna Moellenhoff (biology and German), and Fritz Moellenhoff (psychology). Herminio Portell-Vila, a respected history scholar from Cuba, was hired when he fled the Batista dictatorship. William Zeuch came to teach economics after serving as president of Commonwealth College, a communal educational experiment in Mena, Arkansas, that emphasized technical and intellectual training with a socialist and labor union focus. Literature professor Kenneth Kurtz arrived after teaching at the academically and physically rigorous experimental college and self-supporting ranch, Deep Springs College, in Inyo County, California. Several former Rollins students had managed to raise funds that made it possible to hire Robert Wunsch in 1935, and he had quickly become an important leader among the faculty. Several young faculty members, hired shortly after completing their graduate degrees, in-

1. Adamic, *My America,* 583.

cluded Irving Knickerbocker (psychology), James Gore King (history), Frederick Mangold (romance languages), and Robert Goldenson (philosophy).

Walter Locke, noting that the originally tightly knit group at Black Mountain was now growing more diverse, asked Rice what he would do when an "intriguer" arrived to ply antagonistic schemes and plots. Rice, very confidently in command as rector of a college growing in size and stature, shrugged off the problem. Later he would decide that an intriguer, in the person of Irving Knickerbocker, was already there at the time Locke posed this question.[2]

After several years of close living and working, the college community was ripe for many types of intrigue. It was easy for people to get on one another's nerves. Rumor passing, sniping, griping, and accusing were natural pastimes among group members, who spent twenty-four hours a day together. They found that divisiveness occurred with less effort than consensus. At one end of the spectrum were fairly impersonal but still highly contentious matters about student involvement in decision making and the degree to which "community" should be sought or enforced. At the other end were personal issues about faculty teaching ability, individual temperaments and behavior, and the power of Rice as rector.

Rice knew how to fuel community debate and was ever curious to see how people might react to a loaded issue; if none presented itself, he was ready. Dick Andrews remembered the general meeting Rice called in the lobby of Lee Hall to talk about institutions and their misguided, self-perpetuating natures. "They outlive their purposes," he explained, "but go blindly on." Then, sucking his pipe and digging deep into his repertoire of Socratic challenges, he asked, "Why shouldn't we, this very night, decide to end the college so that it could become unique among all institutions?" Andrews, a relatively new student who had arrived from Bronxville, New York, recalled the general reaction:

> There was a silence. Then someone gasped. After all, this was a time of depression and some had just come from Europe as refugees. The debate began, and of course Rice was ready for all arguments. And he had the most powerful voice. One man who had been in a brutal jail in his native Central American country jumped to his feet and launched a tirade, not necessarily connected at all to the subject of the debate. This was the moral and emotional equivalent of an old-fashioned revival meeting.
>
> Gradually it all wound down. As people stood up and moved around, Rice

2. J. Rice, *Eighteenth Century,* 333; F. Rice, interview with the author, February 13, 1993.

was still sitting by the end of the table, smoking his pipe. On the table by his elbow was a tiny log cabin he had made out of the match sticks struck to keep his pipe going.[3]

In addition to stirring waters that may have appeared too calm for his liking, John Andrew Rice had vividly demonstrated his own ambivalent feelings about personal attachment to any institution. He had repeated in almost identical phrase and style his challenge in Winter Park to the conference of clergy who were asked to ponder the event of waking up to the disappearance of all the church structures. Certain in his conviction that religion was not to be equated with the churches just as education was not to be equated with the colleges, Rice claimed that the only time he ever found himself in agreement with Robert Maynard Hutchins was when he heard Hutchins had stated that colleges should be in tents.[4] For Rice, tents were just fine for almost any purpose, as he developed very little regard for material possessions or for tangible products of ideas put into action. And he thoroughly enjoyed prompting the distress and defenses of those who found comfort in their attachments to structures and institutions.

Rice himself became the issue when he emerged as the heroic focus of an article about Black Mountain by Louis Adamic, a Yugoslav immigrant and writer renowned for his 1934 book *The Native's Return*. Adamic, who, like Rice, had spent a year in Europe on a Guggenheim Fellowship, arrived at the college with his wife Stella in January, 1936, for an afternoon visit suggested by Henry Allen Moe. They stayed nearly two months. While there, Adamic became thoroughly enchanted by the place and the people—especially by John Andrew Rice. Rice struck up an immediate friendship with the Slavic immigrant and enjoyed elaborating his ideas and experiences for Adamic to incorporate into an article he had decided to write for *Harper's*.[5]

Before the Adamics left the college, Louis Adamic read the draft of "Education on a Mountain" to a community meeting. Although it recognized the brave students who had joined the venture and singled out for special notice Josef Albers and Robert Wunsch, the article most prominently extolled the thoughts and actions of John Andrew Rice. Compiling the most comprehensive statement yet made of Rice's educational philosophy, Adamic quoted at length Rice's explanations of the aims and functions of the college. He described Rice as "an idealist-optimist: intelligent, well-informed, fan-

3. Richard Andrews, "John Rice and the Model Log Cabin," 1988 (MS in possession of Richard Andrews, North Waterford, Maine).

4. J. Rice, *Eighteenth Century*, 326.

5. Adamic, "Education on a Mountain," 519.

tastically honest." Continuing up the pedestal, he plotted Rice's stature as "perhaps one of the great teachers of all time," and admired his adherence to his own prescription: "A good teacher is always more a learner than teacher, making the demand of everyone to be taught something. . . . A teacher must have something of humor, a deeply laid irony, and not be a cynic. In the center of his being he should be calm, quiet, tough." In the finished essay Adamic also applauded Rice's vision, insisting, "The majority of the original Black Mountain College faculty had no clearly formed positive ideas, and the questions of educational policy were left almost entirely to the leader, John Andrew Rice, whose head bristled with ideas, and who said at the start that he wanted a new kind of college. The educational policy was left largely to him."[6]

The community discussion that followed the reading was critical of the essay's untempered good news about the effect of community life on student development and about Rice as a teacher and leader. Several students ventured for the first time to voice their impression that Rice was a sometimes insensitive Socrates whose power in the community could be misdirected or misused. Although there were some Rice defenders at the meeting, the detractors agreed with faculty member William Zeuch's impression: "He [Louis Adamic] represents to me the futility of a man without community experience and without educational experience trying to understand Black Mountain College. That was the reason why in the end it was necessary for Mr. Rice, as everyone here knows, to supply the information and the point of view. . . . Mr. Rice was practically ghost writing for Mr. Adamic. That is an open secret."[7]

Rice managed to attenuate the worst of the venom by admitting to some mistakes and to heavy-handedness with some students; and he expressed admiration for those students who were now candidly voicing their opinions. He invited students to continue to approach him with observations that might help him curb his negative tendencies. Insisting he had no taste for the power side of leadership, he told the group they shared some blame for elevating his position by bringing to him problems and issues they could deal with themselves.[8]

Finally, Rice appealed for all to focus on the bright side of Adamic's article. Its publication would attract attention to the college that could ensure a

---

6. *Ibid.*, 526, 518.
7. J. Rice, *Eighteenth Century*, 337; Duberman, *Black Mountain*, 116–17; William E. Zeuch, "The State of Black Mountain College," 1937 (MS in Faculty Files, BMCP, N.C. Archives).
8. Duberman, *Black Mountain*, 118.

healthy infusion of applicants.[9] About that, Rice was correct. The article was published in *Harper's* in April, 1936, just in time to generate applications for the 1936–1937 academic year. It was soon reprinted in *Reader's Digest,* and a slightly revised version of it was included as a chapter in Adamic's book *My America.* Requests for information and applications increased dramatically.

Later, in a very brief chapter about Black Mountain College in his auto-biography, Rice seemed uncharacteristically, but genuinely, humbled by the community furor over the Adamic article. He insisted that he had tried hard to maintain the spirit of democracy at the college. But the incident had taught him something new about himself: "I was also hungry for recognition, for praise. Webb School, Nebraska, New Jersey College, Rollins, all had called me a fool and were glad when I was gone. I knew that discipleship, while maybe, almost certainly, necessary for a time, was in the end wrong, and not only for what it did to the disciple. And yet, when I foresaw my name in print, saw the words 'great teacher,' I became not even a teacher."[10]

Outside Black Mountain, only Bernard DeVoto, in his *Harper's* column, "The Easy Chair," took exception to Adamic's euphoric piece. DeVoto, who likened participation at Black Mountain to participation at Brook Farm, in jails, and in armies, acknowledged, "I have always distrusted the assumptions and the aims of such [experimental] colleges, and as my experience increases, I distrust them more." His list of grudges ranged from the inability of small colleges to achieve large libraries or extensive laboratory equipment, to the tendency of maverick colleges to repeat earlier community experiments (not collegiate experiments) that had failed in the past. DeVoto's vehemence on the subject overcame critical analysis when he characterized Black Mountain as "downright dangerous. It sounds a good deal less like an educational institution than a sanitarium for mental diseases, run by optimistic amateurs."[11]

Adamic wrote to Rice of the DeVoto column, "The guy practically epitomizes what is wrong with education and the world." Rice decided the problem was DeVoto himself, "who had been born in Utah and hated the word community as intensely as I the Methodist Church." Other educators similarly derided DeVoto's point of view. Among those who wrote objections to DeVoto or encouragement to Adamic was Harold H. Anderson of the University of Iowa. Anderson captured the general mood when he attacked DeVoto's sarcasm about student participation in the dining hall and the garden, noting, "He compares the incomparable by giving intellectual

9. J. Rice, *Eighteenth Century,* 338.
10. *Ibid.*
11. Bernard DeVoto, "Another Consociate Family," *Harper's,* CLXXII (April, 1936), 605.

work a pseudo-superiority over physical work. It is like asking one if he would rather read a sonnet or take a bath. . . . Experimental educators are not unmindful of the value of libraries and laboratories. But what kind of a laboratory does one need to discover how human beings can live together, tolerating each other and learning from their differences?"[12]

Just as the controversy over Adamic's article began to ebb as a community issue, another swelled to take its place. In April, 1936, the board of fellows voted to send warnings to psychology professor Irving Knickerbocker at the end of his first teaching year and to philosophy professor Robert Goldenson at the end of his second year, stating it was "quite pessimistic" that either could "develop into the kind of teacher we want here permanently." Five members of the board, including Rice, had voted for sending the warning; two members had voted against.[13]

Goldenson's case was simple. His teaching was not considered up to par. However, he was an avid golfer and a fine golf coach. After he received his warning notice, Rice managed to add insult to injury when he advised Goldenson to give up classroom teaching and become a professional golf instructor. Apparently Rice had support for his position. At a subsequent faculty meeting, when Goldenson brought up Rice's suggestion as an example of his insensitivity, Ted Dreier ventured, "My guess would be that it was very good advice, without meaning anything hostile or unfriendly."[14]

At the same meeting, Bob Wunsch, hoping to take the sting out of Goldenson's situation, mentioned that Rice also had sometimes made insensitive comments about plays he (Wunsch) had produced. Goldenson, not to be comforted, countered to Wunsch, "But not after you had been dismissed from the faculty." Rice explained to Wunsch that his abrupt advice to Goldenson was calculated, saying, "Bob needs to be shocked out of this feeling that . . . he can be a teacher by having a mass of information."[15]

Goldenson, with support from Zeuch and several others, particularly objected that when he received his written warning about his tenuous position on the faculty, none of his colleagues had yet attended his classes. It seemed inconceivable to him that performance could be judged by individuals who

12. Louis Adamic to John A. Rice, March 24, 1936, in Faculty Files, BMCP, N.C. Archives; J. Rice, *Eighteenth Century*, 337; Harold H. Anderson to Louis Adamic, [n.d.] 1936, in Faculty Files, BMCP, N.C. Archives.

13. Frederick Georgia to Irving Knickerbocker, April 15, 1936, in Faculty Files, BMCP, N.C. Archives.

14. Faculty Meeting Minutes, December 7, 1936, in Official Documents, BMCP, N.C. Archives.

15. *Ibid.*

had never witnessed that performance firsthand. After his warning notice, Goldenson challenged, "No one had come to visit my classes or come to me to discuss my teaching. I got the notice in my box. I didn't know what was coming up. Just as a matter of common courtesy, why not give a man a look-over to see what he does at work? Instead, I was judged by things on the fringe. It is like judging a city by its suburbs."[16]

Knickerbocker's case, however, was only somewhat related to his teaching competence. He had lent a sympathetic ear to students who had complaints about the college, in general, and John Andrew Rice, in particular. New and young students especially tended to draw to Knickerbocker, and they could rely on him to agree with their dismay or distress on any number of counts. Inevitably, factions emerged in the college, with groups of students lining up behind Rice or Knickerbocker. Bob Wunsch, who saw that the community was on the verge of splitting into two colleges, believed Knickerbocker was "coddling" students who were unhappy with Rice; and Dreier tended to agree with him. Knickerbocker, however, insisted that he needed to protect some students from Rice's "extremely destructive effect upon personality."[17]

Rice was not particularly reluctant to mention his colleagues to students, but he was inclined to speak of a number of faculty members. Knickerbocker, in contrast, focused fairly exclusively on Rice in discussions with students. His own explanation was that Rice's cutting ways with students gave rise to their need for someone to go to for support. "I have done my best to protect the students," Knickerbocker insisted, "by giving them all the information I could about Mr. Rice and his methods."[18]

Students and faculty who protested the warnings given to Goldenson and Knickerbocker considered themselves to be doing battle with John Andrew Rice. With the group polarized, there was little protection for Rice, even though he was only one of five (Rice, Dreier, Mangold, Albers, and student moderator Mary Beaman) on the board of fellows who had voted to send the two professors warnings (Georgia and Martin had dissented). Disliking this contentious atmosphere, some probably hoped that Goldenson and Knickerbocker might decide to sneak away over the summer. Both teachers returned, however, impelled perhaps by sheer need or by the expectation that their situations would improve.

16. *Ibid.*
17. Faculty Meeting Minutes, October 19, December 7, 1936, in Official Documents, BMCP, N.C. Archives; F. Rice, interview with the author, February 13, 1993.
18. Steinau, interview with the author, May 3, 1993; French, interview with the author, July 27, 1993; Faculty Meeting Minutes, December 7, 1936, in Official Documents, BMCP, N.C. Archives.

In the fall of 1936, Rice suggested that the faculty begin a series of weekly discussions on teaching. He asked Josef Albers to chair the first of these, and the group decided later to pass the meeting leadership around. Early discussions centered on method, especially the value of lecture versus dialogue. Later topics included the "imperialism of teaching," "boundaries and dangers of personalities," and "deduction v. induction."[19]

Black Mountain College faculty were in a unique position to discuss teaching practices as well as philosophy because they often attended one another's classes. The vitality of firsthand information marked these discussions, as when recent Bauhaus transplant Xanti Schawinsky commented, "What I have seen here is that in Mr. Rice's classes they are interested in Mr. Rice. He goes toward what he is interested in but collects every meaning and idea of everyone. This is new for me. I have never seen this before. . . . This kind of teaching, to be interested in one common ideal and to resolve it altogether (not to have a dictator but to follow one idea) is good."[20]

In their classes and during the teaching discussions, Albers, Zeuch, Dreier, and Rice could be counted on to promote dialogue and individual feedback. Portell-Vila, in contrast, was an inveterate lecturer who represented the opposing style. Rice wanted to know why some used one method and some another. Zeuch, to general agreement, explained: "I like discussion because I find out about the various students. I know just what their background is and what their thought is, and when I have a problem to present I usually can tell what the reaction will be. You cannot do that in a big institution. From my point of view there is not 'education' in a large university, but only 'instruction' because they do not know the important factor—the individual."[21]

Portell-Vila, however, defended his strict use of lecture. He insisted: "The message I have in a lecture is useful for the students and for the community and for the people for whom they are going to work. In the lectures, I am all the time trying to expound a thesis. . . . to provoke mental unrest, to see if students start to doubt about what they know of the subject and start to think along the lines I am thinking. I think that I am right, that I have something to say where I am trying to convince, and that the student ought to think as I think about the question I am expounding."[22]

Portell-Vila had some solid support from biology and German professor

---

19. Faculty Meeting Minutes, September 7, 28, October 19, 1936, in Official Documents, BMCP, N.C. Archives.

20. Faculty Meeting Minutes, October 19, 1936, *ibid.*

21. Faculty Meeting Minutes, September 28, 1936, *ibid.*

22. *Ibid.*

Anna Moellenhoff, considered one of the more skilled teachers in the college. And the threatened Knickerbocker also expressed his accord in maintaining that a lecture could "start an interest and be an inspiration." His vivid example of an inspiring lecturer was a geology professor at Harvard who "took the earth up on the platform and it heaved and rocked and lived. . . . I read books because he lectured."[23]

When the issue of feedback to the students surfaced, the group expressed a wide variety of views. Some thought that any feedback—especially the favorable sort—was coddling and pandering; others contended that at least some feedback could sustain or encourage a student. Albers, who often mentioned the need for students to experience "mental unrest," summarized the middle road—infrequent feedback—noting: "The least effort to correct students is best. He [the student] must not say that this is right because the teacher says so. You can prove whether or not you are an imperialist by watching this. Sometimes we must push, but generally we should give the feeling, '*I* did my work,' not the feeling that the teacher did it."[24]

Rice and Zeuch agreed that negative feedback should be used sparingly. Rice even pointed out that when he attended Albers' drawing classes, the most devastating feedback occurred when Albers briefly glanced down at a student's work and walked by without a word. However, they disagreed at length on the issue of positive feedback. Zeuch decided that neither praise nor reproach were particularly appropriate in the classroom. He raised the problem associated with students' insistence on hearing teachers' responses to their views and work: "They want teachers' opinions of what they are doing and are not developing any judgment of their own. After preparing a paper, they seem unable to see whether their own work was good or bad." He insisted, "I never say, 'This is a good paper.'"[25]

Although Rice drilled Zeuch at length about his disdain for "praise getting out," Zeuch would not budge. Eventually, for the sake of argument, an impatient Rice challenged Zeuch to explain why a teacher should withhold his or her view of student work. When Zeuch still would not acknowledge the value of positive teacher commentary, Rice simply sighed, "Zeuch ought to take drawing and have Mr. Albers pass him by once in a while without a word about his work!" Undoubtedly, Black Mountain College had be-

23. Faculty Meeting Minutes, October 19, 1936, in Official Documents, BMCP, N.C. Archives.

24. *Ibid.*

25. *Ibid.*

come one of the few endeavors in higher education where faculty could argue from the perspective of students as well as instructors. Albers voiced the general faculty feeling on feedback, insisting, "We must be able to say 'I do not know' even if we seem dumb. In painting, I give them two or three solutions to choose from."[26]

The meetings about teaching became particularly heated when they touched upon the types of teachers thought to be appropriate for Black Mountain College. Most participants agreed that there was room for faculty who used a variety of methods, but Zeuch stretched the view to suggest that there was room for even the most bizarre personalities. Possibly thinking of the Goldenson and Knickerbocker situations, he asked Rice, "Do you know the right kind of personality to have?" He then opened a debate: "A disintegrated personality can be a strong personality. Should we keep students away from disintegrated personalities?"

Albers observed, "Every school has the right to select personalities that fit their program."

Rice, however, tested Zeuch's limits, asking, "Would you go out and look for poor teachers?"

Not to be cornered, Zeuch replied, "Yes. Get one or two."

Characteristically, Rice squelched further remarks from Zeuch, asking, "Can't you trust the Lord to send them to you?"[27]

Neither the faculty meetings on teaching nor the earlier warnings from the board of fellows changed the situations of Professors Knickerbocker and Goldenson. After Thanksgiving, 1936, the board of fellows voted that those two would not be reappointed to the faculty after the current academic year. The decision had been made with little prodding from Rice. Again, only Martin and Georgia voted against the resolution.

William Zeuch, who was not among the faculty on the board of fellows, led a countercharge. He was especially furious about the decision concerning Knickerbocker and demanded the issue be reconsidered at a faculty meeting. There, Bob Wunsch explained his view, shared by the majority of the board of fellows, stating, "I did hear from students in September that Mr. Knickerbocker was doing well. Then there came to me gradually one fact after another that began to make me doubtful about Mr. Knickerbocker's usefulness here. My information came from students and was not solicited.

26. *Ibid.*
27. Faculty Meeting Minutes, October 12, 1936, in Official Documents, BMCP, N.C. Archives.

The information led me to believe that there were forming here two colleges. There was a group which tended to get away from the center of the college."[28]

Interestingly, although the major concern about Knickerbocker was his role in polarizing students on issues involving Rice, Rice had not assumed a particularly vocal role in ousting Knickerbocker. He had stated his opinion to the board of fellows, cast his vote for the nonreappointment, and left town for a conference shortly afterward. He was not present at the December faculty meeting in which Zeuch appealed for the type of community vitality and healthiness contributed by faculty members such as Knickerbocker, colleagues who were open in their opinions and objections. However, Zeuch, in his argument for a repeal of the decision to terminate Knickerbocker's appointment, included an attack on Rice, charging, "As much as I respect and admire him, the sooner the group faces the dangers in his personality and methods, the better for Mr. Rice and for the school." Zeuch was certain that Rice's personal ill feelings for Knickerbocker constituted the prime force behind his ouster, although Wunsch and Dreier both insisted they had sensed no such animosity on Rice's part.[29]

Zeuch found his most vocal support in Frederick Georgia and James Gore King, but he was unable to move the faculty members who regarded Knickerbocker's active support of anti-Rice students as disloyal and manipulative. Anna Moellenhoff summarized this view, stating, "In such a young institution and such a small one there has to be a certain amount of loyalty to the institution itself. I did not find this in Mr. Knickerbocker. . . . Knickerbocker has not made students part of this place but has made them opponents of Mr. Rice." Apparently, most of the board of fellows agreed with Mrs. Moellenhoff, and they turned down a proposal by Zeuch that their decisions on both Knickerbocker and Goldenson be reversed. Perhaps finding Goldenson's argument that he had little advance warning compelling, embarrassing, or both, the board of fellows did slightly alter their position to allow Goldenson to resign.[30]

Although the decision was final, the dissension had not ended. Those faculty and students who disagreed with an outcome they could not influence predictably shifted their attack to the process. Student discussions and community meetings during late winter and spring, 1937, focused on issues of community governance. Students and several faculty members insisted that

28. Faculty Meeting Minutes, December 7, 1936, *ibid.*
29. *Ibid.*
30. *Ibid.*

such a communal venture demanded greater voice for all, including students, in decision making. Zeuch summarized the argument, saying, "I would much rather trust the community as a whole on the question of reappointment than I would a small group in the community."[31]

Rice countered that Black Mountain College was foremost an educational venture, not a community. With his most active backing from Mangold, Dreier, and Wunsch, he insisted that in a college not all opinions and voices could be equal. When one student claimed that students were in an excellent position to make judgments about teachers, Rice maintained that hiring and firing decisions were not in their purview. Bluntly, he added, "If you want a specific instance, I would say that I am a better judge of who ought to teach on this faculty than you are."[32]

Some of the students, still not satisfied with the situation, determined that resignation in protest was their only viable option. On June 1, 1937, at the final general meeting of the year, eight students announced their intent to leave Black Mountain College. Their charges against the college ranged from "puritanical moral attitudes" to an atmosphere of "malicious gossip." Other complaints were lodged against limitations on student participation in decision making, Rice's heavy-handed treatment of students, and excessive power in the hands of the rector.[33]

The dissident students also mentioned faculty salaries in their statement, charging that low salaries for some were a deliberate attempt to encourage their departures. This contention sparked a heated argument among faculty members as to how salaries were determined. In fact, the board of fellows had, in October, 1936, voted faculty salaries (beyond living expenses) for the first time. Officially, these were to be determined "on the basis of need . . . [including] intangible needs the importance of which varies in individual cases." The salaries varied greatly, with Rice and Wunsch on the high end at $2,100 each and Joe Martin on the low end at $300. Albers received $1,700, the second highest salary, and Georgia received $1,300. With the widely ranging faculty salaries on the table, the discussion of the disgruntled students' resignations quickly became a discussion about faculty complaints and comparisons. Portell-Vila was particularly incensed that others' salaries were higher than his; and Georgia was informed by Rice and several others that his lower salary reflected teaching problems and an unwillingness to partici-

---

31. General Meeting Minutes, February 17, 1937, in Official Documents, BMCP, N.C. Archives.

32. *Ibid.*

33. "Student Statement," June 1, 1937 (Typescript in Student Files, BMCP, N.C. Archives).

pate fully in the community. Shortly after the meeting, Georgia submitted his resignation, and it was accepted. Portell-Vila did the same but Rice persuaded him to stay.[34]

The next fall, true to their word, the eight students did not return. Zeuch and King both found other options over the summer, raising the number of nonreturning faculty to five. Shortly after school started for the 1937–1938 academic year, Rice wrote to his friend Louis Adamic that "the year starts off very well, more quiet and peaceful than ever before. So far I have fairly revelled in the enjoyment of absences."[35]

Rice could well look forward to an enjoyable year. He began to teach a writing seminar that attracted students who were excited about learning and who enjoyed his style. The immediate problems among faculty and students had been removed, and even with the recent student departures, the year began with fifty-five registered students. Furthermore, in June, 1937, the college had managed to purchase a seven-hundred-acre former girls' camp on Lake Eden, three miles north of the Blue Ridge site. Although Rice was not as euphoric as others about the event, faculty had begun planning a permanent campus at Lake Eden that would eliminate the difficulties of a yearly lease and the effort of packing and storing furnishings each June.

Rice's writing seminar was scheduled to meet for two hours after dinner once a week. "But if it was exciting, it went until midnight; and if very exciting, Rice would pull out a case of beer, and it went well past midnight," recalled Emil Willimetz. During the sessions, long or short, approximately six to twelve students sat around Rice's study in Lee Hall and read and critiqued their writing aloud. Still pondering the possibility of publishing articles or a book, Rice read stories about his South Carolina childhood. Eventually, these stories became chapters in his autobiography, *I Came Out of the Eighteenth Century.*[36]

Students agreed that Rice was probably at the top of his masterful teaching form in the writing seminar. He was able to challenge, probe, and inspire criticism about the tangible products of student work, as well as his own work. He was student and teacher, with no exclusive corner on meaningful feedback. The Socratic leader gave way to the facilitative partner in a process that seemed to have a softening effect on Rice's abrasive side. "He mainly

34. Board of Fellows Meeting Minutes, October 23, November 30, December 18, 1936, in Official Documents, *ibid.;* Duberman, *Black Mountain,* 135–37.

35. John A. Rice to Louis Adamic, September 20, 1937, in Faculty Files, BMCP, N.C. Archives.

36. Willimetz, interview with the author, July 1, 1993; Emil Willimetz to Katherine Reynolds, April 11, 1994, in author's possession.

worked with us about making sure whatever you had in your mind, you had gotten it out on paper . . . and about considering what impact it would have on readers," explained Robert Sunley. The seminar included no work on structure or grammar, but a student with special needs might be asked to take a tutorial, such as Sue Spayth Riley did in spelling with Mary Barnes. When Emil Willimetz indicated an interest in literary form, modern language instructor Frederick Mangold and Rice joined forces to tutor him; in the process they critiqued the various incarnations of a brief story he was required to write ten times in the styles of ten different writers. Willimetz later commented, "It was, for me, one of the endearing features of BMC, that two prominent professors would collaborate to invent a class for a single student."[37]

In the writing seminar, Rice's capacity for intimidation rarely surfaced, although his proclivity for humor readily emerged. Sue Spayth Riley recalled a piece she had written that Rice decided to read in class. It was a spoof on abstract contemporary literature that seemed deliberately crafted to make no sense at all, so Riley's story also made no sense. At some point, Rice came to a paragraph about a bowl sliding across ice. Riley explained, "I was a very poor speller, and I had misspelled 'bowl.' Mr. Rice just laughed and laughed. He was such a jolly soul, with a wonderful sense of humor, and he almost shook like Santa Claus. When he got over laughing, he pointed out that I'd put an E in bowl."[38]

A happy rector and the promise of a calm year ahead provided welcome relief to faculty members and students who were weary of the unsettling atmosphere of the previous year. Unfortunately, however, Rice would soon disappoint anyone counting on him to steer clear of controversy. Although the most recent problems at the college had receded, the relationship between Nell and John Andrew Rice was as stormy and strained as it ever had been. Rice's response to this strife would prompt a community furor.

Nell Rice undoubtedly was worn out by her husband's frequent tangles with faculty and students, which, in a small space like Black Mountain, spilled over into every phase of life. She had none of her husband's capacity for gaining energy from the great highs and lows presented by constant embroilment. Her temperament was more controlled, more guided by the search for a patterned existence. According to her son Frank, she rarely laughed, a trait she held in common with her mother and with her brother

---

37. Sunley, interview with the author, May 22, 1993; Sue Spayth Riley, interview with the author, May 24, 1993; Willimetz to Reynolds, April 11, 1994, in author's possession.

38. Riley, interview with the author, May 24, 1993.

Frank. Although she expertly played the role of unofficial college hostess and was an important nurturing presence for many students in need, she also found it possible to disengage or shy away. "A curious, detached, impersonal warmth of manner" was how her son Frank later described her outward demeanor.[39] Nor was Nell Rice given to laying out her grievances to her husband. When she became fed up with his volatility or insensitivity, she found it easiest to pack up herself and daughter Mary and head for the Aydelotte homestead in Sullivan, Indiana.

By the fall of 1937, Frank Rice was attending the University of North Carolina at Chapel Hill, and Mary was applying for a scholarship to Swarthmore. Nell, whose mother had died the year before, took long trips to Sullivan during that spring and fall to assist in disbursing family property while escaping the discord in her marriage. Meanwhile, John Rice, while reveling in the absence of dissension and dissenters, fell in love with one of the Black Mountain College students.

She was young, to be sure, and she was not exceptionally beautiful or brilliant. However, according to David Way, then a second-year student from Montana, "She had perfected the southern girls' demure attention to masculine discourse." Her attention to and from Rice began during a ritual autumn pastime in which male and female students circulated among each other's studies to chat, share a drink, and consider the possibilities. It was not uncommon for Rice also to make the rounds of student studies, frequently accompanied by several circulating male students.[40]

Rice later characterized his feelings for the new student as "a sudden spasm as a result of this unhappiness [in marriage]. I fell in love—or what they call it. I never understood what the ancients meant when they said love was a disease, but it is when it was that kind." He had had previous interests in women outside his marriage, perhaps actual affairs. There had been rumors about his relations with a drama teacher at New Jersey College for Women and with a secretary in Henry Allen Moe's office. But infatuation with such a young woman in such a small community was new to him.[41]

As some students and faculty began to notice the direction of Rice's attentions, they began to talk. "There were rumors," explained Morton Steinau.

39. F. Rice to Reynolds, December 8, 1994, in author's possession.

40. David Jacques Way to Mervin Lane, March 11, 1988, in Student Files, BMCP, N.C. Archives; David Jacques Way, interview with the author, April 23, 1993.

41. J. Rice, interview with Duberman, June 10, 1967; Henry Allen Moe to John A. Rice, September 17, 1932, in J. Rice File, Guggenheim; F. Rice, interview with the author, November 24, 1995.

"It was assumed by most people. It was not an open thing." Furthermore, no one was at all certain that Rice's attentions toward the young lady were being returned. David Way later conjectured that she "was more bewildered than anyone else in Rice's growing infatuation. . . . I think some of us felt a certain sympathy for her, subjected as she was to the full blast of Rice's considerable personality."[42]

Quite naturally, substantial confusion and ambivalence conditioned what was observed and what was rumored. Emil Willimetz explained, "It was not common knowledge whether the relationship was physical. I don't know of anyone who ever saw anything—touching, hand holding, or anything." Many who heard the rumors decided they were fueled by forces who disliked Rice and his behavior, especially those who longed for more structure and authority at the college. Others recognized that the situation was not exceptional. Earlier, another married male faculty member had fallen in love with a college secretary and eventually divorced his wife to marry her. In that case, Rice had acted effectively as a force for quelling gossip and indignation. Still others, however, were genuinely outraged. Norman Weston recalled, "We were a bunch of puritans, of course, sitting up there on the mountain; and many of us had a great love for Black Mountain College and its future and an interest in standards."[43]

Conjecture gave way to conviction when the word passed around that Nell Rice had confided to another faculty spouse that she had caught her husband and his student in the act of making love. The matter then became "a visible anguish," recalled Barbara Dreier. "Conceivably you could keep that sort of thing secret, but Mr. Rice and his wife didn't have that kind of relationship." Indeed, the indiscretion was not secret for long even from then–college student Frank Rice. During the fall, his parents visited him in Chapel Hill and took him out to dinner at a fine restaurant, the Carolina Inn. When Rice left their table to use the restroom, Nell Rice turned to her son with an expression he later described as "like an angry cat—the most anger I'd ever seen in a face." Then, she leaned toward him and hissed, "I caught him at it. I saw him with her." Young Frank silently stood, turned, left the restaurant, walked back to his room, fell onto his bed, and wept. When his

42. Steinau, interview with the author, May 3, 1993; Way to Lane, March 11, 1988, in Student Files, BMCP, N.C. Archives.

43. Willimetz, interview with the author, July 1, 1993; Robert Sunley to Katherine Reynolds, May 1, 1993, in author's possession; J. Rice, interview with Duberman, June 10, 1967; Weston, interview with the author, April 13, 1993.

parents came to his door, he could not speak to them; and he maintained his silence toward them for a number of weeks.[44]

Once again, battle lines were drawn throughout the college community. After Christmas, Rice took to his study, where he sulked and sucked his pipe, while faculty and students registered either repulsion for his poor judgment or sympathy for his predicament. As it became apparent that the girl attracting Rice's attentions was more interested in another student, the infatuation cooled. However, indignation among faculty, students, and family did not. The community had been lulled into the possibility of a year on even keel at Black Mountain. When Rice's actions disrupted the peace, many of them became angry. The college rector had opened up all the old grievances concerning arrogance and insensitivity, all the old tensions about philosophy and style, and all the old animosities toward leadership and power.

Most damaging, Rice had exhausted the support system that once existed among his colleagues and admirers. There were some students who rallied around him and were convinced, as was David Way, "There was no sin involved. Nobody was being immoral. The moments of intimacy between them were almost nonexistent." Robert Sunley recalled that although student opinion was mostly either indifferent toward or critical of Rice, there were still "quite a few" Rice supporters, including himself. Sunley viewed the different positions on Rice as reflective of two distinct philosophies in the college community: one characterized by "valuing the intuitive, inspirational, sensual, taking risks, experiencing, wondering," and one characterized by "constraint, defining limits, carefulness, results oriented, fearfulness, moralism, puritanism."[45]

Supportive friends among the faculty were difficult to find. At the very least, faculty members who saw a personal flaw exposed decided, like Thomas Whitney Surette, "Well, he's self-indulgent." Portell-Vila vocally expressed moral outrage, whereas Josef Albers' deep disdain was more controlled and unemotional. The issue of an undisciplined colleague was as simple as that of an undisciplined student to Albers, who often told his classes, "Who likes not discipline, let him leave suddenly!" Ted Dreier and Bob Wunsch felt let down and fed up. Student David Way recalled Wunsch,

44. Duberman, *Black Mountain,* 140; Weston, interview with the author, April 13, 1993; B. Dreier, interview with the author, April 5, 1993; F. Rice, interview with the author, November 24, 1995.

45. Way, interview with the author, April 23, 1993; Robert Sunley to Martin Duberman, January 3, 1973, in Duberman Papers, N.C. Archives.

in tears, asking him, "How could he, with that great belly, imagine himself in love with a young girl?"[46]

Faculty discussions ranged from addressing the specific incident to debating general issues of Rice's administration and leadership. Several faculty members, tired of uncertainty and upheaval, had begun to believe that perhaps a bit more structure might not prove so loathsome after all. They may have held a view similar to that of an exhausted later faculty member, who finally declared of his Black Mountain experiences: "I began to feel a warm glow at the thought of a department chairman, a dean, a trustee, even a vice-chancellor in charge of development! . . . The demon of Don Quixote was forever dead in my bosom, and Sancho Panza had won."[47]

Rice was in a precarious position to weather another storm concerning college leadership. Even with increased student enrollment, the college never had gotten on secure financial footing. And Rice, as he himself knew, had little patience for stroking a potential donor. Tellingly, in the case of Colonel Arthur Dwight, the first contributor to the idea of a new college, Rice demonstrated even limited patience for existing donors. He visited Dwight at his large estate on Long Island, after Black Mountain College had survived several years but still badly needed additional funding. At breakfast, there was some discussion of an isolationist group called "America First," of which Colonel Dwight was a proud member. Rice, unwilling or unable to hold his tongue, told Dwight bluntly, "I would not let a yellow dog of mine belong to that outfit." The college never received any additional money from Colonel Dwight.[48]

Faculty members were losing confidence steadily in their rector and in his ability to guide the college toward the security, stability, and structure they now sought. Albers was moved to state his anguish in a confidential letter to Rice. In it he attempted to clarify the gravity of faculty feelings toward Rice: "Their criticisms are serious. . . . They come also from people who supported you against the opposition last year. They are a danger for the existence and continuation of BMC. They prove a loss of confidence in you. [They are] of a too heavy weight to be answered by dialectical discussions."[49]

46. Williams, interview with the author, May 10, 1993; Allan Sly to Anna Hines, n.d., in Faculty Files, Way to Lane, March 11, 1988, in Student Files, both in BMCP, N.C. Archives.
47. Aaron Levi, "A Valedictorian Changes His Mind," *Dartmouth Alumni Magazine* (May, 1972), 24.
48. Weston to Reynolds, April 25, 1993, in author's possession.
49. Josef Albers to John A. Rice, January 28, 1938, in John A. Rice File, the Josef and Anni Albers Foundation, Orange, Conn.

By February, 1938, with Rice suffering substantial distress over his failing marriage and his dwindling support at the college, the faculty began to encourage him to consider a leave of absence that might allow a time of calm and possible healing to ensue. Fred Mangold, then serving as college secretary, and Ted Dreier, as treasurer, met with Rice on March 3 to work out conditions of the leave. Rice was granted leave until the first of May, but with the stipulation that he not return at that time unless the faculty had agreed it was appropriate. Mangold and Dreier also elicited Rice's agreement that he would not seek student opinion about whether and when he should return and that students would be told only that Rice "may or may not return before next September."[50]

Rice borrowed a small beach cottage at Folly Beach, South Carolina, near Charleston, where he began to shape his writing about his early life in the South into publishable form. In this endeavor he was prodded and encouraged by Louis and Stella Adamic, whom he visited during the spring at their home in Milford, New Jersey. Nell Rice left for an extended visit to Swarthmore. Rice intended to return to the college no later than May 1, figuring he would then be rested and animosity about him would have subsided. However, when he applied to end his leave, the board of fellows voted unanimously to risk no interruption of the calm they now enjoyed and to extend Rice's leave until September. Rice was furious at the decision. He refused to represent the college at an upcoming meeting of progressive educators in Chicago; and on April 13, 1938, he resigned his position as rector of Black Mountain College. Bob Wunsch, at the final board of fellows meeting of the year, summarized the views and motivations of the faculty: "It was a matter of Mr. Rice's failing, over a period of time, to show good judgment and in so doing to dissipate his leadership and effectiveness. The faculty, in sending Mr. Rice away, was saying, in effect, 'You are in no condition to direct the College affairs now.' . . . Many of us have missed Mr. Rice: the stimulation of his conversations, his common sense wisdom about so many things. And we entertain the high hope that when he returns in the fall, he will be the Mr. Rice we knew at the beginning of the College."[51]

Salaries at Black Mountain were still based on family "budgets of need" and had been cut by 25 percent during the 1937–1938 academic year. As

50. Memorandum of Conversation: Dreier, J. Rice, Mangold, March 3, 1938 (Typescript in Official Documents, BMCP, N.C. Archives); Duberman, *Black Mountain,* 144–45.

51. Board of Fellows Meeting Minutes, June 2, 1938, in Official Documents, BMCP, N.C. Archives; Duberman, *Black Mountain,* 145–46.

treasurer, Ted Dreier felt somewhat responsible for finding enough money to support Rice through the summer; to send Nell Rice to Sullivan, Indiana, and then to Swarthmore, Pennsylvania; and to continue funding the education of Frank Rice at the University of North Carolina. During the spring of 1938, Dreier wrote to Frank Aydelotte for advice and assistance. In that letter, Dreier suggested that perhaps the solution would be to find Nell Aydelotte gainful employment at the college, preferably in starting an on-site elementary school for faculty and local children. Aydelotte's reply indicated the financial problem might be temporary. He informed Dreier that Nell would take over the librarianship at Black Mountain College when the incumbent retired and that he would financially assist her in attending library school during the next year to prepare herself.[52] Just as he financed Nell's trips to Sullivan and supplemented college finances and medical expenses for Mary and Frank Rice, Aydelotte had once again played a key role in assisting, even orchestrating, the Rice family saga. If John Andrew Rice resented Aydelotte's continuing involvement or considered him overly meddlesome, he never let on. He may have understood very well that he himself had always been happy to benefit from Aydelotte's widespread regard among educators, from his hospitable welcome to Rice family members and friends at his Swarthmore mansion, as well as from his financial largesse.

On his extended leave of absence Rice was visited at Folly Beach by several delegations of students and faculty who were interested either in his future plans or in his present well-being. Sharing with him meals of crab, oysters, and beer and conversing with him far into the night, students found a more mellow, reflective Rice. "His attitude was that he'd just sit out this part of the year and come back in the fall, let things cool off," recalled Robert Sunley. "He told the students not to worry, to just relax." However, the exile could not have been easy. When Norman and Nan (née Chapin) Weston visited, Rice took Nan aside and asked if she could lend him five dollars for a bottle of whiskey.[53]

Occasionally, Rice found himself more philosophical than bitter about the events of the preceding year. Later he commented: "The restless sea does something to me: It takes away my restlessness. The endless marshes, too, do something. . . . So the marshes had spoken to Sidney Lanier, and so they

52. Ted Dreier to Frank Aydelotte, April 6, 1938, Frank Aydelotte to Ted Dreier, April 17, 1938, both in Aydelotte Papers, Swarthmore.

53. Sunley, interview with the author, May 22, 1993; Weston, interview with the author, April 13, 1993.

spoke to me in the back reaches of Charleston's Folly Beach. I began to see, but slowly and with reluctance, that I must live apart from people, for their good and mine."[54]

When he returned to Black Mountain College in September, 1938, Rice barely participated. He moved into several rooms in Lee Hall and spent most of his time writing and talking with students who were his most ardent supporters. "He was rather secretive about it," reported Robert Sunley. "If he wanted to see you, he'd say, 'I'm going to be in room so-and-so, but don't tell anyone.'" Only students in the writing seminar saw him regularly. He continued to share with them his own writing, increasing pages of the episodic autobiography that recalled his youth and his perceptions of the post–Civil War South. His wry and literary two-part remembrance of his mother's family, "Grandmother Smith's Plantation," was published in *Harper's* monthly magazine in November and December, 1938. Rice also managed to return to a fairly constant round of speaking engagements about education and the college, including several trips to Charleston and appearances in Greensboro, North Carolina, and Augusta, Georgia.[55]

Nell Rice spent the fall in Sullivan and in Swarthmore, exploring options for university library science programs. She decided to return to North Carolina several months later to serve a library apprenticeship and take some courses at Asheville Normal School in preparation for entering the University of North Carolina, Chapel Hill, library program in the fall. She established cordial communication with her husband, but had no intention of making another try at living as husband and wife. Mary Rice began her freshman year at Swarthmore that fall, and Frank, now job hunting, also spent a good deal of time in residence at the Aydelotte home.[56]

Robert Wunsch was appointed the new rector of Black Mountain College. There were some on the faculty who believed that with Rice removed from the rector position and returned to the faculty only, animosities about him would subside. Apparently, however, Rice's colleagues, especially Josef and Anni Albers and Ted Dreier, found it very difficult to simply return to their prior relationships with Rice, who now seemed more petulant than penitent. Some faculty more supportive of Rice, such as musician Allan Sly, English professor Peggy Loram Bailey, and biology professor Anna Moellen-

54. J. Rice, *Eighteenth Century,* 339.

55. Sunley, interview with the author, May 22, 1993; John A. Rice to Thomas Whitney Surette, January 11, 1939, in Faculty Files, BMCP, N.C. Archives.

56. Frank Aydelotte to Nell Rice, November 8, December 15, 1938, and Nell Rice to Frank Aydelotte, November 3, 1938, June [n.d.], 1939, all in Aydelotte Papers, Swarthmore.

hoff, were not particularly vocal and did not hold appointments on the board of fellows. Later, Rice would decide faculty attitudes against him were inevitable, because "I represented authority, although not statutory. I don't think you can have something like that without someone being the authority. It's bound to be resented."[57]

By the end of the academic year, Rice was negotiating with publishers about his proposed book and with the faculty about another leave of absence for fall semester, 1939. The faculty asked him to consider taking a leave for the entire 1939–1940 academic year instead; but, perhaps to maintain some semblance of control over his own destiny, he refused and renewed his request for a single semester leave. Eventually and grudgingly, this was granted, leaving at least some faculty members angry that they had let Rice have his way.[58]

Although Rice had hoped to follow Nell to Chapel Hill in order to write there and to attempt a reconciliation, she would have none of the plan. When he left Black Mountain in June, it was for Southern Pines, North Carolina. Nell remained at Black Mountain, preparing to finish her work at Asheville Normal School and to move to Chapel Hill. Frank and Mary also returned to Black Mountain for the summer and took jobs at the nearby Lake Eden Inn.[59]

During Rice's fall term leave, the faculty started serious discussions about whether they would ever want him to return to Black Mountain College. Wunsch made several trips to Southern Pines to assess whether Rice would want to return and to encourage him to make a definitive decision—preferably to resign. Because Rice made it clear that his idea of a return would be to restore both his marriage and his teaching, Wunsch asked Nell Rice to accompany him on several visits. Nell Rice was firm in her hurt and in her desire to distance herself from Rice and their marriage. Rice was firm in his desire to return to teaching and to Nell. Wunsch, who had deep affection and admiration for Rice, also understood and per force communicated the position of colleagues who still harbored great animosity toward him. Hence he encouraged Rice to reconsider his determination to return to Black Mountain College.[60]

57. Duberman, *Black Mountain,* 147–49; T. Dreier, interview with the author, April 5, 1993; J. Rice, interview with Duberman, June 10, 1967.

58. Faculty Meeting Minutes, June 2, 1938, in Official Documents, BMCP, N.C. Archives; N. Rice to F. Aydelotte, June [n.d.], 1939, in Aydelotte Papers, Swarthmore.

59. N. Rice to Aydelotte, June [n.d.], 1939, in Aydelotte Papers, Swarthmore; F. Rice, interview with the author, February 13, 1993.

60. Duberman, *Black Mountain,* 149–51.

Finally, in February, 1940, when Rice had extended his leave but could not be prodded into resignation, Wunsch, as rector, wrote the letter that concluded the struggle: "We should appreciate very much your sending us your resignation. You remember, you told me if your resignation were needed to keep the College from closing, you would willingly send it to me. I think that it is necessary now, for we are at a standstill with plans for next year and the subsequent years until we hear from you. Half the members of the faculty are unwilling to face, in addition to economic insecurity, the possibility of another enervating internal struggle. . . . It all boiled down to the fact that we have lost confidence in your ability to work effectively in a small community such as this one." In a separate letter to Nell Rice, Wunsch explained, "Mr. Rice is responsible for our losing confidence in him. God knows, we didn't want to lose confidence in him. . . . We believe, as a matter of fact, that we shall feel less whipped down, less fretted, more self-reliant without him."[61]

In a brief memo dated February 17, 1940, John Andrew Rice submitted his resignation from the faculty of Black Mountain College, effective at the end of the academic year 1939–1940. After a final trip by Wunsch to Southern Pines, details of financial arrangements for Rice and his family were settled, as were promises on both sides to publicly announce only that Rice had resigned of his own volition to pursue a writing career. Rice was devastated by a sense of terrible failure and terrible fate. Later, he gave voice to his emotions, claiming, "Athens, a pure democracy, had a device. Black Mountain, a pure democracy, used it, but the name was changed to 'leave of absence.' Ostracism, by any name, I reminded myself, was very old, but so is heartache, even older."[62]

Rice's resignation brought great relief, but little rejoicing, among the faculty. Most recognized that Black Mountain College had closed a chapter of its history that could never be revisited. Rice's absence meant the college had lost a certain kind of paternal leadership and charismatic presence, even while it gained in the direction of normalcy in faculty relationships. Rice had been domineering, unyielding, cynical, and insensitive to colleagues who felt the essence of academic life was collegiality and cordiality. But Rice also had been brilliant, innovative, open, and involved. He was challenged little by long-term ambition for himself, but greatly by day-to-day curiosity about people and their behavior. This had prompted him, holding court in

61. W. R. Wunsch to John A. Rice, February 16, 1940, and W. R. Wunsch to Nell Rice, February 16, 1940, both in Faculty Files, BMCP, N.C. Archives.

62. John A. Rice, memo, February 17, 1940, *ibid.*; J. Rice, *Eighteenth Century,* 340.

the cavernous main lobby of Lee Hall, to be either the great manipulator or the great listener. He knew very well that he could make others furious with him, and he seemed to enjoy experimenting with that power. But he could not understand why some colleagues and students—and even his wife—truly became fed up, tired of dealing with him, and unwilling to come back for more; and because he could not understand, he mistakenly arrived at the view that the problem was within themselves.

Yet, for many—possibly most—early faculty members and students, John Andrew Rice had stood above others as the crucial and positive force at Black Mountain College. Allan Sly, music professor from 1935 to 1939, captured this sentiment perfectly nearly fifty years after he left Black Mountain:

> My most persistent recollection of those years is the pervasive presence of John Andrew Rice. I can see him now, in his comfortable rocking chair, smoking his pipe, and seeming to relay the style of an Oxford don to a receptive audience. There was always an audience, and he always had something to say—gadfly-wise. The offering and scrutinizing of ideas was at center stage at all times. . . . I recall he often spoke against ambition, and referred to the human wreckage he'd seen in the trail of ambitious people. I think that's made quite an impression on me over the succeeding years. And I think that this kind of thing that Rice put out so much, was just as important as anything one might have learned in a classroom.[63]

63. Allan Sly to Mervin Lane, "Taped Reminiscence of Black Mountain," n.d. (Typescript in Faculty Files, BMCP, N.C. Archives).

8

Down from the Mountain: New Beginnings

Departing from his college, his profession, and his marriage, John Andrew Rice harbored profound anguish and a deep sense of failure, but little remorse. Consequently, he mirrored his scholarly understanding of Greek tragic heroes, human beings whose flaws inexorably draw them to commit irreversible actions. If there was a tragedy occasioned by Rice's rise and demise as an educator, it turns on the notion that his career was finished but not complete. Writer and critic Malcolm Cowley commented later that Rice's history as an educator "makes me think of a train plunging through the night with its curtains drawn and ending its run at what should be only a way station."[1]

Rice found his feelings shifting back and forth between anger and sadness when he considered the circumstances of his forced resignation from Black Mountain College. He felt that Ted Dreier had betrayed him and that Josef Albers had resented his influence and his spontaneity. However, especially in the case of Bob Wunsch, he also was capable of navigating a philosophical high road. Within days of penning his resignation, he sent Wunsch a reassuring letter maintaining, "In the long reach of time this thing that now seems earth-shaking will not so much as stir a blade of grass, only a little laughter, at least over the second Old Fashioned. Please do not think that it has lessened my affection for you; rather, that it has deepened."[2]

Rice's view of his situation likely was tempered by his familiarity with a life marked by periodicity, having spent his boyhood relocating from one Methodist parish to the next and his adult life moving from one educational

---

1. Malcolm Cowley, "Lost Worlds," *New Republic,* CVII (1942), 614.
2. W. R. Wunsch to Fred Mangold, February 21, 1940 (letter containing his hand-written copy of John A. Rice to William R. Wunsch, February 19, 1940), in Faculty Files, BMCP, N.C. Archives.

endeavor to the next. Experiences had become episodes unfettered by pattern, continuity, or planned direction. Additionally, the frequent moves early in life may very well have contributed to Rice's limited grasp of the means necessary to form and sustain human relationships and, in some instances, to his limited appreciation for such long-term relationships.

Rice's Black Mountain experience drew to a close at an appropriate moment in the college's evolution. The original campus utilizing the Blue Ridge Assembly grounds evoked a spirit that was pure Rice. As reminiscent of the Old South as Grandmother Smith's plantation, Robert E. Lee Hall had enchanted Rice with its stately white columns and long views, the perfect backdrop for lingering conversation on the front veranda. The founder's departure coincided with the start of the second Black Mountain College campus in its new setting among the pines at Lake Eden—six miles and at least one hundred years removed from the original location. Only a month before Rice penned his resignation, the faculty commissioned former Bauhaus architects Walter Gropius and Marcel Breuer to design contemporary main buildings for the Lake Eden campus.

Delicate verbal negotiations at the time of Rice's resignation determined that the college would pay Rice through the end of the academic year, would contribute unspecified amounts directly to Swarthmore for Mary Rice's tuition, and would recognize Rice's interest in the Lake Eden property should the college ever close and sell its land. All parties understood that the several thousand volumes that Rice left at the Black Mountain library were on indefinite loan until he decided to retrieve or dispose of them. These included a large selection of classics, some rare eighteenth-century manuscripts collected as part of his research on Swift, and an original edition of the Oxford *New English Dictionary*.[3]

At his borrowed bungalow in Southern Pines, North Carolina, Rice wrote. His approach entailed hours of silent thought followed by hours of longhand composition. His goal was a book-length collection of autobiographical narratives, mostly about his youth in the South. Through the earlier publication of "Grandmother Smith's Plantation" in *Harper's*, he already had demonstrated his keen understanding of human relationships in the South—among the young and the old, men and women, Confederates and carpetbaggers, African Americans and Anglo-Americans. The masterful storyteller in conversation proved an equally masterful storyteller in print. He also demonstrated his capacity for profound observation and powerful descriptive writing, exemplified in this passage about his arrival, as a small

3. John A. Rice to William R. Wunsch, December 24, 1941, *ibid.*; F. Rice, interview with the author, November 24, 1995.

boy, at his grandmother's home for a visit: "When we finally came to a halt before the pillared porch my grandmother stood at the top of the steps waiting for us, to be reached through a swarm of delighted dogs, tremendous pointers and setters, whose cold muzzles left sticky patches on my face and hands. It was a mighty task to climb the gigantic steps, knee bumping chin, but to be managed unassisted. At last my face was hidden in the folds of my grandmother's apron and the top of my head pushed into her warm stomach. I was home, the only home I ever knew."[4]

In "Grandmother Smith's Plantation," Rice also exhibited his bold and stinging candor in describing people, mostly his own relatives, whose names and personalities he eagerly identified. One of his mother's brothers, Uncle Charlie, was exposed as "always angry, with himself and with the world" and as prone to "a rage that was nearly madness." Uncle Ellie, familiar to readers as powerful U.S. senator Ellison Durant ("Cotton Ed") Smith and widely loved by generations of voters in his native South Carolina, was labeled "an evangelical politician" who "never had the courage completely to accept or reject anything."[5] However, Rice's biting phrases stemmed as much from a commitment to honest opinion as from a desire to vent anger. In narration and in anecdotes, the author also expressed great affection for his Smith relatives and noted some favorable quality in each one.

Given Rice's own respect and affection for the African Americans whom he had encountered and his liberal leanings concerning race relations, he was probably even more outraged than his writing indicated by his overtly racist Uncle Ellie. Senator Smith was still serving his marathon in Congress (1908–1944) when Rice's comments were published. An archetype of the southern demagogue, this uncle was a loud proponent of states' rights, white supremacy, and farm support. He pinned a cotton boll to his lapel and stumped across South Carolina through six successful senatorial campaigns atop a mule-driven cotton wagon. Several years before Rice began writing about his family experiences, Cotton Ed Smith had led two walkouts of southern delegates to the 1936 Democratic convention in Philadelphia—one to protest a black preacher giving the invocation and the other to protest a black congressman being presented as a speaker. He was widely quoted as saying he voted against women's suffrage because it would have included black women in the vote.[6]

4. J. Rice, "Grandmother Smith's Plantation," Part 1, p. 573.
5. *Ibid.*, 581, 577.
6. Mary Louise Gehring, "Cotton Ed Smith: The South Carolina Farmer in the United States Senate," in *The Oratory of Southern Demagogues*, ed. Cal M. Logue and Howard Dorgan (Baton Rouge, 1981), 143–44.

Predictably, most of the Smith family members who read the two-part *Harper's* article were outraged. Uncle Charlie's son, William H. Smith, penned a long letter to the editor, published in the April, 1939, *Harper's*, describing a number of factual errors in Rice's work, especially concerning the physical layout of the plantation and certain incidents that were said to have taken place there, but actually occurred elsewhere. He particularly defended his Uncle Ellie against the article's contention "that Senator Smith advocated the sacred right of a white man to lynch. This is so palpably false that I should not comment. Senator Smith has always condemned lynching both in public addresses and privately."[7]

William Smith's lynching comments gave Rice a fine opportunity in his own letter to supply the defense that he had "made no willful mis-statements of fact." As an example, he quoted from the April 16, 1935, Congressional Record, which transcribed Senator Smith's vehement speech against an anti-lynching bill. The senator had insisted on the "necessity of going outside the law at times to vindicate the sanctity of our firesides and the virtue of our women. Senators should not hurry to reflect on the glorious traditions and history of the section to which I belong, beleaguered by influences and forces with which most Senators have not been familiar and with which they have not had to reckon." Referring to the legislation as "this infamous bill," Smith, overcome by oratorical drama, had insisted that lynching was necessary in cases involving "the purity and sanctity of our womanhood" and termed it "the just penalty which should be inflicted upon the beast who invades that sanctity." The libel suit threatened by Rice's cousin William never materialized.[8]

Although a number of Rice's male relatives detested the piece, a few of his aunts and female cousins very much approved of it, possibly because Rice in print, like Rice in the classroom, usually reserved the worst of his sting for the male population. In passing or pointed reference, with good humor or sarcasm, he was determined to let men know their place was less than exalted. He mentioned his grandmother's earliest days on the plantation as a time "when her children were small and she had to run the place under the slight handicap of a living husband." In the second installment for *Harper's*, he attempted to summarize his thoughts about women, explaining, "Try as I will, and I have tried very hard, I have never been able to rid myself of the belief, of a something deeper than belief, that women are superior to men, that

7. William H. Smith, "Protest," *Harper's*, CLXXVIII (1939), 558–64.
8. John A. Rice, "Dr. Rice's Reply," *Harper's*, CLXXVIII (1939), 564–65; *Congressional Record*, 74th Cong., 1st Sess., 5749; John A. Rice to Liston M. Rice, January 19, 1939, Faculty Files, BMCP, N.C. Archives.

men are pretty common and cheap stuff compared to them. . . . I know as well as anyone what a shoddy thing Southern chivalry is, what an insult to women, how it has been used by politician and ecclesiastic to keep the world in the hands of men, and by women to sneak from men some of their power, coiling and slithering around with their perpetual charm, to what rotten ends it can be put in the war between black and white." Rice, characteristically, decided that the outcry from his male relatives was "good proof" of additional observations he intended some day to make in print about what he viewed as the particularly weak and insincere nature of southern men. One female cousin, attempting to sum up the view of various female kin, told Rice, "You have gotten all the facts wrong, but you have told the truth."[9]

In September, 1940, *Harper's* published more of Rice's recollections in a piece titled "My Father's Folks," which described his experiences at Grandmother Rice's home. This time Rice let loose the full force of his scorn, not sparing women in his indignant account of his coarse relatives. Without a hint of fondness for his father's mother, he explained, "Grandmother Rice was a vegetable. In the morning after breakfast she planted herself in a split-bottom chair in the chimney corner and sat rooted there the livelong day, with an occasional excursion into usefulness, when she moved heavily about the kitchen helping Aunt Mollie; but as a rule things were brought to her where she sat, beans to string, potatoes to peel, anything that could be done with inattention. . . . She seldom spoke, and at length even I with all my love of talk grew grateful for the infertile silence; her little sample of speech held no promise of the wisdom I had learned to expect from the very old."[10]

Urged on by his friends Louis and Stella Adamic, whom he visited regularly at their home in Milford, New Jersey, Rice had approached Adamic's publisher, Harper and Brothers, about publishing an autobiography. The proposed book would include chapters about life on the plantations of his two grandmothers as well as about other circumstances and events of his childhood, his higher education, and his early teaching career. After Rice submitted two sample chapters, Harper senior editor Cass Canfield replied immediately that the publishing house wanted to buy the book and reported enthusiastically, "It is certainly rare for us to receive a manuscript with so much charm."[11]

9. J. Rice, "Grandmother Smith's Plantation," Part 1, p. 577; J. Rice, "Grandmother Smith's Plantation," Part 2, p. 89; Dikka Moen Rice to Katherine C. Reynolds, July 20, 1994, in author's possession.

10. John Andrew Rice, "My Father's Folks," *Harper's*, CLXXXI (1940), 428–29.

11. Cass Canfield to John A. Rice, October 20, 1939, in Harper's Collection, Harry Ransom Humanities Research Center, University of Texas, Austin.

Rice received a contract for a five-hundred-dollar advance from Harper and Brothers, along with advice to delete several personal opinion chapters and instead to integrate the views explored into the narrative of key episodes in his life. Among the portions that Rice had planned but now would scuttle were a chapter on progressive education, a movement he called "the latest thing in band wagons"; a chapter on teachers' colleges and teachers at the elementary and secondary levels; a chapter on the people and culture of the Middle West; and a chapter with the working title, "The Gentleman, the Lady, and the Negro: Three Teachers of the South and Three Fictions." Many of the ideas that he had in mind for those chapters he eventually did incorporate into the exposition about his youth and early career. In particular, chapters about Webb School, Tulane, Oxford, the University of Nebraska, and Rollins provided platforms for a wide range of general commentary on education and culture.[12]

Rice agonized some over a title for his book and was not at all satisfied with his working title, "From South Carolina to the Present." Canfield finally found a title for him and found it close to home. In a speech several years earlier, Rice had told a group in Cambridge, Massachusetts, "I was born in the eighteenth century in South Carolina." He echoed the thought in a letter to Canfield, mentioning his belief that he had "come out of the eighteenth century." Canfield underlined the phrase and by return mail informed him that *I Came Out of the Eighteenth Century* was an ideal book title. It is tempting to recall Rice's research on Swift and assume that Rice considered himself most suited for sparring with the wry skepticism and keen wit of eighteenth-century intellectuals; however, Rice explained in his book that his heart was moved by the values, beliefs, and unconditional human relationships he imagined in Charleston, South Carolina, in the eighteenth century.[13]

Rice's writing progressed slowly throughout 1940, much of which he spent holed up in Southern Pines, only making occasional visits to New York and New Jersey. Both his son Frank and his daughter Mary visited him. In June, 1940, Mary and Frank drove with their father to Bella Vista, Arkansas, for a visit with Rice's stepmother, Launa Darnell Rice, who had a summer cottage there. They were accompanied by Rice's dachshund, Nicky. On the way, they stayed overnight in Asheville, North Carolina, where Frank Rice

12. J. Rice to Canfield, November 3, 1939, *ibid.*

13. Allan Sly to Mervin Lane, "Taped Reminiscence of Black Mountain," n.d. (Typescript in Faculty Files, BMCP, N.C. Archives); J. Rice to Canfield, November 3, 1939, and Cass Canfield to John A. Rice, November 10, 1939, both in Harper's Collection, University of Texas; J. Rice, *Eighteenth Century,* 340–41.

happened upon Ann Craig Sutton, whom he had met earlier in Havana, Cuba, while working there with the American Friends Service Committee. The chance meeting had enormous consequences. Frank proposed to Ann Sutton by letter, and she came to Bella Vista to visit him in August. Ann Rice later recalled her first dinner in Arkansas with the Rice family, an occasion when John Andrew Rice's unrelenting Socratic challenges eventually drove her from the dinner table in tears. Only later did father and daughter-in-law establish a fond and friendly relationship. When Frank and Ann Rice married in 1941 in Haverford, Pennsylvania, John Andrew and Nell Rice saw each other for the last time.[14]

A habitual procrastinator and no stranger to unfinished projects, Rice waged an uphill battle in producing a complete manuscript for Harper and Brothers. He was frequently distracted by his uncertain living situation. Attracted to the intellectual excitement of New York City, he sometimes stayed just outside its boundaries with the Adamics or in short-term rental situations. In the past, he had proved adept at garnering offers of houses to share or borrow rent free, but now offers in New York City were only for brief visits. Making the rounds of various former Black Mountain College students in the New York area, he stopped at a house shared by Dick Andrews, David Way, and some other former students in Cornwall, New York, on the Hudson River. However, according to Way, "He found our situation much too tenuous. There were no rich people to tide him over."[15] Although Rice was not in the least acquisitive and did not mind that his situation never allowed him the possessions of the rich, he very much liked living around individuals who would include him in the activities of the rich. He enjoyed being waited upon, dining in style, and participating in cultural events; but he had little use for owning expensive clothes, cars, or artwork.

While in the New York area, Rice frequently visited or was visited by Black Mountain students who had moved there, including Sue Spayth Riley, Betty Young Williams, and Hope Stephens Foote. Eventually, however, he began to carve out his own circle of friends, many of them writers, artists, and musicians. Just as it became apparent that his separation from Nell would end in divorce, Rice met the woman who would become his second wife, Dikka Moen. A striking blond of Norwegian descent, she had attended St. Olaf College before moving to Manhattan, taking a secretarial job, and pursuing a singing career with part-time engagements in small ensembles. Mary

14. Ann C. Rice, interview with the author, February 13, 1993; Frank A. Rice to Katherine C. Reynolds, November 30, 1994, in author's possession.

15. Way, interview with the author, May 3, 1993.

Rice, although sympathetic to her mother and never entirely comfortable with her father's new life, credited Dikka Moen with successfully pushing Rice to finish *I Came Out of the Eighteenth Century.*[16]

During 1941 and 1942 Rice lived at various times in Hampton, New Jersey, Clinton, New Jersey, and New York City. He stretched thin his final payments from Black Mountain College, the largesse of friends, and returns from a few magazine articles (in *Harper's* and *Common Ground*) to scrape by financially. Although his advance from Harper and Brothers was due on submission of a completed manuscript, Rice persuaded his editors to dole out several partial payments ahead of schedule. He had promised Canfield a manuscript in August, 1941. He delivered it in May, 1942. He had added a chapter about Black Mountain, which had not been in his original plan, after Canfield insisted, "After all, you are well known for your activities at Black Mountain, and the experiment itself is certainly one of outstanding importance."[17]

In August, 1942, with the book now complete, the advance spent, and any new writing projects still far from certain, Rice moved to his stepmother's cottage in Bella Vista, Arkansas, with his new wife, Dikka Moen Rice. Shortly after the move, the son of his second marriage, Peter Nicolai Rice, was born. The new career proved as solidly underway as the new family when Rice's book was published in November, 1942, to enthusiastic reviews. *Newsweek*'s praise was typical: "Rice quit [Black Mountain College] to become a writer. Judging by *I Came Out of the Eighteenth Century*, a skilled and deadly writer he is."[18]

Time magazine's review, titled "Brilliant Critic," hailed Rice's outspoken and eloquent discourse concerning the state of American education: "Having thus spanned a half-century and a cross section of U.S. education, Professor Rice, who knows where the educational skeletons, real and imaginary, are hidden, has turned state's evidence against his profession."[19]

Orville Prescott, reviewing for the New York *Times,* astutely characterized Rice as "two different persons inhabiting one flesh and writing one book. One is a small town Methodist preacher's son from South Carolina who is a fascinated, critical, wryly detached observer and commentator on Southern life; the other is the questioning, searching, controversial teacher

16. D. Rice to Reynolds, July 20, 1994, in author's possession; Roger D. Marshall, interview with the author, February 23, 1993.

17. Canfield to J. Rice, November 10, 1939, in Harper's Collection, University of Texas.

18. F. Rice, interview with the author, February 13, 1993; "Down the Mountain," *Newsweek,* November 30, 1942, p. 71.

19. "Brilliant Critic," *Time,* November 23, 1942, p. 88.

whose fierce independence and experimental views about education have made him an academic stormy petrel for years. In either capacity he writes well, with vigor, ease, a deft hand at characterizing other people and a sputtering chain of epigrams. . . . He writes with zest, freshness and constant evidence of a mind that is questioning, original, strongly opinionated."[20]

Harper and Brothers added materially to the glow of favorable reviews when they named *I Came Out of the Eighteenth Century* a winner of the Harper 125th Anniversary Prize for the best nonfiction book submitted before May 1, 1942. Rice shared the honor with French immigrant Julian Green for his book *Memories of Happy Days*. The two authors split the $12,500 prize, each receiving an amount approximately five times greater than the average per capita income in America that year.

In his approach to his subject, Rice had added his voice to those of other southern writers who had only recently begun to challenge the reigning literary bias for antebellum culture. In the romanticized accounts that Rice despised, the Old South possessed bountiful plantations, cultured ladies and gentlemen, and black slaves best remembered for their banjoes and watermelons. The dearth of candid and critical literary commentary by southern writers and thinkers had been widely broadcast by H. L. Mencken in his 1920 essay "The Sahara of the Bozart," a caustic diatribe characterizing the South as "a vast plain of mediocrity, stupidity, lethargy, almost of dead silence."[21] Even as Mencken fumed, a number of southern writers stood poised to challenge the puritanism and sentimentality that had enjoyed widespread escapist appeal following the reality of Appomattox. Candid portraits of southern personalities who knew hardship, poverty, ignorance, and bigotry signaled a fresh and pragmatic commitment among writers of the 1920s like Julia Peterkin of South Carolina, James Branch Cabell of Virginia, and Frances Newman of Georgia. Of course, these early beacons of a new southern literary presence soon would be eclipsed by the illuminating prose of Thomas Wolfe and William Faulkner.

Southern white autobiography had also begun to find a voice far removed from the unabashed ancestor worship that had become commonplace since the Civil War. As the last surviving witnesses of the waning days of southern agrarian life styles—from plantations to hard-scrabble farms—a number of writers, John Andrew Rice among them, experienced a collective urge to set the record straight. Their aim was not necessarily to expose the secret hypocrisies of southern gentility or to shock their readers with tales of cruelty and

---

20. Orville Prescott, "Books of the Times," New York *Times,* November 4, 1942, p. 21.
21. Mencken, "The Sahara of the Bozart," in *Prejudices, Second Series,* ed. Mencken, 141.

dysfunction in southern families and commercial interests. The more subtle and personal purpose for many of these writers was to come to terms with the South. They sought to understand how it was possible to know the region's many flaws and love it still; to ponder the shaping influences of its contradictions; or, in the words of Mississippi Delta poet William A. Percy, "to watch the spread and pattern of the game that is past."[22]

Percy's *Lanterns on the Levee,* first published in 1941, proved to be the most commercially successful southern autobiography of the time. Direct and unguarded, Percy wrote of teachers, grandmothers, plantation owners, sharecroppers, black nannies, and adored parents in a descriptive prose that intermingled family legend, local color, and personal opinion. His discussions of the kinds of people encountered in the South revealed a variable mixture of reactions. He expressed disgust for the poor whites who moved from mountain areas to the cities or fertile farmland, reverence for southern plantation women who managed grace and grit in equal measure, anger for Ku Klux Klan members and others who resorted to overt racism, and moral indignation for southern blacks, whom he characterized as "not disciplined, but tragic, pitiful, and lovable."[23]

Among southern-born writers who could reach back to their youth to create remarkable works of literature, James Agee stood apart with his Pulitzer Prize–winning *A Death in the Family.* A novel of people more than place, the final manuscript was pulled together by editors after Agee's death in 1955. However, the book's prologue, "Knoxville: Summer 1915," had already appeared as a story in the *Partisan Review* in 1938 as if to demonstrate the motherlode of descriptive material that collected during a southern childhood.

Other southern autobiographers gave voice to their recollections and opinions in quick succession. Two women from Georgia, Lillian Smith and Katharine DuPre Lumpkin, penned vivid narratives that did much to explain how a white child's experience with and tutoring in racial issues could mark the future of race relations. Indeed, Smith's *Killers of the Dream,* published in 1949, was only in occasional anecdote a volume about her particular southern upbringing. It quickly reinvented itself as a stirring essay advocating the human need for equality of the races and sexes; to this end it demonstrated existing inequalities in education, employment, criminal justice, and social interactions. Lumpkin reached back several generations into her distinguished middle Georgia family, which included a governor and a senator,

22. Percy, *Lanterns on the Levee,* i.
23. *Ibid.,* 309.

in writing *The Making of a Southerner* (1946). In it she presented a brief social and economic history that chronicled the region's difficult adaptation from slavery to freed labor after the Civil War. Like Smith's book, Lumpkin's autobiography eventually transcended literary or historical purposes in several late chapters that call for a new order in race relations.

With the publication of his coming-of-age autobiography, *Black Boy*, in 1945, Richard Wright exposed the most oppressive effects of southern racism and revealed the scars of emotional and cultural deprivation that marked even the brightest and most determined black youths. He described a boy with a quick and curious mind confronting the inability of whites to see past his color and the inability of a racist system to accommodate a black youth's desire even for a small opportunity, such as borrowing a library book. In contrast to Wright, Zora Neale Hurston withheld any personal positions she may have had about race relations in writing her 1942 autobiography, *Dust Tracks on a Road*, a book that has since been roundly criticized for leaving readers with only a one-dimensional view of her complex persona. While she did opt to celebrate her supporters and ignore the cruel social and economic realities of segregation, Hurston managed to demonstrate in this book her substantial anthropological expertise as well as her distinctive literary style rich in fanciful symbolism. Her autobiography became a metaphorical rock on a front porch from which to tell stories about her Eatonville, Florida, youth and her student days in Baltimore, Washington, D.C., and New York City. Along the way, she acknowledged John Andrew Rice, Robert Wunsch, and several others at Rollins College who encouraged her earliest writing. The book's discussion of race is confined to observations about similarities and differences under the skin; Hurston maintained that she "did not have to consider any racial group as a whole. God made them duck by duck and that was the only way I could see them."[24]

In *I Came Out of the Eighteenth Century* Rice favored storytelling as a device to move around in time without accumulating facts and forcing transitions. Like Hurston, he was more concerned with individual acts of bigotry or courage by whites or blacks than with the system that perpetuated segregation or its effects. He loved to relate small but telling stories about well-known figures, especially those he could dethrone for the ignorance that matched their racism. Thus, he turned his boyhood memories of Columbia, South Carolina, into opportunities to take cynical potshots at former governors Wade Hampton and Ben Tillman as well as his uncle Ellison Durant.

24. Hurston, *Dust Tracks*, 235.

From early teachers and childhood friends of no renown to Edwin Hubble and the Prince of Wales, Rice managed to parade hundreds of personalities across the pages of his book, often with just a phrase, occasionally with a paragraph, but sometimes with the better portion of chapters.

One such chapter, titled "Rollins Was Holt," eventually chilled the book's success with the threat of legal action. Still president of Rollins College, Hamilton Holt was angered to find himself portrayed as "driven in unpredictable turn by ambition, sentimentality, charity, Yankee shrewdness, pride, humility, and childlike wonder; but somewhere nearby was always ambition." Harper's lawyers, however, had insisted the publisher delete Rice's descriptive "sycophancy" from the list of the Rollins president's attributes. Rice relished recounting the publicity-conscious days of Rollins' "golden personalities" and "professor of books." He also detailed the most absurd—only the most absurd—charges against himself during the AAUP investigation.[25]

Both Holt and Rollins College professor of books Edwin Grover contacted Harper and Brothers shortly after publication of Rice's book to challenge what they perceived as damaging and malicious falsehoods. When confronted with the allegations and his editors' fears of a libel suit, Rice held firm, advising his editors, "I suspect that this is a sort of commando raid on the part of general Hammie [Holt]." Attorneys for Harper and Brothers, however, were convinced Holt would take legal action and possibly even win a libel suit, if he could not be placated. In May, 1943, with approximately 8,200 copies sold from a press run of just over 10,000, Harper and Brothers withdrew the remaining stock from circulation. When Rice requested ten additional personal copies from his publisher a year later, the Harper and Brothers editors refused, citing anxiety about any move that could be construed as further publication of the book.[26]

Hamilton Holt apparently was satisfied with the gesture and did not pursue legal action. In his own copy of *I Came Out of the Eighteenth Century,* he scribbled marginal notes about passages whose veracity or accuracy he challenged, frequently penning denials like "never said it," "not true," "implication quite false," and "do not remember." Where Rice described the meetings with the AAUP investigators and noted, "Holt was determined to

---

25. J. Rice, *Eighteenth Century,* 302; Elizabeth F. Lawrence, memo to files, August 20, 1942, in Harper's Collection, University of Texas.

26. John A. Rice to Elizabeth F. Lawrence, December 11, 1942, Elizabeth F. Lawrence to John A. Rice, June 25, 1943, June 8, 1944, all in Harper's Collection, University of Texas.

destroy me," Holt inserted in the margin, "Until the last, I tried in every way to save him." Taking a high road showing more ambivalence than anger, he also finally inserted, "Rice had a good side in not a few respects."[27]

With the cash from the Harper anniversary prize, Rice and his family were able to move to Sarasota, Florida, in the spring of 1943. There Rice continued to write, although slowly and in fits and starts, trying his hand at fiction. In 1944 he sold his first short story, "The Metamorphosis of Mr. Cracovaner," to the *New Yorker;* and for the next three years he maintained a first-reading arrangement with that publication which gave the *New Yorker* first refusal rights on all his short fiction.

Many of his stories told of relations between the races in the South, generally portraying African Americans as shrewd and dignified, capable of almost uncanny understanding of realities that often escaped the Anglo-American members of the community. Other stories described simple incidents within families or among friends—small dramas that guided the reader to larger thoughts. Fiction for Rice was a zoom lens trained on a minute detail, gesture, or figure of speech to illustrate the parts that eventually composed the whole of a person. Small, ordinary incidents told in Rice's keen prose became important examples of how people related to one another and to their situations in life.

Rice's most finely drawn characters were African Americans. Whether honest youngsters or hardened criminals, all surfaced as engaging individuals whose life stories, neither particularly uplifting nor tragic, produced small metaphors for conditions they shared with all humanity. Razor Belle, a crafty black murderess hiding in a South Carolina swamp, reflected Rice's respect for wit and patience. In the story "Monday Come Home," appearing in *Collier's* in 1949, Belle quickly learned the art of defending herself from male attackers when she acquired a set of shaving razors, one marked for each day of the week. The sheriff's deputy who captured her in the swamp took her to the nearby home of his aging mother and enslaved her as a cook and companion to the quarrelsome old lady.[28]

Belle slept on the floor of a cold, squalid cabin on the property and was guarded and threatened. Rice did not allow Belle a complaint, a thought of violence, or a plan for escape. He did allow her patience. Belle waited out her keepers until the son died and the mother was infirm. Then, through a combination of luck and stealth, she was able to turn the tables. The reader's last

---

27. Marginal notes in Hamilton Holt's handwriting are in his personal copy of *I Came Out of the Eighteenth Century,* in Hamilton Holt Papers, Rollins.

28. John A. Rice, "Monday Come Home," *Collier's,* September 3, 1949, pp. 22–31.

glimpse of Belle finds her dragging her blankets into the big house and mak-ing plans for a comfortable life. She expresses no smugness in her triumph, no "gotcha." In Rice's hands, Belle and her fellow fictional African Americans were, above all, pragmatic. Belle used razors in defense; she accepted her fate when she was caught. But when she found a chance to improve her lot, that is what she did. She saw nothing extraordinary in these circumstances.

Nonviolence, dignity, patience, and shrewdness are qualities found in ample supply among Rice's fictional African Americans. Passive resistance was often the behavior that drew on all these qualities, and it was the center-piece of the story "Miss Hattie," which appeared in the *New Yorker* in 1947 and was later anthologized in *South Carolina in the Short Story*. Old Miss Hat-tie was living out her few remaining years in a crumbling family home, for-merly a thriving plantation, near Charleston, South Carolina. She was ac-companied by a black housekeeper named Millie and by occasional paying visitors who wanted to see a real plantation. Although she thought it rather ridiculous, her nephew sent her the first modern convenience she knew: an electric refrigerator.

After Miss Hattie and Millie determined what should go into the refrig-erator, Miss Hattie fretted a bit about security. Finally, she had a lock installed and pocketed the key. This arrangement, of course, was not convenient for Millie, who did all the cooking. Millie, rather than say anything about the situation, simply requested regular unlocking from Miss Hattie—more and more often as time went on and at more and more inconvenient times for her employer. As could be expected, Miss Hattie finally decided to turn the key over to Millie. She considered herself defeated in her effort to assure security, for "Miss Hattie knew when she gave the key up that there would be no more locking. In all her years of knowing Negroes, she had never known one who would lock anything."[29] The following day, heated after some gardening, Miss Hattie came into the kitchen to find that Millie had surprised her by leaving a cool fresh salad and homemade dressing out on the counter for her lunch. Just to see if she might want something else to accompany it, Miss Hattie then turned to the refrigerator. It was locked.

Not all Rice's African Americans improved their lives or even won small victories. Many simply survived possible defeat or learned valuable lessons, but carried on as before in a world where the white men and women still held economic, political, and legal power. Rice's works did not raise objections to this unequal balance of power, only to unequal treatment in day-to-day rela-tionships among the black and the white. Those relationships rarely exposed

29. John A. Rice, "Miss Hattie," *New Yorker,* October 11, 1947, pp. 57–63.

anything so obvious as physical abusers or helpless victims; rather, they revealed some people who should have known better and some who did know better. When in 1955 a number of Rice's short stories were collected into a paperback book, *Local Color,* Erskine Caldwell authored the volume's Foreword. There Caldwell proclaimed:

> John Andrew Rice, the author of these many wise and knowing insights into the lives and living habits of Americans—Americans who happen, fortunately, to be Negroes and whites—is one of those uncommon writers of fiction who has within himself the basic requirements of authorship. One of these essentials is the ability to tell a meaningful story in an interest-gripping manner, and another essential is the perception to understand and reveal the lives of the people being brought to book. . . . His love for and his understanding of the Negro and the white—which here means a social and economic relationship—is only the first evidence of his talents. Next in evidence is his insight into the delicate and subtle way that Negroes and whites in the South have of comprehending each other's unspoken thoughts and unrevealed deeds.[30]

Regardless of his expertise, John Andrew Rice was not a prolific writer. He was readily distracted by the siren calls to read, to converse, to fish, to garden, to create succulent sour-orange marmalades, or just to sit still and ponder ideas. As he was not prodded to action by any desire for material things, he thus had trouble pushing himself toward earning steady income. The Rice family, grown to four members with the birth of Elisabeth in 1944, lived on a shoestring. Money from one or two published stories each year was stretched through living simply, and the big dream of so many writers—the best-selling book or the movie contract—never materialized.

After the favorable critical reception of *I Came Out of the Eighteenth Century,* Rice planned to follow up with another book, and editors at Harper's assured him that they looked forward to his next manuscript. He wanted to write a biography of former South Carolina white supremacist governor and U.S. senator Ben Tillman, telling a social and political story of the South while tracing Tillman's rise to and use of power. When Rice pitched the idea to Harper and Brothers, he insisted that he would need approximately $3,600 in advance to pursue two years of research and writing. The editors at Harper's told him this amount was not financially feasible, given their estimates of sales, but encouraged him to come back if he could not find another

---

30. Erskine Caldwell, Foreword to *Local Color,* by John Andrew Rice (New York, 1955), 8–9.

publisher and if he decided he could alter his financial terms. Rice never found another publisher and never went back to Harper and Brothers.[31]

Rice had longed one day to settle again in his native South Carolina, and in 1945 he moved his family to the coastal area near Charleston. George Grice, president of the College of Charleston and an old friend to Rice from his days on the academic conference circuits, found the Rice family an old home in the country that could be secured for little rent while the owners were away for a year. Residing in a classic rural southern home, with large fireplaces, wide verandas, and an interesting and hard-working black family down the road, Rice was in his element. When the year was up, Grice again found the family accommodations: this time in a tiny, plain frame cabin on the property of Boone Hall Plantation, an eighteenth-century establishment whose main mansion was rebuilt in 1935. Located six miles north of Charleston, the grounds held ample pecan and fig trees, as well as a healthy garden and good crabbing from a nearby dock, all of which helped supplement the family's meager income and savings. The expert culinary abilities that John Andrew Rice had developed allowed him to stretch their own harvests into acceptable meals. Nine one-room brick slave cabins remained from the plantation's earliest days, and Rice used one of these for his writing. Frank and Ann Rice also had moved to the Charleston area, with Frank teaching German at the College of Charleston. Ann had her hands full with their own two young children in a Charleston apartment, but John Andrew and Dikka Rice also left Peter, a pre-schooler, and Elisabeth, a toddler, with her while they went into Charleston. Occasionally the younger Rice family traveled to Boone Hall for Sunday dinner.[32]

When Frank Rice left Charleston in 1947 after accepting an offer to teach German at Black Mountain College, he knew his father was furious with his decision. But the exact cause of the anger can only be guessed at. The anger may have meant it was inconvenient for the senior Rice to be without family support in the area. It may have meant that Rice sensed a slight to his friend George Grice, who had hired Frank Rice. Or Rice might have been stung by recollections of his bitter memories of Black Mountain College.[33]

The Black Mountain College that Frank Rice returned to in 1947 was

31. John A. Rice, "Prospectus" n.d. (Typescript), Elizabeth F. Lawrence to John A. Rice, March 4, 1943, June 22, 1945, all in Harper's Collection, University of Texas.

32. D. Rice to Reynolds, July 20, 1994, in author's possession; A. Rice, interview with the author, February 13, 1993.

33. F. Rice, interviews with the author, February 13, 1993, November 24, 1995.

both very different from its predecessor and somewhat the same. The campus on Lake Eden was a showcase for functional architecture, dominated by the large contemporary studies building at lakeside. The original architectural designs for the new campus, developed by Gropius and Breuer, had proved too complex and expensive to pursue. Instead, the college had turned to architect Lawrence Kocher, a noted proponent of both historic preservation efforts and Bauhaus ideas, who was managing editor of the *Architectural Record* from 1928 to 1938. Designed by Kocher and constructed by students under his direction throughout the 1940–1941 academic year, the studies building, along with refurbished existing lodges and various smaller dwellings and studies, established architectural and interior design as important learning at the college. Summer music and art institutes had been developed, giving the college a reputation as a school that focused on teaching and workmanship in the arts. Buckminster Fuller experimented with raising huge geodesic domes on the Lake Eden campus, Merce Cunningham choreographed musicals, and Robert Motherwell critiqued painting workshops. The summer institutes, which brought to Black Mountain notable faculty and substantial renown, were associated with the years after Rice's departure when Josef Albers assumed greater influence at the college. In fact, however, it had been Rice, in 1937, who first proposed the idea of summer music and art institutes lasting from four to five weeks. After receiving some general agreement, he had directed the music and art faculty members to begin planning for the sessions and to report back to the full faculty as soon as possible.[34]

Students on the GI Bill of Rights swelled the dormitories and classrooms on the Lake Eden campus to reach an enrollment of ninety students during the immediate postwar years. Yet some things had not changed. Nell Rice still served as librarian but worked in a larger library occupying its own building. Finances were still unstable. Community schisms and uproars still occurred. One such fracture, in 1944, was occasioned by friction concerning a decision not to admit African American students. Another, in 1945, occurred tragically when Bob Wunsch suddenly departed Black Mountain after being arrested in Asheville for homosexual acts with a marine. Josef Albers soon was elected rector of the college.

By 1949, with pent-up postwar demand for higher education leveling off and with faculty salaries increasing, Black Mountain College faced another huge deficit. Discussions of what to do about dwindling funds evolved into

---

34. Duberman, *Black Mountain,* 154–56; Faculty Meeting Minutes, September 13, 1937, in Official Documents, BMCP, N.C. Archives.

a community furor when Rector Albers and Treasurer Dreier proposed the unthinkable: a board of trustees. Further fueling community discord was the rumor that the still-married Ted Dreier was having an affair with a female faculty member. By the end of the 1948–1949 academic year, the faculty gave voice to their discontent with financial crises and new policy proposals. They requested Ted Dreier's resignation and witnessed the resignations that Josef Albers and several others gave in protest. Faculty members Ray Trayer and Natasha Goldowski, temporarily acting as rector and secretary, respectively, proposed that the college consider bringing back John Andrew Rice. Rice had, after all, held the community together longer than anyone since.[35]

When hearing of possible renewed interest in Rice, Frank Aydelotte, then director of the Institute for Advanced Study in Princeton, New Jersey, wrote to his sister, "Nothing would be more disastrous for the college. It would end my interest in it." Rice, although he never seriously pursued the possibility, said of the suggestion that he return, "For a moment the clouds seemed to open."[36]

With his son Frank having departed from Charleston for Black Mountain, John Andrew Rice desired to be closer to his New York publishing contacts. Thus he moved his family again, to a small low-rent house that a friend found for him in Shrub Oak, New York, on the Hudson River, about fifty miles north of New York City. Peter Rice later recalled of his young life, "I remember we were one step ahead of the landlord, always moving. We were in terrible poverty with no money at all." Concerning their varied living conditions, Peter later decided that his father "just didn't seem to care if we were cold or hungry. Clothes wore out. I had one pair of shoes, hand-me-down pants and shirts." After two cold winters in New York, the family left for a summer at the old Rice retreat in Bella Vista, Arkansas, and then moved to an apartment in St. Lucie, Florida.[37]

Peter was an active boy whose capacity for rebellion grew as his father's stubborn brilliance gave way to stormy arrogance. Although Rice maintained his skill at provoking stimulating conversation among adults, he had limited patience with his young son. Peter recalled him as "very pushy, very domineering," and "very impatient" at home. The son began erasing and changing the grades he brought home on his report cards to try to avoid his

35. Nell Rice to Frank Aydelotte, September 12, 1949, in Aydelotte Papers, Swarthmore.

36. Frank Aydelotte to Nell Rice, June 16, 1949, *ibid.*; W. Rice, interview with the author, January 6, 1993.

37. Peter N. Rice, interview with the author, February 13, 1993; John A. Rice to George Grice, December 5, 1951, in George Grice Papers, Robert Scott Small Library, College of Charleston, Charleston, S.C.

father's wrath. His eventual suspension from school led to the inevitable and intimidating confrontation.[38]

When the Rice family alighted at places where Dikka Rice could find employment, or when Rice sold a story or reprint rights, some money became available. In 1949, for example, Simon and Schuster published a book of the decade's best *New Yorker* magazine fiction entitled *55 Short Stories from the New Yorker.* Because his story "Content with the Station" appeared in the anthology, Rice found himself in company with a group of authors that included E. B. White, James Thurber, J. D. Salinger, Carson McCullers, Jessamyn West, Marjorie Kinnan Rawlings, and Vladimir Nabokov. The same year, Rice was included in *Prize Stories of 1949: The O. Henry Awards.* In 1952 a chapter from *I Came Out of the Eighteenth Century* was used as a model in a book titled *Reading for Writing,* and "Miss Hattie" was anthologized in *South Carolina in the Short Story.*

During the 1950s Rice was asked to be one of fifteen authors to write reviews of great American books for a Carnegie Corporation project to put fine American literature into overseas libraries, with an accompanying review volume entitled *American Panorama.* Again Rice was part of an impressive group, with other authors for the project including Jacques Barzun, Clifton Fadiman, Mark Van Doren, and Lionel and Diana Trilling. In 1955 Dell Publishing Company anthologized Rice's short stories about the South in the paperback *Local Color;* and in 1957 Hillary House brought out a new edition of *I Came Out of the Eighteenth Century* that deleted chapters beyond Webb School, thus eliminating those on Rollins College and Black Mountain College.

Rice had kept in touch only sporadically with Louis and Stella Adamic during the years of moving about with his young family. However, he still considered the couple to be his closest friends. When Adamic died in 1951, at age fifty-two, Rice was devastated. Adamic's death, from a gunshot wound he received at his farm in New Jersey, was officially pronounced a suicide. Rice knew Louis Adamic too well to believe he could have taken his own life, and he was convinced Adamic had fallen victim to a violent crime. Many of Adamic's friends also believed that although he had been working hard on a new book, he was under no particular stress that might have led him to suicide. He had been investigated in 1948 by the House (of Representatives) Committee on Un-American Activities for association with left-wing organizations. However, a clear motive for suicide was never advanced,

38. P. Rice, interview with the author, February 13, 1993.

and Adamic left no suicide note. Clues indicating foul play also were difficult to unearth, as Stella Adamic had been out of town and the farmhouse was set on fire at approximately the same time as her husband's death.[39]

The Rice family's second residence in Florida also proved to be temporary. In 1954 the family moved to Montgomery County, Maryland, adjacent to Washington, D.C. Dikka Rice took a job with the Montgomery County library system and enrolled in the graduate library school of Catholic University in Washington, D.C. She eventually became a branch librarian, which provided not only a welcome steady income but also a steady supply of books for her husband, a voracious reader. Like his father, John Andrew Rice filled his home with piles of books perched on tables, floors, and even stairs. Rice particularly enjoyed southern writers and believed that as a group they constituted the finest literary figures in America. He was an avid reader of William Faulkner, Eudora Welty, Thomas Wolfe, Truman Capote, and James Baldwin (the last of whom Rice insisted was as southern as Faulkner, although Baldwin had been born in Harlem).[40]

When Rice became a consulting reviewer for Guggenheim Fellowship applications, he gained an opportunity to read fiction by many new young writers. He spent hours reading fellowship applications and drafting his evaluation reports; and once each year he attended meetings in New York City to finalize the selection of fellowship winners. Rice was later amused to recount that upon reading Joseph Heller's application for support to finish *Catch 22,* he had decided the project had little chance of success and recommended it be rejected.[41]

While living in Maryland, Rice began to establish more frequent contact with his son Frank and his daughter Mary Aydelotte Marshall. Frank became an Arabic language and linguistics expert and was living in the Washington, D.C., area, where he eventually taught Arabic for the Foreign Service Institute. Mary, living in Arlington, Virginia, was a political activist who was elected and reelected to serve twenty-seven years in the Virginia House of Delegates. When Rice visited either his son or daughter, he trailed the usual ashes from his pipe and instigated the usual challenging conversation and southern storytelling. His son-in-law, Roger Marshall, called him "a superb

39. Meyer Berger, "Adamic Dies of Shot, Home Aflame," New York *Times,* September 5, 1951, pp. 1, 12; D. Rice, interview with the author, March 17, 1993.

40. John Andrew Rice, "*Go Tell It On The Mountain,* by James Baldwin," in *American Panorama,* ed. Eric Larrabee (New York, 1957), 89; D. Rice to Reynolds, July 20, 1994, in author's possession.

41. F. Rice, interview with the author, November 24, 1995; D. Rice to Reynolds, July 20, 1994, in author's possession.

conversationalist. He could talk on almost any subject and usually did. He was the center of attention, but also interested in any contribution anyone else made."[42]

Rice's brother Mike, a successful entertainment lawyer in Dallas, visited on occasion and proved equally adept at telling humorous stories of the South. A man of dry wit who was considered the most successful and financially stable family member, Mike once received a telegram from his youngest brother, Coke, stating, "Need $1,500 immediately." Mike's return wire simply stated, "So do I!" Coke Rice, at one time a member of the U.S. Foreign Service and consul to Malta, later became an aluminum blind and door salesman in the Washington, D.C., area. When the brothers got together, conversations about their shared experiences inevitably included discussions of their father. When the senior John Andrew was at issue, observers could notice the brothers' voices raise and faces redden collectively, as they described youthful experiences with great vehemence.[43]

Rice's son Peter maintained that his father's humor and expert conversation could compose a public face that changed to anger and bitterness at home. "My father had the ability to charm your socks off," he recalled. "But that was a game. How far can I go here? How far there?" As John Andrew Rice eventually recognized that he had been afraid of his own father, Peter Rice also found himself fearful. "I didn't know what he was going to be like when I got home from school. There was a lot of tiptoeing around him." Peter Rice briefly ran away from home several times during his early teens. At age eighteen, he left for good, returning only occasionally to visit.[44]

The youngest son of Frank and Ann Rice, William, generally enjoyed an affectionate relationship with his grandfather and recalled many hours spent helping him tend his large garden or listening to him tell stories of the family and the South around a dinner table. However, he also knew the sting of the intimidating side of John Andrew Rice. He recalled this incident:

> When I was a kid, I had a set of strawlike pieces you made little sculptures from. When my grandfather, mother, and father were sitting around talking about ideas, I came in to show them some of my sculptures. I didn't realize how I'd annoyed grandfather, but when he came to our house a week or two later he really started berating me about it. He yelled about how I shouldn't have interrupted. I should be reading books or out running around, but not bothering adults. He pointed this out as a character flaw because I wasn't con-

---

42. Marshall, interview with the author, February 23, 1993.
43. *Ibid.;* F. Rice, interview with the author, February 13, 1993.
44. P. Rice, interview with the author, February 13, 1993.

centrating on more important things. I was looking for approval instead of just doing things for themselves. . . . This was a typical pattern, how one little thing could set him off. It was incredible how tiny you felt. I didn't go to his place for quite a while after that. My mother was rather annoyed too.[45]

The John Andrew Rice family's years in Maryland took them to several locations in small, rural towns just beyond the suburban fringe circling Washington, D.C. They first rented an old farmhouse on five acres at the foot of Sugarloaf Mountain. There they raised Rhode Island Red chickens, tended a garden, and picked gallons of wild strawberries for jams and pies. After a year, they moved to a tiny rented home in the enigmatic town of Washington Grove, originally an enclave for summer cottages owned by otherwise urban residents. The cottages of Washington Grove, convenient to a nearby railroad station, faced a central meadow and turned their backs to the road. In addition to gardening, canning, and cooking, John Andrew Rice took up caning when he and his wife brought back from a flea market a set of antique straight-back chairs that needed new seats. In 1959 the Rice family moved from Washington Grove to a rented house in nearby Gaithersburg, where Elisabeth and Peter spent their middle school and high school years. Elisabeth Rice had several friends who enjoyed her father's company and quick wit, and the feeling was mutual. Rice enjoyed those youngsters who seemed creative and talented, and he entertained them with conversation and much listening.[46]

Finally, John Andrew Rice, at age seventy-six, and Dikka Rice became first-time homeowners when they purchased a 150-year-old farmhouse in rural Barnesville, Maryland, just outside Gaithersburg. It included several acres of established cherry trees, apple trees, raspberries, gooseberries, currants, and rhubarb. Rice added a large vegetable garden and an asparagus bed. His grandson William C. Rice later fondly recalled the hours spent at what he considered to be his grandfather's "farm." But, he noted, "Grandfather really loved best planning the garden each year, thinking about it, planting it, and conversing about it. When it came to the hot summer work of tending it—weeding and harvesting—he would prefer to leave that to us kids."[47]

While living in Gaithersburg, Rice struck up a close friendship with his neighbors, artist Bob Chambers and Chambers' wife, well-known concert pianist Helen McGraw. Coincidentally, McGraw had performed at Black Mountain College shortly after Rice's departure from the school. Cham-

45. W. Rice, interview with the author, January 6, 1993.
46. D. Rice to Reynolds, July 20, 1994, in author's possession.
47. W. Rice, interview with the author, January 6, 1993.

bers and Rice talked about everything from race relations to politics to education. Both were solid liberals who, according to Chambers, "agreed on everything. [Senator Joseph] McCarthy was one of our great mutual hates." Chambers saw mostly the brilliant conversationalist in Rice but occasionally observed his ability to be combative and argumentative. As an avid audience for Rice's stories about the South, he found that although Rice granted the African Americans much wisdom and dignity, he did not particularly applaud the notion of desegregation. Chambers recalled, "He had some old-fashioned views about the colored folks; he was very fond of them, but he thought the process of giving them real freedom should be taken slowly."[48]

Rice often appeared at the Chamberses' house simply to hear Helen McGraw play the piano. Claiming Beethoven as his favorite composer, he could sit still for hours, except for movements necessary to keep his pipe going, and listen in silence. He never refused an invitation afterwards to stay for dinner. In exchange, Rice presented his hosts with jars of sour-orange marmalade he made from Seville oranges ordered once each year from Florida. Eventually, Chambers painted a small portrait of John Andrew Rice, which he later gave to Dikka Rice, who eventually donated it to the National Portrait Gallery.[49]

After he took up residence in Maryland, Rice frequently was visited by former Black Mountain students, and even a few from Rollins, although none of his former faculty colleagues kept in touch. During the first decade after his departure from the college, Rice noted, "It must have had something people wanted, because it's still going." Later, however, as Rice heard news of financial instability, departures among the veteran faculty, and continued interpersonal turmoil, his assessment of the college became less sanguine as he observed, "Institutions seem to acquire a life of their own. They keep on going long after they have outlived their usefulness."[50]

Black Mountain College's ability to survive the turmoil and resignations of 1949 seemed to verify that it indeed had some life of its own. By selling off some campus acreage, the remaining faculty managed to keep the college afloat and to retain its original mind-set of freedom from outside control. In 1951 the faculty expanded to include Charles Olson, a poet and author who had attained popular acclaim for his book *Call Me Ishmael* and who had taught during two summer institutes at the college. Olson soon became a

48. Robert Chambers, interview with the author, April 26, 1993.

49. *Ibid.;* D. Rice, interview with the author, March 17, 1993.

50. Andrews, interview with the author, May 11, 1993; F. Rice interview with the author February 13, 1993.

driving force among the faculty and was quickly elected rector. His presence alone, at six feet seven inches and 250 pounds, accounted for some of his instant elevation in status; his dominant personality and natural charisma mixed with keen intellect accounted for the rest. His ideas about education leaned decidedly toward the arts and literature, with an emphasis on literature. He was known as an exciting teacher, but his administrative desires and abilities could be ranked well below those of Rectors Rice, Wunsch, and Albers, his predecessors.

What Albers lacked in administrative ability he had made up for in tenacity and sense of duty. That which Rice lacked he had made up for in ideas and charisma. When Olson could not manage the administrative functions of financial development, planning, and student recruitment, he retreated. In the face of difficulties with finding funding sources, he stopped development efforts. In the face of a discouraging student enrollment, he ended recruitment attempts. He concentrated his talent and energy on literature and writing programs, initiating in 1952 a fine journal, the *Black Mountain Review.* However, the school was running without financial management or administrative leadership. By 1954 Olson also was embroiled in personal problems that further hastened his retreat from addressing college issues. Although his wife, Connie, was still with him on campus, a Black Mountain student, Betty Kaiser, had given birth to his son in New York. Olson commuted between the two places until his wife finally left Black Mountain and his student and son returned.[51]

Nell Rice left Black Mountain College in 1955 and joined her ailing brother in Princeton, New Jersey. In the fall of 1956, with only a handful of faculty and students returning to the college and much of its land sold off piecemeal to pay various bills, Olson and the remaining faculty decided to close the twenty-three-year experiment in higher education. Without fanfare or public announcement, the college quietly failed to open for the winter quarter. Only Olson and his new wife and child stayed on to oversee the legal disbursement of property.

During 1956 and 1957 John Andrew Rice corresponded with Charles Olson from Washington Grove about the books and bookcases he had left on loan at Black Mountain College. As soon as he heard rumors of the college's closing, he asked that they be shipped to him, naming in particular a ten-volume *Oxford New English Dictionary,* a *Jewish Encyclopedia,* a hundred-volume collection of antique and rare books by and about Jonathan Swift,

51. M. Harris, *The Arts at Black Mountain,* 202; Tom Clark, *Charles Olson: The Allegory of a Poet's Life* (New York, 1991), 260–65.

and a very rare first printing of *Purely Original Verse* by Joel Chandler Harris. Olson's fairly obscure replies to Rice's inquiries addressed the issue of the books less than the college's situation and Rice's founding role. On April 1, 1957, he wrote of the closing of Black Mountain College: "This may sound like the wolf this time, this time, John Rice, the wolves have got your sheep. On the face of it we didn't make it, that is, we have closed the collegiate operation on this site, and I am instructed to sell everything against debt. But you are one of the few, and so far as we are concerned Papa. You'd guess maybe education at this date might abandon that part and still have plenty of program."[52]

Early in this correspondence, Olson had sent Rice a handful of volumes, but he found a variety of reasons to put off the complete disbursement of Rice's books. He explained at various times that they could not be found, could not be identified, or were mired in the drawn-out process of cataloging for potential sale of the entire library. He also insisted that Nell Rice had much earlier removed several of the books specifically mentioned by Rice. Later he charged that most or all of the Rice volumes had been systematically removed, and that perhaps Rice should check with his former wife.[53]

Exasperated, after the college's closing Rice provided Olson with a list of those volumes he could remember as his. Additionally, he asked for any that had his name inscribed in them, although these represented only a handful of the approximately two thousand items Rice recalled having on loan at the library. As the correspondence between these two Black Mountain College rectors continued, so did Olson's activities to dispose of all college property. In September, 1957, Olson informed Rice that any of his books that might have been there had been packed for storage and sold with the Black Mountain College library to interests in a new college being planned: North Carolina Wesleyan College in the town of Rocky Mount. Although Nell Rice may have removed books, Olson himself undoubtedly took away some Black Mountain College library books during his work to finalize legal and financial issues. He sent a number of these to his longtime friend and lover, Frances Boldereff, and, in a letter alerting her of packages of books soon to arrive, mentioned that he had "gutted Black Mountain College Lib." Additionally, during the 1950s students and faculty at the chaotic and impoverished col-

52. John A. Rice to Charles Olson, March 19, 1956, August 21, 1957, Charles Olson to John A. Rice, April 1, 1957, all in "The Olson-Rice Correspondence, 1956–1957" (MS in private collection of William C. Rice, Boston).

53. Charles Olson to John A. Rice, March 21, 1956, April 1, 1957, May 8, 1957, August 1, 1957, all *ibid.*

lege often took with them on their departure library books and various other items belonging to the college.[54]

John Andrew Rice was furious about the loss of his books, although he did not attach particular blame. After a decade, however, still fuming, he remarked on his correspondence with Charles Olson: "I received Olson's responses and, well, they were practically the writings of an illiterate!" Years later, when his grandson William C. Rice visited Black Mountain, family friend and Black Mountain College graduate Francis A. ("Faf") Foster took him to a garage at a house in the town of Black Mountain. There they found many books from the college library which had been dropped off by Charles Olson on his way out of town. "J. A. Rice" was penned inside some of their covers.[55]

At various times, Olson indicated his substantial respect for Rice, whom he viewed as a great educator. Olson judged that Rice was treated as unfairly at Black Mountain as he had been at Rollins. At Beloit College in 1968, in an informal talk to students that was peppered with incoherent rambling and inaccuracies, Olson eulogized Rice in this way:

> There's three Black Mountains: The Rice Black Mountain, the Albers Black Mountain, and then this ragged-arse place that I and others were part of. And it was Albers and Dreier, that treasurer I mentioned, who eventually sort of maneuvered Rice out. In other words, again, he lost because his mouth was so. But he talked well, and he thought well, and spoke out and believed in the—in fact, actually, the Socratic method. He cared for human beings' minds—no question. . . . [Rice said] that this place shall be that place in the world in which the arts shall share the center of the curriculum with the more usual studies. And he meant it. And curiously enough, I suppose if you talk in terms of education—literally as such a curriculum—this was why I suppose Black Mountain still sort of has blood for others. Because in some sense Rice is the chief, I would think the chief, reformer of education since the Middle Ages.[56]

Only an occasion like the closing of Black Mountain College could provoke John Andrew Rice to spend much time dealing with that chapter of his past. Wesleyan Press at Wesleyan University in Connecticut had published works of several former Black Mountain faculty members. In 1963 Wesleyan

54. Charles Olson to Frances Boldereff, June 9, 1957, in Charles Olson Papers, Homer Babbidge Library, University of Connecticut, Storrs; M. Harris, *The Arts at Black Mountain,* 177.

55. J. Rice, interview with Duberman, June 10, 1967; W. Rice, interview with the author, January 6, 1993.

56. Charles Olson, "On Black Mountain: A Conversation at Beloit College, March 26, 1968," in *Muthologos: The Collected Lectures and Interviews,* ed. George F. Butterick (2 vols.; Bolinas, Calif., 1977), II, 60.

Press editor J. R. de la Torre Bueno asked Rice to consider writing about Black Mountain. Rice promised to consider such a project but warned it would not constitute a history of the college, but "the record of one man's trying to find what he knows is there but not knowing what it will be when he finds it." Trying to jog his memory, he even wrote to Ted Dreier for information on some early details he wanted to recall. However, when he began to put his thoughts on paper, he got only as far as noting on two legal pads his ideas about art and artists, his impressions of Josef Albers, and some other memories and thoughts about education and Black Mountain College. He simply was not up to the writing task. He tried speaking his memories into a tape recorder, but found that in transcript they sounded artificial and forced.[57]

On one other occasion during his retirement Rice decided to devote some time to addressing issues in education. He was appointed to a Montgomery County, Maryland, commission on teachers and teacher preparation in 1960. As the deliberations proceeded, however, he became known as more troublesome than helpful when he could not agree with the conclusions being reached by his fellow commissioners. Finally, the commission report included an appendix by John Andrew Rice—a minority statement made up of a rambling narrative that gave his indictment of schools and teaching. In it he reserved his harshest criticism for administrators at any level of education, representing them as uncreative drones who hinder the accomplishments of teachers. Although the topic ranged far from the commission's charge, he expressed his particular scorn for those working in colleges and universities, "Administrators are noncreative. They, too, are adult delinquents. And yet, there is evidence that the administrator can be creative: Gilman at Hopkins, Harper at Chicago, Meiklejohn at Wisconsin, Joseph Wheeler, Director of the Enoch Pratt Free Library, and in the beginning Jefferson. Old Dean Briggs of Harvard gave the clue, 'It is the business of a dean to break rules; any stenographer can keep them.' "[58]

At seventy-three years of age, Rice had not lost his sting or his penchant for candid observation about the ills of education. His discussion of requirements for students to certify as teachers concluded, "The excellent student who is not afraid to match his intellect, intelligence, and knowledge with others discovers, on application for certification, that these are not consid-

57. D. Rice to Reynolds, July 20, 1994, in author's possession; J. R. de la Torre Bueno to John A. Rice, April 19, 1963, John A. Rice to J. R. de la Torre Bueno, May 25, 1963, both in possession of William C. Rice, Boston, Mass.; T. Dreier, interview with the author, April 29, 1994.

58. J. Rice, "Appendix," *Report on Teachers and Teacher Preparation,* 49.

ered. The question is, 'How many hours, how many days, how many months—never mind that I'm not asking how you feel. How long were you chair-borne, where, and have your several professors of education recorded that you were chair-borne at the alleged times and places to their satisfaction?' Not the sticky question, 'What do you know that you didn't know before you became chair-borne?' " In terms of preparation, he particularly objected to the Ed.D. degree, claiming, "A doctorate in education is to the world of learning as a doctorate in chiropractic is to the world of healing."[59]

Life for Rice slowed down substantially during the 1960s. For the most part he remained at home, where he tended his garden, read from the stacks of books accumulated around the house, conversed with friends, and sat very still while nursing his thoughts and his pipe. In 1967, at age seventy-nine, he granted a six-hour interview to Black Mountain College historian Martin Duberman. His wonderful southern voice—free from a drawl—never wavered as he recalled in detail even very brief anecdotes. His opinions about people were still strong. Upon hearing from Duberman that a man who had been the resident farmer had died, he responded, "Oh that's good. I approve of that." Of Ted Dreier and of Bob Wunsch, he did not hesitate to state, "I loved Ted" and "I loved Bob."[60]

The following year, on November 17, 1968, John Andrew Rice died in a hospital in Bethesda, Maryland, after fighting an illness for several months. Although bone cancer had spread widely, he did not appear to be in great pain during his final hospitalization. He was not a complainer, and he was alert nearly to the end, conversing with nurses and visitors. His son Frank recalled that just days before he died, his father told him, "I had a curious dream last night. I dreamed that I had to review a book; but first I had to write it."[61]

Although John Andrew Rice had voiced little regret about the twists and turns of his life, he had ended his autobiography, *I Came Out of the Eighteenth Century*, with a homily about the context he would have preferred:

> I should choose to be born in South Carolina in the eighteenth century. . . . I should choose the eighteenth century for its violence, yet touched with grace; for its near escape from Catholicism, while keeping the Catholic view, everything in one and one in everything, without the impost of piety; for its long, clockless days; for its child's world for children; for its passionate belief that the world would be better, perhaps tomorrow; for old ladies who were queens

59. *Ibid.*, 41, 43.
60. J. Rice, interview with Duberman, June 10, 1967.
61. F. Rice, interview with the author, April 9, 1994.

compared to whom Victoria was a scullery maid; for curds, fresh cane syrup, cracklings hot out of the pot, rain on the roof and the roof of split shingles, quilts, mud chimneys cracked from the heat of light 'ood knots, muzzle-loaders, calico, fire crackers at Christmas, puppies; for its simple faith in simple words, justice, freedom, happiness; and belief in the rights of man, and faith in man.[62]

62. J. Rice, *Eighteenth Century,* 340–41.

CONCLUSION: Rebel in Retrospect

John Andrew Rice wrote and spoke about the South of his youth as a place where conversation, activity, and achievement focused almost singularly on people. Tales of who did what, who knew whom, and whose kin were whose created the patterns to be explored on front porches and around kitchen tables. Discussions of abstract ideas were no competition for accounts of the complex and unpredictable drama of human behavior. On the infrequent occasions when talk started with generalities about issues, it quickly reverted back to the specifics of individuals. Politics was about politicians; sports was about athletes; technology was about inventors; education was about teachers.

Because such a South was so well suited to John Andrew Rice's own nature, it is tempting to think that he used his impressive creative talents to invent the place—or at least to embellish parts of its reality to suit the lens through which he filtered his view of his life. That may be the case. But what is most evident is that Rice himself—as a teacher, a thinker, a conversationalist, and a writer—was intensely personal in all he did. His ideas drew from personal experience. His teaching soared when it could rely on personal connections with individual students. His best writing focused minutely on people, describing in detail the nose of University of Nebraska president Sam Avery or the coiled braid atop his grandmother's head.

Rice's instinctive concentration on individuals and their actions may have contributed much to his transience as an educator by masking from him the more abstract realities of institutions and the complexities of group behavior and by leaving him unwilling or unable to master the arts of negotiation and compromise. Rice could not bring himself to play either the organizational politician or the visionary strategist in his institution-building role. Where his nemesis Robert Maynard Hutchins sought (yet did not always achieve) acquiescence for his plans at the University of Chicago by attending to networks of powerful alumni and by nominating friendly outside scholars to the university faculty, Rice was far too impatient to undertake the demands of such maneuvering. Where his brother-in-law Frank Aydelotte traveled and lectured throughout the country in his determination to garner widespread adoption of the honors system, Rice was far too rooted in the immediacy of his experiment to plan for its future growth or transference.

Rice's success in founding a formidable endeavor in higher education owed much to his uncompromising candor, his brilliance, and his inflexible audacity. But those qualities were suited best to high principles like the defense of academic freedom, the pursuit of more complete student development, and the establishment of a democratic learning community. When the same qualities were applied to less lofty, day-to-day interactions with individuals—the part of life that loomed so large in Rice's beloved southern heritage—they did not serve him nearly so well. Yet Rice could not adjust his behavior to avoid unfavorable long-term consequences for himself or even to spare short-term feelings of hurt or anger in others. From his father he had acquired a capacity for argument, for playing the devil's advocate, that could easily slide from intellectual debate to petty criticism. From the adolescent experience of his mother's death, followed by his temporary separation from his brothers and placement in an orphanage, he may well have acquired a defensive shell of arrogance and cynicism in the face of grief unresolved. From his southern predicament, as a highly educated intellectual in a time and place of anti-intellectualism, he may have developed the need to prove himself by taking the offensive in dealings with others. The roots of his complex behavior are subject to numerous speculative theories.

What is certain, and somewhat sad, is that Rice himself recognized something of the darker side of his demeanor, even while he could not manage to change it. "I learned too late that I really was arrogant," he admitted a year before his death. Reflecting in *I Came Out of the Eighteenth Century* about the qualities he brought to the position of rector at Black Mountain College, he admitted, "I had learned and perfected one thing that unfitted me: I had learned the technique of opposition; that is, of irresponsibility, for criticism without chance or obligation to act is irresponsible. Whether in graduate school or in classroom, I had opposed not only the administration—every professor does that—but also my colleagues. . . . I had known only one teacher, John Webb, whom I was willing to call master, only one whom I did not in some measure despise—poor preparation for what I now undertook."[1]

1. J. Rice, interview with Duberman, June 10, 1967; J. Rice, *Eighteenth Century,* 323.

Rice's embrace of the immediate and the personal led him to consult frequently, often selfishly, only his personal preferences and impulses in making decisions about his life and the life of Black Mountain College. For example, a sudden personal interest in Jonathan Swift steered him far afield of his doctoral studies in Greek and Latin; and he pursued research on Swift even though only inquiry within his own discipline would have been likely to lead to a dissertation. When he lost interest in teaching Latin and Greek after only a few years at Black Mountain, he stopped offering the language training. He had become much more interested in writing chapters of his book, so he began holding a writing workshop. He was happy to set up a tutorial for a single student who wanted specialized work in writing, but made no such offer when a student wanted to pursue Latin. Some of the same traits that enabled Rice to take an apparently unselfish interest in a student or colleague when he felt some personal connection also made it possible for him to allow self-guided impulses to supercede other claims on his time and attention.

Guided by his own preferences, Rice was drawn to people as appealing human beings, rather than as representatives of what they were or did. He revered John Dewey because Dewey was a brilliant individual with fine human qualities, but Rice believed progressive education itself far too doctrinaire. After visiting some experimental colleges, he wrote of his admiration for Arthur Morgan of Antioch and Scott Buchanan of St. John's; but he dwelled only briefly on the colleges themselves, and then not particularly favorably. At Black Mountain College, he had great affection for Ted Dreier, even though he felt Dreier was only a marginal teacher with a misplaced desire to launch a college work program. He also cared deeply for Robert Wunsch, but decided the most "important" people he ever knew there were faculty wife Mary Barnes and cooks Rubye and Jack Lipsey.[2] Those three were elevated by some human qualities that apparently struck a chord in Rice.

It was from years of personal observation and experience that Rice formed an instinctive philosophy of education that emerged more as a group of notions than as a coherent theory. Some of his ideas stemmed from his opposition to widespread practices he viewed as injurious or incomprehensible. Thus, he experimented with eliminating credit hours for students and any outside controlling board for the college. Other ideas stemmed from observing how student experiences—including his own—were shaped by the process and context of learning. Thus, he worked to create a small and close environment that elevated teacher-pupil relations as the crucial factor in learning, and he promoted senior-level studies that were self-propelled but

2. J. Rice, interview with Duberman, June 10, 1967.

rigorously examined. After seeing his son Frank suddenly become a disciplined student when given free rein to study art in London and after discussing with Ted Dreier his experiences with music at Thomas Whitney Surette's summer institute, Rice determined that artistic endeavor, as a process of creative discipline, could make an important contribution to learning in any area.

While Rice's distinctly home-grown ideas and their implementation may have exercised his self-motivated willfulness, they also managed to reverberate far beyond the scope of his own pursuits. A number of observers have noted that Black Mountain College did not actually terminate in 1956, but simply dispersed. Some groups of former students gravitated to New York and San Francisco, where they met as small communities of supportive friends who exchanged ideas about various creative endeavors in music, drama, fiction, and art. Olson and the other poets who had published in the *Black Mountain Review* during the 1950s became widely known as the "Black Mountain poets." In the years that followed, many former students and faculty managed to remain remarkably connected and interested in the college, with a number of formal and informal reunions in New York, San Francisco, and North Carolina. Four major books about the college appeared, starting with Fielding Dawson's memoir, *The Black Mountain Book* (1970). Martin Duberman's comprehensive history of the college, *Black Mountain: An Exploration in Community,* was originally published in 1972 and brought out in paperback in 1993. In 1987 a thorough and scholarly treatment by Mary Emma Harris recounted the creative aspects of the college and included fine color reproductions in *The Arts at Black Mountain College.* Finally, an anthology of personal accounts, edited by Mervin Lane, was released in 1990, with memories penned by former faculty and students including John Cage, Kenneth Noland, Francine du Plessix Gray, Helen Frankenthaler, Eric Bentley, and Josef and Anni Albers. In 1994 the Black Mountain College Museum and Arts Center was established in the town of Black Mountain and began to host exhibits of the work of Black Mountain College artists, as well as symposia and a 1995 reunion at the Lake Eden campus. The *North Carolina Literary Review* produced a "Black Mountain College Issue" in the summer of 1995.

Students who did not make names for themselves in the arts were no less influenced by their education at Black Mountain College, and many found occasions to spread that influence widely. Some stayed in education, as teachers or administrators. Others found their niches in the social services. Still others founded small businesses based on craftsmanship ranging from woodworking to book binding. The fact that yet others opted for more conventional careers supports the conclusion of former student David Way, who maintained, "Black Mountain has always seemed to me to conform to that description of poetry: A poem makes Nothing happen. That was what John Andrew was trying to do, make nothing happen—so that anything could happen. That is, so that the student could with freedom become."[3]

John Andrew Rice, of course, never wholly involved himself again in education after leaving Black Mountain College. While his ability to sustain his own forward momentum as an educator was impaired by personal flaws he could not or would not overcome, his influence ranged from his positive impact on a number of young lives to his achievement in demonstrating the reaches, as well as the limits, of innovative higher education ideas put into practice. Through the Black Mountain College example and through his (albeit sparse) writing, he helped to invigorate the public debate among educators and scholars who continue to deliberate the means and aims of education. This contribution is perhaps the most appropriate legacy for a man whose long-time profession was teaching and education but whose foremost love was for ideas and the conversations they provoke.

3. David Jacques Way to Katherine Reynolds, April 27, 1993, in author's possession.

BIBLIOGRAPHY

PRIMARY SOURCES

Manuscript Collections

Josef and Anni Albers Foundation. Orange, Conn.
    Rice, John A. Correspondence, 1938–40.
College of Charleston. Robert Scott Small Library, Special Collections. Charleston, S.C.
    Grice, George. Papers, 1951.
Columbia College Library. Archives. Columbia, S.C.
    Rice, John A., Sr. Presidential Files, 1885–1900.
Fisk University Library. Special Collections. Nashville, Tenn.
    Jones, Thomas Elsa. Papers, 1934.
John Simon Guggenheim Memorial Foundation. Archives. New York.
    Rice, John Andrew. Files, 1925–47.
Howard University. Moorland-Spingarn Research Center. Washington, D.C.
    Locke, Alain. Papers, 1933.
Montgomery County Historical Society, Inc. Rockville, Md.
    Burial records, Monocacy Cemetery, John Andrew Rice, November 20, 1968.
Museum of Modern Art. Archives. New York.
    Barr, Alfred H. Papers, 1933–35.
National Register of Historic Places. U.S. Department of the Interior, Washington, D.C.
    "Inventory and Nomination Form: Tanglewood Plantation." September 22, 1977.
North Carolina State Division of Archives and History. Department of Cultural Resources. Raleigh, N.C.
    Black Mountain College Papers.

Board of Fellows Meeting Minutes, 1933–36.

Faculty Meeting Minutes, 1933–42.

Faculty Files.

Official Documents.

Student Files.

Duberman, Martin. Papers. Personal Collection 1678.

Princeton University Libraries. Rare Books and Special Collections. Princeton, N.J.

Adamic, Louis. Papers.

Rollins College. Archives and Special Collections. Winter Park, Fla.

Curriculum Conference, 1931. Records and Minutes.

Faculty Files, 1930–34. T. Dreier, J. M. Forbes, R. Lounsbury, E. O. Grover, J. A. Rice, R. Wunsch.

Holt, Hamilton. Papers, 1925–40. Includes personal copy, with marginal notations, of *I Came Out of the Eighteenth Century.*

Hurston, Zora Neale. Papers, 1932–34.

Rice Case File, 1933–35.

South Carolina Department of Archives and History. Columbia, S.C.

Federal Censuses of South Carolina: Abbeville and Sumter Districts, 1860–90, and Colleton and Richland Counties, 1890–1900.

"Inventory of Historic Places in South Carolina."

Southern Methodist University. Bridwell Library. Dallas, Tex.

Oklahoma Conference. Meeting minutes, 1930.

Texas Christian Advocate files, 1921–28.

Swarthmore College. Friends Historical Library. Swarthmore, Pa.

Aydelotte, Frank A. Personal Papers, 1925–45.

Tulane University. Office of the Registrar. New Orleans, La.

Rice, John A., Jr. Official Record, 1908–11.

University of Chicago. Office of the Registrar. Chicago, Ill.

Rice, John A., Jr. Official Record, 1916–25.

University of Connecticut. Homer Babbidge Library. Storrs, Conn.

Olson, Charles. Papers, 1957.

University of Florida Libraries. Special Collections. Gainesville, Fla.

Hurston, Zora Neale. Papers, 1932–35.

University of Nebraska Archives. Special Collections. Lincoln, Nebr.

Rice, John A., Jr. Faculty Biographical File, 1925–33.

University of South Carolina. Archives. Columbia, S.C.

Euphradian and Clariosophic Societies. Joint Programs Files, 1885.

University of South Carolina. South Caroliniana Library. Columbia, S.C.

Rice, John A., Sr. File, 1884–1926.

University of Texas. Harry Ransom Humanities Research Center. Austin, Tex.

Harper's Collection. Correspondence of Cass Canfield, Elizabeth Lawrence, and John Saxton with John Andrew Rice, Jr., 1939–45.

Webb School Archives. Bell Buckle, Tenn.
   Webb, William R. Correspondence.
Yale University. Sterling Memorial Library. New Haven, Conn.
   Albers, Josef. Papers, 1933.

Unpublished Memoirs, Letters, and Private Collections

Andrews, Richard. "John Rice and the Model Log Cabin," 1988. In the possession of Richard Andrews, North Waterford, Maine.
Cramer, Doughten. "I Went to Black Mountain College," 1940. In the possession of William C. Rice, Boston, Mass.
Rice, Frank A. "Black Mountain College: The Middle Years," August, 1985. In the possession of Frank A. Rice, Arlington, Va.
———. Correspondence with Lewis Shelly and others, In the possession of Frank A. Rice, Arlington, Va.
———. "Farce Poetica, or The Last Black Mountain College: A Drama in Three Acts with an Epilogue," August, 1985. In the possession of Frank A. Rice, Arlington, Va.
Rice, John Andrew. Correspondence with Launa Darnell Rice; with John Andrew Rice, Sr., 1912–13; with J. R. de la Torre Bueno, 1963; from Oxford, 1912–14. In the possession of William C. Rice, Boston, Mass.
Rice, William C., ed. "The Olson-Rice Correspondence, 1956–57." In the possession of William C. Rice, Boston, Mass.
Riley, Sue S. "John Andrew Rice at Black Mountain College," 1992. In the possession of Sue Spayth Riley, Charlotte, N.C.
Sunley, Robert. "Untitled Script," 1940. In the possession of Robert Sunley, Port Washington, N.Y.
Warren, Katherine Smith. "An Account of Arthur Smith, Sumter County, South Carolina, and Some of His Descendants," 1985. In the possession of William C. Rice, Boston, Mass.

Interviews

With the author

Andrews, Richard. May 11, 1993, April 3, 1994.
Bailey, Margaret Loram. May 10, 1993.
Bliss, Robert. February 1, 1993, May 5, 1993, January 5, 1994.
Carruthers, Richard. March 14, 1996.
Chambers, Robert. April 26, 1993.
Dreier, Barbara L. April 5, 1993.
Dreier, Ted. April 5, 1993, April 28, 1994.
Foote, Hope Stephens, May 13, 1993.
French, John R. P., Jr. July 27, 1993.

French, Sophie. July 27, 1993.
Johnson, Philip. January 16, 1996.
Marshall, Roger D. February 23, 1993.
Page, Donald. June 14, 1993.
Rice, Ann C. February 13, 1993.
Rice, Dikka Moen. March 17, 1993.
Rice, Frank A. February 13, 1993, April 9, 1994, December 7, 1994, November 24, 1995.
Rice, Karen. February 13, 1993.
Rice, Peter N. February 13, 1993.
Rice, William C. December 18, 1992, January 6, 1993, March 15, 1993, March 29, 1994, April 15, 1994.
Riley, Sue Spayth. May 24, 1993.
Smith, Dorothy Shepherd. April 2, 1993.
Steinau, Morton. May 3, 1993.
Sunley, Robert. May 22, 1993.
Teeter, Marian Nacke. May 12, 1993.
Way, David Jacques. May 3, 1993.
Weston, Norman. April 13, 1993.
Williams, Elizabeth Young. May 10, 1993.
Willimetz, Emil. July 1, 1993.

Other

Rice, John Andrew, Jr., by Martin Duberman. June 10, 1967.

Correspondence to the author

Bailey, Margaret Loram. May 13, 1993, April 9, 1994.
Huntington, Scott. April 27, 1993.
Marshall, Roger D. May 25, 1993.
Rice, Dikka Moen. July 20, 1994, August 1, 1994, October 4, 1995, December 1, 1995.
Rice, Frank A. January 8, 1993, February 15, 18, 22, 1993, May 24, 1993, July 14, 1993, April 11, 1994, November 30, 1994, December 2, 4, 8, 1994, March 20, 1995, October 25, 1995.
Rice, Karen. March 5, 1993.
Rice, Peter. December 5, 1994.
Rice, William C. January 6, 1993, March 9, 1993, June 7, 1993, August 2, 1993, October 16, 18, 1993, April 27, 1994, December 19, 1994, August 21, 1995.
Riley, Sue Spayth. May 3, 28, 1993.
Steinau, Morton. April 9, 1994.
Sunley, Robert. May 1, 1993.

Way, David Jacques. April 27, 1993, May 4, 1994.
Weston, Norman. April 25, 1993, April 14, 1994.
Willimetz, Emil. April 11, 1994.

Newspapers

Asheville *Citizen Times,* 1933–40, November 28, 1968.
Atlanta *Constitution,* August 25, 1933.
Charlotte *News,* April 7, 1929, 1933–38.
Christian Science Monitor, December 17, 1966.
Dayton *Daily News,* November 16, 1934.
New York *Evening Post,* September 30, 1933.
New York *Herald Tribune,* January 21, 1931, August 26, 1933.
New York *Times,* 1931–42, September 5, 1951, November 28, 1968.
Orange County (Fla.) *Chief,* 1933.
Orlando *Morning Sentinel,* 1931–33.
PM Weekly, 1940–43.
Raleigh *News and Observer,* October 29, 1933, October 3, 1937.
Rollins College *Sandspur,* 1931–33.
St. Petersburg (Fla.) *Independent,* 1933.
Southern Christian Advocate, February 25, 1882.
Sullivan (Ind.) *Daily Times,* December 30, 1914.
Texas Christian Advocate, September 8 and 22, 1921.
Winter Park (Fla.) *Herald,* January 26, 1933.
Winter Park (Fla.) *Reporter-Star,* June 7, 1933, September 7, 1933.

Published Writings of John Andrew Rice, Jr.

"*Admiral of the Ocean Sea: A Life of Christopher Columbus,* by Samuel Eliot Morison." In *American Panorama,* edited by Eric Larrabee. New York, 1957.
"*All the King's Men,* by Robert Penn Warren." In *American Panorama,* edited by Eric Larrabee. New York, 1957.
"Appendix." In *Report on Teachers and Teacher Preparation,* compiled by the Montgomery County (Md.) Special Commission on Teacher Preparation. Rockville, Md., 1961.
"Aunt Lettie and the Absolute." *New Yorker,* March 3, 1945, pp. 56–60.
"*Benjamin Franklin's Autobiographical Writings,* edited by Carl Van Doren." In *American Panorama,* edited by Eric Larrabee. New York, 1957.
"*The Bent Twig,* by Dorothy Canfield Fisher." In *American Panorama,* edited by Eric Larrabee. New York, 1957.
"Black Mountain College." *Progressive Education,* XI (April–May, 1934), 271–74.
"Black Mountain College." *School and Home,* XVI (April, 1935), 655–58.

"Black Mountain College Memoirs," edited by William C. Rice. *Southern Review,* XXV (July, 1989), 573–85.

"*Caste and Class in a Southern Town,* by John Dollard." In *American Panorama,* edited by Eric Larrabee. New York, 1957.

"*The Collected Writings of Ambrose Bierce.*" In *American Panorama,* edited by Eric Larrabee. New York, 1957.

"Content with the Station." *New Yorker,* January 27, 1945, pp. 23–26. Anthologized in *55 Short Stories from The New Yorker.* New York, 1949.

"*Crazy Horse,* by Mari Sandoz." In *American Panorama,* edited by Eric Larrabee. New York, 1957.

"Dr. Rice's Reply." *Harper's,* CLXXVIII (1939), 564–65.

"*The Enormous Room,* by e. e. cummings." In *American Panorama,* edited by Eric Larrabee. New York, 1957.

"The Exceptional Student in the Middle West." *School and Society,* October 31, 1925, pp. 543–47.

"*From Slavery to Freedom: A History of the American Negroes,* by John Hope Franklin." In *American Panorama,* edited by Eric Larrabee. New York, 1957.

"*From the American Drama,* edited by Eric Bentley." In *American Panorama,* edited by Eric Larrabee. New York, 1957.

"Fundamentalism and the Higher Learning." *Harper's,* CLXXIV (May, 1937), 587–96.

"The Genuine Article." *Collier's,* October 25, 1952, pp. 24–25.

"*George Washington Carver,* by Rackham Holt." In *American Panorama,* edited by Eric Larrabee. New York, 1957.

"*Go Tell It on the Mountain,* by James Baldwin." In *American Panorama,* edited by Eric Larrabee. New York, 1957.

"*Gone with the Wind,* by Margaret Mitchell." In *American Panorama,* edited by Eric Larrabee. New York, 1957.

"Grand Shoes." *Collier's,* July 5, 1950, pp. 28–29.

"Grandmother Smith's Plantation." Part 1. *Harper's,* CLXXVII (November, 1938), 572–82. Part 2. *Harper's,* CLXXVIII (December, 1938), 88–96.

"*Great Tales of the American West,* by Harry E. Maule." In *American Panorama,* edited by Eric Larrabee. New York, 1957.

"Homage to the Porpoise." *Common Ground* (Summer, 1941), 86–87.

I Came Out of the Eighteenth Century. New York, 1942.

"Inside the South." *Common Ground* (Spring, 1941), 26–34.

"Island of Fear." *Collier's,* May 27, 1953, pp. 76–77.

"*Java Head,* by Joseph Hergesheimer." In *American Panorama,* edited by Eric Larrabee. New York, 1957.

"*Jefferson the Virginian,* by Dumas Malone." In *American Panorama,* edited by Eric Larrabee. New York, 1957.

"*The Just and the Unjust,* by James Gould Cozzens." In *American Panorama,* edited by Eric Larrabee. New York, 1957.

"*Lanterns on the Levee,* by William Alexander Percy." In *American Panorama,* edited by Eric Larrabee. New York, 1957.

"The Last Maltby." *Collier's,* August 18, 1951, pp. 22–23.

Local Color. New York, 1955.

"*Look Homeward Angel,* by Thomas Wolfe." In *American Panorama,* edited by Eric Larrabee. New York, 1957.

"Man Possessed." *Collier's,* November 11, 1955, p. 58.

"The Metamorphosis of Mr. Cracovaner." *New Yorker,* October 14, 1944, pp. 70–72.

"Miss Hattie." *New Yorker,* October 11, 1947, pp. 57–63. Anthologized in *South Carolina in the Short Story,* edited by Katharine M. Jones and Mary V. Schlaefer. Columbia, S.C., 1952.

"Monday Come Home." *Collier's,* September 3, 1949, pp. 22–31. Anthologized in *Collier's Best.* New York, 1951.

"My Father's Folks." *Harper's,* CLXXXI (September, 1940), 426–36.

"*Porgy,* by DuBose Heyward." In *American Panorama,* edited by Eric Larrabee. New York, 1957.

"*The Portable Faulkner,* edited by Malcolm Cowley." In *American Panorama,* edited by Eric Larrabee. New York, 1957.

"*The Promised Land,* by Mary Antin." In *American Panorama,* edited by Eric Larrabee. New York, 1957.

"*The Saturday Evening Post Treasury,* edited by Roger Butterfield." In *American Panorama,* edited by Eric Larrabee. New York, 1957.

"*Selected Stories of Eudora Welty.*" In *American Panorama,* edited by Eric Larrabee. New York, 1957.

"*Selected Writings of Gertrude Stein,* edited by Carl Van Vechten." In *American Panorama,* edited by Eric Larrabee. New York, 1957.

"*Sister Carrie,* by Theodore Dreiser." In *American Panorama,* edited by Eric Larrabee. New York, 1957.

"A Small Boy in a Female College." Part 1. *Harper's,* CLXXX (May, 1940), 578–86. Part 2. *Harper's,* CLXXXI (June, 1940), 86–93.

"*A Stillness at Appomattox,* by Bruce Catton." In *American Panorama,* edited by Eric Larrabee. New York, 1957.

"*Theodore Parker,* by Henry Steele Commager." In *American Panorama,* edited by Eric Larrabee. New York, 1957.

"Two School Teachers." *Harper's,* CLXXXIV (January, 1942), 201–209.

"*Up from Slavery,* by Booker T. Washington." In *American Panorama,* edited by Eric Larrabee. New York, 1957.

"*The Virginian,* by Owen Wister." In *American Panorama,* edited by Eric Larrabee. New York, 1957.

"Where Love Begins." *Collier's,* February 3, 1951, pp. 22–23, 46–47.

"*Winesburg, Ohio,* by Sherwood Anderson." In *American Panorama,* edited by Eric Larrabee. New York, 1957.

"The Yankee." *Collier's,* April 4, 1953, pp. 28–29.

"You Can Only Get Just So Much Justice." *Collier's,* October 30, 1948, pp. 18–19. Anthologized in O. *Henry Memorial Award Prize Stories of 1949.* New York, 1949.

Other Published Primary Sources

Adamic, Louis. "Education on a Mountain." *Harper's,* CLXXII (April, 1936), 516–30.

———. *My America.* New York, 1938.

Albers, Josef. "Art as Experience." *Progressive Education,* XII (October, 1935), 391–93.

———. "Concerning Art Education." *Black Mountain College Bulletin,* II (June, 1934), 1–3.

Black Mountain College: 1933–1934. N.p., 1933.

Black Mountain College Bulletin, I (Fall, 1933), II (June, 1934).

"Brilliant Critic." *Time,* November 23, 1942, p. 88.

Caldwell, Erskine. Foreword to *Local Color,* by John A. Rice, Jr. New York, 1955.

Congressional Record, 74th Cong., 1st Sess., 5749.

Cowley, Malcolm. "Lost Worlds." *New Republic,* CVII (November, 1942), 614.

"The Curriculum Conference." *Rollins College Bulletin,* XXVI (1931), 2–12.

DeVoto, Bernard. "Another Consociate Family." *Harper's,* CLXXII (April, 1936), 605–608.

———. "Terwillinger in Plato's Dream." *Harper's,* CLXXII (April, 1936), 493–96.

"Down the Mountain." *Newsweek,* November 30, 1942, pp. 71–72.

Elliott, Randolph. "Old Sawney's." *Atlantic Monthly,* CXXVI (August, 1920), 231–36.

Foster, Francis A. *Black Mountain College.* Montreat, N.C., 1987.

Frisbie, Josephine. "Rice *v.* Socrates." *Time,* December 14, 1942, p. 9.

Goldenson, Robert. "Some Approaches to the Teaching of Philosophy." *Progressive Education,* XIV (May, 1937), 323–29.

Hull, Lewis C. "Athletics at Oxford." *American Oxonian,* I (April, 1914), 21–26.

Hurston, Zora Neale. *Dust Tracks on a Road.* Philadelphia, 1942.

———. *Jonah's Gourd Vine.* Philadelphia, 1934.

"Individualization in Education." *Rollins College Bulletin,* XXVII (1931), 4–7.

Levi, Aaron. "A Valedictorian Changes His Mind." *Dartmouth Alumni Magazine* (May, 1972), 24–26.

Lovejoy, Arthur, and Austin Edwards. "Academic Freedom and Tenure: Rollins College Report." *Bulletin of the American Association of University Professors,* XIX (November, 1933), 416–38.

Mellen, Chase B. "The Organization of the University of Oxford." *American Oxonian,* II (January, 1915), 16–20.

Miller, Henry. *The Air-Conditioned Nightmare.* New York, 1945.

Oklahoma Annual. Methodist Episcopal Church, South. Tulsa, 1930.

Olson, Charles. "On Black Mountain: A Conversation at Beloit College, March 26, 1968." In *Muthologos: The Collected Lectures and Interviews,* edited by George F. Butterick. Vol. II of vols. Bolinas, Calif., 1977.

―――. *The Special View of History.* Lectures delivered in 1956 at Black Mountain College, edited by Ann Charters. Berkeley, 1970.

"Personal News." *American Oxonian,* I (April, 1914), 114–23, II (April, 1915), 108–20.

"Professor Rice Receives Guggenheim Award." *Nebraska Alumnus,* April, 1927, p. 167.

"Report of the Committee on Fraternities." Rollins College, Winter Park, Fla., 1932.

Rice, John A., Sr. "Dr. Rice and the Bible." Letter to the *Texas Christian Advocate,* September 22, 1921, pp. 8–9.

―――. *Emotions Jesus Stirred.* Tulsa, 1950.

―――. *The Old Testament in the Life of Today.* New York, 1920.

―――. *What Science Has Done for My Religion.* Tulsa, 1926.

"Rollins College." *New Republic,* January 17, 1934, p. 265.

"Rollins College Versus the American Association of University Professors." *Rollins College Bulletin,* XXIX (December, 1933), 3–28.

"Rumpus at Rollins." *Time,* June 19, 1933, p. 33.

Smith, William H. "Protest." *Harper's,* CLXXVIII (April, 1939), 558–64.

Stevens, A. M. "Social Phases of Oxford Life." *American Oxonian,* II (January, 1915), 21–27.

"Synopsis of Requirements for the Rhodes Scholarships." *American Oxonian,* II (January, 1915), 3.

Thayer, William W. "Comments on Rhodes Scholarships in American Periodicals." *American Oxonian,* II (January, 1915), 35–48.

Wallis, William D. "The Oxford System Versus Our Own." *Pedagogical Seminar* (June, 1912), 5–15.

Wylie, Francis. *The First Fifty Years of the Rhodes Trust and the Rhodes Scholarships, 1903–1953.* Oxford, Eng., 1955.

―――. "Rhodes Scholars and Athletics." *American Oxonian,* I (April, 1914), 33–35.

YMCA Graduate School Bulletin. Young Men's Christian Association, Nashville, Tenn., 1934.

SECONDARY SOURCES

Articles and Essays

Aydelotte, Frank. "Honors Courses in American Colleges and Universities." *Bulletin of the National Research Council,* VII (January, 1924), 1–18.

Bailey, David. "The Student Is the Curriculum." *Progressive Education,* XVI (January, 1939), 38–43.

"Bauhaus." *Museum of Modern Art Bulletin* (June, 1933), 4.

Bentley, Eric R. "Report from the Academy: The Experimental College." *Partisan Review,* XII (Summer, 1945), 422–30.

Buchanan, William. "Educational Rebels in the Nineteen Thirties." *JGE: The Journal of General Education,* XXXVII (1985), 4–33.

Cadwallader, Mervyn L. "The Uses of Philosophy in an Academic Counterrevolution: Alexander Meiklejohn and John Dewey in the 1980s." *Liberal Education,* LXX (Winter, 1984), 275–92.

Childs, John L. "Democracy and Educational Methods." *Progressive Education,* XVI (February, 1939), 119–23.

de Kooning, Elaine. "de Kooning Memories." *Vogue* (December, 1983), 323–34.

Dewey, John. "Art in Education and Education in Art." *New Republic,* February 24, 1926, pp. 11–13.

———. "The Meiklejohn Experiment." *New Republic,* August 17, 1932, pp. 23–24.

———. "President Hutchins' Proposals to Remake Higher Education." *Social Frontier,* III (January, 1937), 103–104.

———. "Why Have Progressive Schools?" *Current History,* XXXVIII (July, 1933), 441–48.

Ellert, JoAnn C. "The Bauhaus and Black Mountain College." *JGE: The Journal of General Education,* XXIV (October, 1972), 145–52.

Emerson, Ralph Waldo. "The American Scholar." In *Ralph Waldo Emerson: Selected Essays,* edited by Larzer Ziff. New York, 1982.

Evarts, John. "Black Mountain College: The Total Approach." *Form,* VI (December, 1967), 20–25.

French, John R. P. "The Bases of Social Power." In *Studies in Social Power,* edited by D. Cartwright. Ann Arbor, 1959.

Grant, Gerald. "Whither the Progressive College?" *Liberal Education,* LXX (Winter, 1984), 315–21.

Gray, Francine du Plessix. "Campus Correspondence: Summer at Black Mountain." *Mademoiselle* (July, 1952), 10.

Hall, James. "Black Mountain College: Wild, Woolly, Artsy, Gutsy." *Berkshire Sampler,* February 6, 1977, pp. 11–14.

Harris, Joel Chandler. "How Mr. Rabbit Was Too Sharp for Mr. Fox." In *The Complete Tales of Uncle Remus,* edited by Richard Chase. Boston, 1955.

Hill, Patrick J. "A Deweyan Perspective on Higher Education." *Liberal Education,* LXX (Winter, 1984), 307–10.

Hutchins, Robert M. "The Confusion in Higher Education." *Harper's,* CLXXIII (October, 1936), 449–58.

———. "President Hutchins' Proposals to Remake Higher Education." *Social Frontier,* III (January, 1937), 103–104.

———. "Prospects of Higher Education." *School and Society,* January 7, 1933, pp. 1–4.

———. "A Reply to Professor Whitehead." *Atlantic Monthly,* CLVIII (November, 1936), 582–88.

————. "What Is a General Education?" *Harper's,* CLXXIII (November, 1936), 602–609.

Lane, Jack C. "The Rollins Conference, 1931, and the Search for a Progressive Liberal Education: Mirror or Prism?" *Liberal Education,* LXX (Winter, 1984), 297–306.

Little, Clarence Cook. "Inaugural Address of the President of the University of Michigan." *School and Society,* November 7, 1925, pp. 569–72.

Luthin, Reinhard H. "The Flowering of the Southern Demagogue." *American Scholar,* CC (Spring, 1951), 185–95.

McKee, Lily Byrd. "They Made Their Mark . . . Balance at Black Mountain." *Mountain Living,* II (Summer, 1971), 15–18.

Meiklejohn, Alexander. "Educational Leadership in America." *Harper's,* CLX (March, 1930), 440–48.

————. "Who Should Go to College?" *New Republic,* January 16, 1929, pp. 18–26.

Orr, Kenneth. "Higher Education and the Great Depression: An Introduction to the Early Thirties." *Review of Higher Education,* II (1979), 1–10.

Patterson, Tom. "The Success of Its Own Accident: An Opinionated, Encapsulated History of Black Mountain College." *North Carolina Literary Review,* I (Spring, 1995), 17–31.

Pfnister, Allan O. "The Role of the Liberal Arts College: A Historical Overview of the Debates." *Journal of Higher Education,* LV (March/April, 1984), 145–70.

Reynolds, Katherine C. "Socrates and Serendipity: Ungainly Beginnings of an Uncommon College." *North Carolina Literary Review,* I (Spring, 1995), 33–44.

Rice, William C. "Introduction to Black Mountain College Memoirs." *Southern Review,* n.s., XXVI (July, 1989), 569–73.

Shelley, Lewis. "The Founding of Black Mountain College." *Form,* IV, April 15, 1967, pp. 4–7.

Swift, Jonathan. "A Tale of a Tub" (1710). In *Gulliver's Travels and Other Writings.* New York, 1958.

Tindall, George B. Review of *Black Mountain: An Exploration in Community,* by Martin Duberman. *North Carolina Historical Review,* L (April, 1973), 197–99.

Tussman, Joseph. "Remembering Alexander Meiklejohn." *Liberal Education,* LXX (Winter, 1984), 323–42.

Veysey, Laurence. "Experiments in Higher Education." Review of *Black Mountain: An Exploration in Community,* by Martin Duberman. *Harvard Educational Review,* XLIII (May, 1973), 258–64.

Whitehead, Alfred N. "Harvard: The Future." *Atlantic Monthly,* CLVIII (September 1936), 260–70.

Books

Adams, George P., and William P. Montague, eds. *Contemporary American Philosophy.* New York, 1930.

Agee, James. *A Death in the Family.* New York, 1967.

Archambault, Reginald D., ed. *Dewey on Education: Appraisals.* New York, 1966.

Ashmore, Harry S. *Unseasonable Truths: The Life of Robert Maynard Hutchins.* Boston, 1989.

Aydelotte, Frank. *The American Rhodes Scholarships.* Princeton, 1946.

———. *Breaking the Academic Lock Step.* New York, 1944.

———. *"The Oxford Stamp" and Other Essays.* New York, 1917.

Barzun, Jacques. *Teacher in America.* Boston, 1945.

Bayer, Herbert, Walter Gropius, and Ise Gropius. *Bauhaus, 1919–1928.* New York, 1948.

Betts, Alfred D. *History of Southern Methodism.* Columbia, S.C., 1952.

Blanshard, Frances. *Frank Aydelotte of Swarthmore.* Middletown, Conn., 1970.

Bloom-Feshbach, Jonathan, and Sally Bloom-Feshbach. *The Psychology of Separation and Loss.* San Francisco, 1987.

Borsodi, Ralph. *Flight from the City: The Story of a New Way to Family Security.* New York, 1933.

Bowers, C. A. *The Progressive Educator and the Depression: The Radical Years.* New York, 1969.

Bowlby, John. *Loss, Sadness, and Depression.* London, 1980. Vol. III of Bowlby, *Attachment and Loss.* 3 vols.

Boydston, Jo Ann, ed. *John Dewey: The Later Works, 1925–1953.* Carbondale, Ill., 1988.

Brockway, Thomas P. *Bennington College: In the Beginning.* Bennington, Vt., 1981.

Brubacher, John S., and Willis Rudy. *Higher Education in Transition: A History of American Colleges and Universities, 1636–1968.* 3rd ed. New York, 1976.

Butterick, George F., ed. *Charles Olson, Muthologos: The Collected Lectures and Interviews.* Vol. II of 2 vols. Bolinas, Calif., 1977.

Cash, W. J. *The Mind of the South.* New York, 1941.

Clark, Tom. *Charles Olson: The Allegory of a Poet's Life.* New York, 1991.

Clarke, Burton R. *The Distinctive College: Antioch, Reed and Swarthmore.* Chicago, 1970.

Counts, George S. *Dare the School Build a New Order?* New York, 1932.

Cremin, Lawrence A. *American Education: The Metropolitan Experience, 1876–1980.* New York, 1988.

———. *The Transformation of the School: Progressivism in American Education, 1876–1957.* New York, 1962.

Davis, Edwin A. *Louisiana: The Pelican State.* Baton Rouge, 1959.

Dawson, Fielding. *The Black Mountain Book.* New York, 1970.

Demarest, William H. S. *A History of Rutgers College, 1766–1924.* New Brunswick, N.J., 1924.

Dewey, John. *Art as Experience.* New York, 1934.

———. *Democracy and Education.* New York, 1916.

———. *Experience and Education.* New York, 1938.

———. *Experience and Nature.* New York, 1929.

————. *The Quest for Certainty: A Study of the Relation of Knowledge and Action.* New York, 1929.

Duberman, Martin. *Black Mountain: An Exploration in Community.* New York, 1972.

Duncan, Watson B. *Twentieth Century Sketches of the South Carolina Conference, Methodist Episcopal Church.* Columbia, S.C., 1901.

Dyer, John P. *Tulane: The Biography of a University.* New York, 1966.

Dzuback, Mary Ann. *Robert M. Hutchins: Portrait of an Educator.* Chicago, 1991.

Edgar, Walter B. *South Carolina in the Modern Age.* Columbia, S.C., 1992.

Federal Writers' Project. *Nebraska: A Guide to the Cornhusker State.* New York, 1939.

Flexner, Abraham. *I Remember: The Autobiography of Abraham Flexner.* New York, 1940.

————. *A Modern College and a Modern School.* New York, 1923.

————. *Universities: American, English, German.* London, 1930.

Gideonse, Harry D. *The Higher Learning in a Democracy.* New York, 1937.

Glassman, Steve, and Kathryn Lee Seidel. *Zora in Florida.* Orlando, 1991.

Grant, Gerald, and David Riesman. *The Perpetual Dream: Reform and Experiment in the American College.* Chicago, 1978.

Grimes, Lewis H. *A History of the Perkins School of Theology.* Dallas, 1993.

Grover, Edwin O., ed. *A Professor of Books.* Winter Park, Fla., 1929.

The Handbook of Private Schools. 73rd ed. Boston, 1992.

Harmon, Nolan B., ed. *The Encyclopedia of World Methodism.* 2 vols. New York, 1974.

Harris, Mary Emma. *The Arts at Black Mountain College.* Cambridge, Mass., 1987.

Hemenway, Robert E. *Zora Neale Hurston: A Literary Biography,* Urbana, Ill., 1977.

Hofstadter, Richard, and Wilson Smith. *American Higher Education: A Documentary History.* Chicago, 1961.

Holsten, George H., Jr. *Bicentennial Year: The Story of a Rutgers Celebration.* New Brunswick, N.J., 1968.

Hutchins, Robert M. *Education for Freedom.* Baton Rouge, 1944.

————. *The Higher Learning in America.* New Haven, 1936.

James, William. *Pragmatism.* New York, 1907.

————. *Principles of Psychology.* New York, 1890.

Jarausch, Konrad H., ed. *The Transformation of Higher Learning, 1860–1930.* Chicago, 1983.

Jencks, Christopher, and David Riesman. *The Academic Revolution.* New York, 1968.

Jones, Barbara. *Bennington College: The Development of an Educational Idea.* New York, 1946.

Knoll, Robert. *A Prairie University.* New York, 1994.

Koch, Raymond, and Charlotte Koch. *Educational Commune: The Story of Commonwealth College.* New York, 1972.

Kuehl, Warren F. *Hamilton Holt: Journalist, Internationalist, Educator.* Gainesville, Fla., 1960.

Lane, Mervin, ed. *Black Mountain College, Sprouted Seeds: An Anthology of Personal Accounts.* Knoxville, Tenn., 1990.

Logue, Cal M., and Howard Dorgan, eds. *The Oratory of Southern Demagogues.* Baton Rouge, 1981.

Lumpkin, Katharine DuPre. *The Making of a Southerner.* Athens, Ga., 1946.

McMillin, Laurence. *The Experimental College.* New York, 1932.

————. *The Schoolmaker: Sawney Webb and the Bell Buckle Story.* Chapel Hill, 1971.

————. *What Does America Mean?* New York, 1935.

Manley, Robert N. *Centennial History of the University of Nebraska.* Lincoln, Nebr., 1969.

Mencken, Henry L. *Prejudices: Second Series.* New York, 1920.

Metzger, Walter P. *Academic Freedom in the Age of the University.* New York, 1955.

Mims, Edwin. *The Advancing South.* Garden City, N.Y., 1926.

————. *History of Vanderbilt University.* Nashville, 1946.

Morgan, Arthur. *A Compendium of Antioch Notes.* Yellow Springs, Ohio, 1930.

Moxon, Rosamond S, and Mabel C. Peabody. *Twenty-five Years: Two Anniversary Sketches of New Jersey College for Women.* New Brunswick, N.J., 1943.

Neumann, Eckhard, ed. *Bauhaus and Bauhaus People.* New York, 1993.

Newman, John Henry. *The Idea of a University.* London, 1852.

Nicholes, Cassie. *Historical Sketches of Sumter County: Its Birth and Growth.* Columbia, S.C., 1975.

Ohles, John F., ed. *Biographical Dictionary of American Educators.* 3 vols. Westport, Conn., 1978.

Oleson, Alexandra, and John Voss. *The Organization of Knowledge in Modern America, 1860–1920.* Baltimore, 1979.

Olson, James C. *History of Nebraska.* Lincoln, 1966.

Percy, William Alexander. *Lanterns on the Levee: Recollections of a Planter's Son.* New York, 1941.

Pollock, George H. *The Mourning-Liberation Process.* 2 vols. Madison, Wis., 1989.

Robertson, Ben. *Red Hills and Cotton: An Upcountry Memory.* Columbia, S.C., 1942.

Rudolph, Frederick. *The American College and University: A History.* 2nd ed. Athens, Ga., 1990.

————. *Curriculum: A History of the American Undergraduate Course of Study Since 1636.* San Francisco, 1977.

Savory, Jerald J. *Columbia College: The Ariail Era.* Columbia, S.C., 1979.

Schlipp, Paul A., ed. *Higher Education Faces the Future.* New York, 1930.

Schmidt, George P. *Douglass College: A History.* New Brunswick, N.J., 1968.

Sinclair, Upton. *The Goose Step.* Pasadena, Calif., 1922.

Smith, J. Winfree. *A Search for the Liberal College: The Beginning of the St. John's Program.* Annapolis, Md., 1983.

Smith, Lillian. *Killers of the Dream.* New York, 1949.

Snider, William D. *Light on the Hill: A History of the University of North Carolina.* Chapel Hill, 1992.

Stein, Gertrude. *Lectures in America*. New York, 1935.

Storr, Richard J. *Harper's University: The Beginnings*. Chicago, 1966.

Thomas, Mary M. H. *Southern Methodist University: Founding and Early Years*. Dallas, 1974.

Tindall, George Brown. *The Emergence of the New South, 1913–1945*. Baton Rouge, 1967.

Townsend, Barbara, L. Jackson Newell, and Michael Wiese. *Creating Distinctiveness: Lessons from Uncommon Colleges and Universities*. Washington, D.C., 1992.

Veblen, Thorstein. *The Higher Learning in America: A Memorandum on the Conduct of Universities by Business Men*. New York, 1918.

Veysey, Laurence. *The Emergence of the American University*. Chicago, 1965.

Wagner, Paul A. *Rollins College and Dr. Hamilton Holt*. Philadelphia, 1951.

A Walker's Guide to Rollins College. Winter Park, Fla., 1988.

Wall, Bennett H., ed. *Louisiana: A History*. Arlington Heights, Ill., 1984.

Wallace, David D. *The History of South Carolina*. Vols. II and III of 4 vols. New York, 1934.

Ward, F. Champion, ed. *The Idea and Practice of General Education: An Account of the College of the University of Chicago*. Chicago, 1950.

Warren, Constance. *A New Design for Women's Education*. New York, 1940.

Weber, Nicholas Fox. *Patron Saints: Five Rebels Who Opened America to a New Art, 1928–1943*. New York, 1992.

Whitehead, Alfred North. *"The Aims of Education" and Other Essays*. New York, 1929.

Whitford, Frank. *Bauhaus*. London, 1984.

Wingler, Hans Maria. *The Bauhaus: Weimar, Dessau, Berlin, Chicago*. Cambridge, Mass., 1969.

Woodward, C. Vann. *Origins of the New South*. Baton Rouge, 1951.

Wright, Richard. *Black Boy*. New York, 1945.

Other

Leong, Linda-Mei. "John Andrew Rice, Jr.: Visionary." B.A. honors thesis, Harvard University, 1969.

INDEX